Hopkins

MINNESOTA

Through the Years

By The Hopkins Historical Society
Beverly O. Ewing, Editor

Cover Photo. This is a group photo of all the Hopkins Junior and Senior High School students taken in May 1919. The photo is taken in front of the Senior High School building located on the south side of Excelsior Boulevard (now Mainstreet) between 15th and 16th Avenues. Today, the Central Park Manor apartment building sits on this site.

Inside front cover. This plat map is taken from Wright, George B., *Map of Hennepin County, Minnesota, 1874*. From the Minnesota Historical Society's Map Collection.

Inside back cover. This street map is taken from an M.B. Hagen Realty Company brochure about 1970.

All photos and illustrations are from the Hopkins Historical Society archives unless otherwise noted. Additional information about the history of Hopkins can be found at the Hopkins Historical Society Museum, Hopkins Activity Center, 33-14th Avenue North, Hopkins, Minnesota 55343. (952) 979-0447.

ISBN 0-9727014-0-0

Editor's Preface

In 1987, the Hopkins Centennial Committee compiled an interesting town history in a surprisingly short time. A committee of writers incorporated over 125 historic photographs with text and called it an "album," styling it after a family photo album. The book did a fine job of telling the town's history, but as soon as it was done, omissions started to be noticed, a few errors too, but mostly it was too short and people wanted more of the same.

It is a credit to the authors of the original *Hopkins Centennial Album* that they produced such a fantastic book in the first place. Thanks to Larry Gardiner, Hugh Strawn, Svante Severson, Reid T. Burns, John DeVeau and Lyman (Ham) Hamilton, Harold "Frenchy" Faucher and editor Jeff Wagner, the *Hopkins Centennial Album* is still being requested 15 years after it was originally written.

Since publication, members of the Hopkins Historical Society Board have been faithfully recording items they want to change or include in the "next book." This book, then, incorporates much of the same material as the 1987 *Hopkins Centennial Album*, with additions to the year 2002. It includes improvements where they were needed and many more topics are covered. Over 200 photographs and some maps have been included and much more history has been chronicled.

Now, we have all these wonderful photographs of Hopkins… with a few MORE words.

Special thanks to the Board of the Hopkins Historical Society—Dean Empanger, Jim Zdrazil, Henry Pokorny,

> "We have all these wonderful photographs, all we need is a few words."
>
> —Jim Marvy of the Hopkins Centennial Committee as quoted by Jeff Wagner, Editor of the *Hopkins Centennial Album 1887-1987*

Marlene (Blake) Dvorak, Therese (Feltl) Glatt and Mary (Anderson) Raabe. They gave me the opportunity to edit this book and fall in love again with the town in which I grew up. It has been a pleasure to dig in the Hopkins archives and explore the lives of some of the men and women who helped build this town.

I could not have completed this book without the patience and wisdom of Henry Pokorny, former Hopkins mayor and lifeblood of the Hopkins Historical Society. He answered all my minute questions with grace and wit. Special thanks also goes to Kenneth and Harriet Ahlstom, of Daniels Photography, for electronically scanning the photos used in this book and to Vern Wigfield, for his railroad knowledge. And words cannot express how thankful I am for my family, who exhibited great patience this past year.

My hope for the book is that it contributes to civic pride and encourages the younger generations to have the same citizenship and ownership of their town that the older generations did.

Bev (Ophoven) Ewing, Editor

Dedication

We all owe a huge debt of gratitude to Clint Blomquist, Hopkins Historical Society's first curator. One of the six founders of the Hopkins Historical Society, Clint knew more about Hopkins History than anyone else in town, mainly because he acquired, cataloged, wrote about and stored virtually everything in

Clint and Vivian Blomquist.

the museum and archives, now housed in the former band room of South Junior High; in the Hopkins Activity Center.

As we were assembling this book, Clint's writings on many subjects were available to provide the needed dates and context. Clint wrote historical articles that appeared in the *Hopkins Review* and each of his articles we found in the files was concise, clear, historically accurate and well documented.

Clinton K. Blomquist was born on December 21, 1903 in the house at 246 12th Avenue North where he lived his entire life. He was the son of Charles Blomquist and Nancie J. McClure. Charles Blomquist came to Hopkins in 1892 and worked at the M.T.M. Company, owned a shoe business with Oscar Quist, then ran Anderson and Blomquist grocery store on the main street in Hopkins until he died in 1922. Clint married Vivian Mahoney on June 12, 1937. Clint was a member of the charter commission in 1947 that structured the document that governs Hopkins to this day. Clint was Hopkins' building inspector under Mayor Henry Pokorny, who today is Treasurer of the Hopkins Historical

Society. Clint was the leading force behind the Hopkins Historical Society and served as its president and archivist from 1972 until 1996.

If Clint was "Mr. Hopkins Historical Society," Vivian Blomquist was "Mrs. Hopkins Historical Society." Offering hospitality at historical society meetings, and working together with the original founders of the society to assemble and store acquisitions, Viv was much beloved by all who knew her. The Blomquists were honored with a recognition party in 1995. The Hopkins city council passed a proclamation honoring them and WCCO radio named Clint Blomquist its "Good Neighbor." Clint passed away in 1996 and Viv in 1998.

To see the story of Hopkins and Clint Blomquist in action, borrow a copy of the videotape from the Hopkins Public Library "A Walk Back in Time" that Clint helped produce. The Hopkins Historical Society also has a copy of this video. Or simply enjoy this book, much of which originated with Clint Blomquist, the tireless keeper of Hopkins history.

House at 246-12th Ave. N. where Clint Blomquist grew up. Pictured are Mrs. Charles Blomquist, Clinton, and Quentin in 1905.

Contents

Cir.1907. This photo was found on a postcard inside of the fireplace mantel of the Dow house just prior to its demolition. Looking north along 9th Avenue, the Dow house is the large home on left (now the site of the Hopkins Post Office).

CHAPTER 1

Overview and Timeline

Hopkins, Minnesota, was originally incorporated as the Village of West Minneapolis, population 1,105, on November 27, 1893. Before that, it was a part of Minnetonka and Minneapolis (formerly Richfield) Townships in Hennepin County. Before that, it was part of Dakota Territory. On July 7, 1928, it became the Village of Hopkins. Originally, Hopkins was about three square miles in size (1,920 acres). It has been enlarged by annexation to its present size of about four square miles. It was named after a pioneer and its first postmaster, Harley H. Hopkins, who made an arrangement with the railroad that the depot on his property be called "Hopkins." Today, the City of Hopkins is a balanced community of businesses, residences and open space, an integral part of the bustling metropolitan Minneapolis-St. Paul area, while still preserving its hometown atmosphere. As we will explore in this book, Hopkins has an interesting and rich past.

Soon after the treaties of Traverse des Sioux and

Mendota of 1851, European-Americans started claiming former Native American lands west of the Mississippi River. Beginning in 1852, while Minnesota was still a Territory, the Hopkins area was settled by Yankee and Bohemian farmers. Strategically located near a trail established by Native Americans that followed the high ground from Lake Calhoun to Shakopee on the Minnesota River, Hopkins was settled as mills

"Hopkins has been a very nurturing place to live and to raise a family. I am pleased to see all the new activity on main street, and pleased with the continuing excellence of our schools and hopeful that Hopkins will continue to provide a safe and good environment for the generations to come."

—Margaret Lapic

Hopkins in 1890, three years after the M.T.M. factory (left) was built.

were being built on Minnehaha Creek to the north in what later became known as Minnetonka Mills. Hopkins was also centrally located between the Village of St. Anthony and the newly explored beautiful Lake Minnetonka and became a stopping off place to rest horses.

From 1854-1870 settlers continued to migrate into the area, staking out claims and clearing land for farming and raising cattle. A big change came for Hopkins when between 1871 and 1881 three railroads were built through the area, opening its potential for industrial growth. The Minneapolis Threshing Machine Company factory was built to make farm equipment in 1887 and soon became the largest employer in western Hennepin County. The factory brought more Bohemian and Scandinavian workers into the area and a company to supply housing to the new settlers was established.

Merchants and services began to spring up to accommodate the growing population. Soon, Excelsior Avenue became a thriving main street and the primary market hub for the neighboring communities of Eden Prairie, Edina, St. Louis Park and Minnetonka Township. Hopkins became a hometown for many factory workers as worker houses and tenements were built. Churches and schools were built. It became the center of higher education and social activity for the rural population from the neighboring townships.

Between 1887 and 1945, the Hopkins area continued to grow as a farming area and prosper as a small busi-

ness community. A gigantic business and population boom following World War II saw the Twin Cities spread to the west—to Hopkins and all around it and beyond. Surrounded by urban activity, the small town of Hopkins put on some of the glamour of the big city. After all, until about 1950, Hopkins was the largest city in the western suburbs and its downtown was the area's major shopping district. Hopkins acquired new stores, new businesses, new services and more government as its population increased. By the mid-1950s, the pastures and prairies were covered by modern dwellings and the modern businesses that served the new inhabitants.

Transportation was one of the reasons Hopkins was such a focal point. Hopkins was always easy to get to, first by trails, then by dirt roads and railways, next by street cars connecting to Minneapolis and Lake Minnetonka and after the automobile was introduced, by the major north-south and east-west roads running through it. The streetcar era (1899-1951) was Hopkins' heyday. The streetcar allowed Hopkins residents easy access to the big cities. If you needed a job, higher education or services only available in the city, you could live in or near Hopkins, get on a streetcar and have access to all these facilities in Minneapolis or St. Paul.

Hopkins' Mainstreet (formerly Excelsior Avenue) distinguishes it from neighboring communities and other newer suburbs. Over the years, businesses of all types have lined the now 16-block stretch of Mainstreet. In the early years there were necessary services such as a general store, lumber yard, meat market, milk depot, blacksmith shop, livery stable, barber shop and public bath. Saloons, an opera house and lodges provided various leisure time activities. Schools and churches were built alongside homes and businesses.

In the early to the middle of the twentieth century, Hopkins' thriving merchants provided all needed services such as doctor and dental services, banks, drug stores, grocery and hardware stores, bakeries, shoe and millinery stores, restaurants and mortuaries. Car dealerships, theaters, photography studios, jewelry stores and a library were concepts hardly imagined by the early settlers of the 1800s, but they were part of Hopkins throughout much of the twentieth century. Hopkins merchants outgrew the main street and built on adjoining side streets, thus creating "Downtown" Hopkins.

On Dec 2, 1947, Hopkins became a city through the adoption of a city charter. Then, as now, the city leaders had a challenge to grow with the times. Many more city services were required such as sewer and water service, better roads and more police and fire coverage. The post World War II building boom created multiple new neighborhoods and the need for new schools. Hopkins

Looking west from 8th Street down Mainstreet Hopkins, about 2000. Photo from the City of Hopkins.

Hopkins looking south in 1949. The large Minneapolis Moline plant is at the top, flanked by farmland; the stores of downtown Hopkins run along Excelsior Ave., the horizontal street lined with larger buildings in lower half of photo.

Night scene along Excelsior Avenue looking east from 11th Avenue, cir. 1955.

was no longer just a small town; it was an integral part of the thriving Minneapolis-St. Paul metropolitan area.

Downtown Hopkins underwent rapid changes in the latter half of the twentieth century. Cars became the predominant mode of transportation and Hopkins became the "car capital of the world"—in auto sales, that is. For a while, there was a gas station on every corner and auto lots lined parts of Excelsior Avenue. Cruising the drag was a major pastime for several generations of teens. For adults, there was always plenty of entertainment at the local bars lining the strip. That's how Hopkins got the reputation as the "cars and bars" town.

During the late 1950s and early 1960s, new shopping centers were built in surrounding suburbs. As each new shopping center was built—Miracle Mile and Knollwood in St. Louis Park and Southdale in Edina—customers were lured away from Hopkins' shops. Nothing equaled the changes set off when Ridgedale Center opened in the early 1970s less than a 10-minute drive from downtown Hopkins. A number of the buildings in the Hopkins shopping district were over 70 years old and needed renovation and Hopkins merchants could not compete with the convenience of the modern shopping center. Small, specialized stores were no longer profitable and many old Hopkins establishments closed. The mix of services available in Hopkins began to change and the Hopkins downtown was no longer a necessary destination for many of its residents.

But Hopkins' population continued to increase, its industrial base continued to be strong and it became a desirable location for affordable housing. Urban sprawl

from the growth of the western suburbs of Minneapolis created an intense need for housing and, along with that, yet even more city services. The population of Hopkins in 1950 was 7,595; by 1980, it had more than doubled to 15,336; as of the 2000 U.S. census, there were 17,145 people living in Hopkins. Land once used for agricultural purposes has become fully developed and is now used for multi-unit housing, sprawling industrial complexes and recreation space.

The city leaders, in addition to its industrious people, have kept Hopkins alive and well. The downtown area has been revitalized several times, often to the dismay of preservationists. In the 1970s, a grand experiment was tried but failed. Excelsior Avenue was narrowed, curved and transformed into a compact shopping district named the "Welcomall." It had trees, bus bays and decorative lighting and was very attractive, but did not produce the desired results of turning Hopkins once again into a major retail district.

Throughout the 1980s and 1990s, Hopkins' leaders kept plugging away at creatively financing and planning "urban renewal" projects and the fruits of their labor can be seen today. Excelsior Boulevard was re-routed south of town and the main road through town is now straight again and named "Mainstreet." County Road 18 became a major connecting north-south freeway, Highway 169.

Now, the Hopkins Center for the Arts, a multi-screen movie theater and Stages Theatre grace Mainstreet. Antique and thrift shops abound. A library, senior activity center and new restaurants and coffee shops ensure that Hopkins is once again a place to spend time and not just pass through. Apartment and condominium homes near Mainstreet provide a desirable living situation for its population. Still providing most of the necessities for its residents, Hopkins' Downtown has a unique feel of old-time hometown, while providing the cultural extras for its cosmopolitan residents.

The award winning Hopkins School District 270, with beginnings as far back as 1862, sprawls well beyond the borders of Hopkins. Only three of its seven elementary schools are in Hopkins proper; its state-of-the-art high school and two Junior Highs are located in Minnetonka and the school district serves all of Hopkins and parts of Minnetonka, Golden Valley, Eden Prairie, Edina, Plymouth and St. Louis Park. While Hopkins' borders are no longer distinct, many of its residents are no longer of similar heritage. Hopkins boasts a rich diversity of cultures within its borders. Five percent of the school population are ESL (English as a Second Language) students, representing 58 countries and 50 languages. Just as new community members were welcomed to Hopkins with substantial opportunities from the 1850s through the twentieth century, its newer population is today welcomed into the existing culture with open arms and open minds. Jobs are available at Hopkins' huge Super Valu grocery wholesale warehouse and the high-tech companies of Hopkins join with those in neighboring communities to offer its citizens many opportunities to reach their full economic potential.

The major highways that run near Hopkins allow easy access to the large metropolitan area of the Twin

A note about the use of the name "Hopkins"—It wasn't until 1928 that the village was officially named "Hopkins." The post office was named "Hopkins" and the train depot was called "Hopkins Station." Many people referred to the area as "Hopkins," but the village was actually named "West Minneapolis" from 1893-1928.

In writing about the early years, it seemed confusing to continually write "the area now known as Hopkins," or "West Minneapolis, now known as Hopkins," or even worse, "rural Hennepin County, later known as West Minneapolis and later known as Hopkins." To avoid unnecessary confusion, the term "Hopkins" will simply be used regardless of the official name at the time.

Cities of Minneapolis and St. Paul, to the large international airport and thus to the world.

The first settlers of Hopkins could not have imagined what life would be like for us as we are perched at the beginning of the twenty-first century. Likewise, we cannot imagine what life will be like 100 years from now, but we look forward with hope and wonder about what changes the new century most certainly will bring.

But first, we pause to consider what wonder and changes the past century and a half have brought to the village, now city, of Hopkins.

Timeline of Hopkins History

1849	**March 1849**	Minnesota Territory is established.
	July & August 1851	Treaties of Traverse des Sioux and Mendota cede lands west of the Mississippi River to the government and open up Indian Territory to white settlement.
	1852	Mary Gordon and George Andrews become Hopkins' first white settlers.
	1853	First Bohemians, Francis Pesek and Joseph Prib, settle near Shady Oak Lake.
	1854	Harley H. Hopkins settles in what is now Hopkins.
	1857	Mrs. Fairchild conducts a 3-month school; Mrs. Lamb preceded her.
	1858	Minnesota becomes a state and Minnetonka Township is platted.
1860	1862	Mr. Allison teaches school in Harley H. Hopkins' granary.
	1862	First school building, Burnes School, is built.
	1863	Harley H. Hopkins builds a 15-room house.
	4 Jan. 1865	Hennepin County Poor Farm opens.
1870	1870	The Railroad begins to buy land through the Hopkins area.
	25 Nov 1871	Inaugural run of the M.&St.L. train through Hopkins to Excelsior, MN.
	26 Feb 1873	Harley H. Hopkins is appointed postmaster.
	1879	First Catholic Church in the area opens—St. Margaret's on Shady Oak Rd.
1880	1880s	Empangers lead the way to establish the raspberry growing industry.
	July 1882 thru August 1886	The "Motor Line" narrow-gauge railway runs through Hopkins.
	1885	The Methodist-Episcopal congregation begins to organize in Hopkins.
	1886	John Feltl develops the concept of covering raspberry plants to protect them over winter.
	1887	The Minneapolis Threshing Machine Company factory opens.
	1887-1888	First Protestant church is built, known as the Bohemian Presbyterian Church, later called John Hus Church on County Road 3 west of Shady Oak Road (now is Faith Presbyterian Church.)
	1889	The West Minneapolis Methodist-Episcopal Church is built at 28 Ninth Ave. S.
	17 Nov 1889	Mizpah Congregational Church is dedicated at Eighth and Excelsior Ave.
	1888-1889	Brick grade school is built on Ninth Avenue, north of Excelsior Avenue.

1890

1889-1890	Swedish Lutheran Church of West Minneapolis builds on 2nd Street and Ninth Avenue North.
1892-1895	The Bushnell Post Office operates in addition to the Hopkins Post Office.
1893-1895	Severe depression. M.T.M. has huge lay-offs. Tourist trade on Lake Minnetonka wanes.
27 Nov 1893	Village of West Minneapolis is incorporated. Population: 1,105.
9 December 1893	First Village of West Minneapolis election is held. Chester L. Hopkins is elected president, Fred Souba, Andrew A. Olson and William Hosp are elected Trustees; E.A. Close is elected recorder.
1894	Daniel & Belinda (Hamilton) Dow finish building their large house on the site of the current Post Office.
1895	St. Mary's Catholic Church is built at 51 Sixth Avenue S.
1897	Only two telephones are in Hopkins. Later in the year, Smetana Drugstore installs a pay station so people can phone into the city.
1898	East End Grade School is built near Jackson Ave and First St. S.
16 June 1899	Streetcar service comes to Hopkins and runs to 6th Avenue and 1st St. N.

1900

1900	Village of West Minneapolis' population is 1,648.
1902	Another frame grade school is built on Ninth Avenue North.
1902	First High School Graduation – Opera Hall, 9 grades.
1905	The Twin City Rapid Transit Company begins streetcar service between Minneapolis and Hopkins.
September 1905	Fifty telephone subscriptions are sold in Hopkins.
1907	Village holds first Agricultural Fair. Later becomes the Hennepin County Fair.
1908	First "High School" building opens on south side of Excelsior Ave. between 15th and 16th Avenues.

Panorama photograph of Hopkins looking north on 9th Avenue South in 1903.

1910

1910	Village of West Minneapolis' population is 3,022.
1912	Hopkins residents could take advantage of 390 miles of streetcar service running from Stillwater to Tonka Bay. 39 round trips came through Hopkins each day with more on Sunday.
1915	The German Lutheran Church (later, Zion Lutheran) takes over the former Norwegian Lutheran Church property at 41 Twelfth Ave N.

1920

1920	West Minneapolis' population is 3,055.
1921-1923	Merger of St. Mary's and St. Margaret's Churches into St. Joseph Catholic Church; parochial school is built; also used as a church.
1925	Junior High School is built on north side of Excelsior Ave. between 13th and 14th Avenues. Known as South Junior High for some time, this building is still used as community center and Raspberry Ridge Apartments.
2 June 1925	Devastating tornado hits M.T.M. and other east-side properties.
1926	East End School is replaced by new school named Harley Hopkins.
7 July 1928	The Village of West Minneapolis becomes the Village of Hopkins.
1929	The Minneapolis Threshing Machine Co. (M.T.M.) becomes "Minneapolis Moline."

1930

1930	Village of Hopkins' population is 3,834.
1932	All streetcar rails west of Hopkins are removed.
1935	Hopkins business people organize the first Raspberry Festival.
1937	Artist David Granahan's murals are installed in the Hopkins Post Office.

The Hopkins Water Tower in 1938.

1940

1940	Village of Hopkins' population is 4,100.
1941	The Engler Brothers build the Hopkins Theater on 5th & Excelsior Avenues.
1946	Katherine Curren Grade School is built on Excelsior Avenue between 16th and 17th Avenues.
1946	National Tea and Red Owl grocery businesses move to Hopkins. The former Harley H. Hopkins home is torn down.
2 December 1947	By Charter, the Village of Hopkins becomes a City.
January 1948	First television in Hopkins is at the M.B. Hagen Appliance Store. In March of 1948, the first bona fide broadcast by a KSTP transmitter is received.
20 May 1948	The library is moved to the Dow House and opens to the public on 24 June 1948.

View of Mainstreet Hopkins looking west from 7th Avenue in the 1970s.

1950	1950	City of Hopkins' population is 7,595.
	July 1951	Streetcar service to Hopkins discontinues.
	1949 & 1952	Interlachen Park neighborhood is annexed to Hopkins.
	1952	Alice Smith Elementary School opens.
	1952	Super Valu moves to Hopkins.
	16 April 1953	Hennepin County Poor Farm closes and its main building is sold to Honeywell.
	1956	A new Hopkins High School is built north of Highway 7. Known as Eisenhower High School for 12 years, it is now called Eisenhower Elementary School and Eisenhower Community Center.
1960	1960	City of Hopkins' population is 11,370.
	January 1963	Minneapolis Moline becomes a subsidiary of White Motor Co.
	17 July 1963	The library is moved from the Dow House to 25 9th Ave, N. and opens to the public on 28 January 1965.
	April 1965	The Dow House is demolished.
1970	1970	Hopkins Lindberg High School is built north of Cedar Lake Road in Minnetonka.
	1970	City of Hopkins' population is 13,428.
	1972	Hopkins' main street becomes the "Welcomall."
	4 January 1973	The Hopkins City Library becomes part of the Hennepin County Library System.
	1977	South Junior High closes as a school; it reopens in 1981 as apartments and community activity center.

1980

1980	City of Hopkins' population is 15,336; 98% are Caucasian. There are 7,257 dwelling units, none vacant; 4,345 are rented, 2,716 are owner occupied.
1980	White Motor Company, owner of the former Minneapolis Moline, files for bankruptcy.
1981	Harley Hopkins School is converted to a Family Center.
1981	Hopkins Historical Society moves into the newly remodeled former South Junior High band room in the new Hopkins Activity Center.
1982	Eisenhower High School closes and becomes a community center.
1985	Engler's Hopkins Theater on 5th and Excelsior Avenues closes.
1987	Hopkins celebrates its centennial. *Hopkins Centennial Album 1887-1987* is published.

1990

1990	Hopkins' population is 16,536. Average age is 31.
1997	In winter, the Hopkins Cinema 6 opens at 1118 Mainstreet. In April, groundbreaking for Hopkins Center for the Arts and construction of Glenrose floral block begins.
9 November 1997	The Hopkins Center for the Arts celebrates its grand opening.

2000

2000	Hopkins' population is 17,145. 82.6% are Caucasian.

Hopkins Centennial postmarked envelope, 1887-1987.

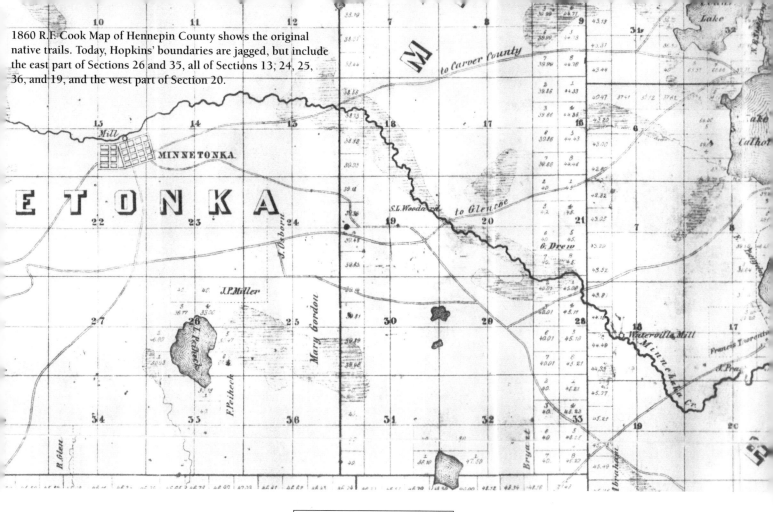

1860 R.F. Cook Map of Hennepin County shows the original native trails. Today, Hopkins' boundaries are jagged, but include the east part of Sections 26 and 35, all of Sections 13, 24, 25, 36, and 19, and the west part of Section 20.

CHAPTER 2

Territory to 1900

Before European-American Settlement

When the first white settlers came to the Hopkins area in 1852, the world was much different than it is today. Physically, the land was untamed; in its wild, natural state, it must have been spectacularly beautiful.

Minnetonka Township, of which Hopkins is a part, was covered with a heavy growth of timber in the western portion of the township, with a light growth of underbrush in the eastern part where Hopkins was located. The surface was rolling, with occasional mounds of considerable height. The soil was principally a sandy loam, while in some portions of the eastern part, a clay loam appeared. A number of lakes were scattered about, the principle one being Shady Oak Lake, which is described in an 1881 history book as a beautiful body of water, located in the southeast part. Minnehaha Creek flows through the north-central part of

the township on its way from Gray's Bay in Lake Minnetonka to the Mississippi River north of Fort Snelling. Of significance to Hopkins is the north fork of Ninemile Creek, which emerges from a wetland near what is now Central Park in Hopkins and flows southeast to the Minnesota River Valley in Bloomington near Black Dog Lake.

In 1849, the Minnesota Territory was established. Land west of the Mississippi River belonged to various native tribes. East of the Mississippi, land was available for white settlement. As late as 1842, the United States Senate had seriously considered making southern Minnesota a permanent Indian land and keeping white immigrants out. However, the times were quickly changing.

In the 1840s, the United States had acquired Texas to California from Mexico via war and the Oregon Territory from Great Britain by peaceful means. By 1849, the California gold rush had started. In people's minds, the

Mississippi River didn't seem like a boundary anymore. The U.S. government and its growing number of European-American citizens were anxious to expand the country from coast to coast. The Native Americans living in Minnesota were soon to be squeezed off land that was exclusively theirs west of the Mississippi River.

As soon as he was elected, the new territorial governor, Alexander Ramsey, started to push for the acquisition of the "Suland," which was what the Sioux territory west of the Mississippi was called in the newspapers.

In July 1851, Governor Ramsey and others met with the Sisseton and Wahpeton bands at Traverse des Sioux, near present-day St. Peter, to negotiate the land away from them. When the bargaining was finished, the two bands found themselves confined to a strip of country extending 10 miles on each side of the Minnesota River above the Yellow Medicine River. Below that, another 20-mile strip was reserved for the Mdewakanton and Wahpekute bands, with whom a separate treaty would be made. The United States had now acquired land as far west as Lake Traverse and the Big Sioux River for its own citizens. For their land, the natives were to be paid about 7.5 cents an acre.

We can hardly imagine how exasperating this was for the native people. Just 10 years earlier, these Dakota groups had agreed to a treaty making this area an all-Indian territory. In the meantime, there had been lean years and some of their people were close to starvation, while others had survived only on credit from traders. They desperately needed the government's money to feed their people.

Shortly after this, in August of 1851, a separate treaty was signed at Mendota with the Mdewakanton and Wahpekute bands. Having already received some treaty money from ceding their land east of the Mississippi, the Mdewakanton were less hungry and desperate than the others. They were also more determined and suspicious, since they had learned from experience that government payments were always late and that many promises were never kept. But there was nothing they could do except protest. They were trapped by the fact that the western bands had already given in.

Rhoda R. Gilman, in her historical paper, "Territorial Imperative, How Minnesota Became the 32nd State," published in *Minnesota History*, Winter 1998-99, speaks eloquently about the vast changes taking place:

"With the signing of the treaties a subtle but profound change had already taken place. Prairie and oak openings had become acres; forests had become timber stands; tumbling rivers had become water rights. A world of natural features once invested with mystery and power of their own had become resources for human manipulation…

To nineteenth-century Americans, too, land had an almost holy quality. The sacred element they saw was not the land itself, with its ancient layers of interwoven plant and animal life, but the dream of what human labor could produce from it…

Even more alluring and powerful than the natural bounty of land was the meteoric rise in its value as population poured into an area. A tract bought from Indian people for 7.5 cents and resold by the government to its own citizens for $1.25 might be worth hundreds if platted as a town lot or even thousands if it became the business block of a rising city. Successive waves of land speculation built great fortunes and fueled the U.S. economy through much of the nineteenth century, and one of them was created just at the time Minnesota became a territory…"

The population of non-Indians in Minnesota territory as shown in the 1850 census was 6,077; the U.S. Department of Indian Affairs estimates there were 31,700 Indians living in and near the territory in the early 1850s. Of the non-Indians counted, many (37-57%) were of mixed-Indian ancestry. The Indians had traded goods and shared lives with the French traders for many years. What they had no experience with were the American pioneers from the east coast who remained separate and apart from them and who had such strange new ways.

Settling the Hopkins Area

The first white settlers in the township of Minnetonka were Simon Stevens and James Shaver, Jr., who came in the spring of 1852. This was before land claims could be entered and these men came with the intention of setting up a mill on Minnehaha Creek. The mill area was slightly north of the area that eventually became Hopkins.

The first settler in Hopkins was Mrs. Mary Gordon and her five sons, who settled on what was later the Hennepin County poor farm. She came in the year 1852 and so did George Andrews, who sold his claim early the following spring to John P. Miller. Proximity to the mill being built was one of the reasons for these early settlers to locate where they did.

The newcomers did not yet have legal claim to the land. They were squatters that occupied some acreage, built a dwelling and started to subsistence farm. They did this under the Preemption Act of 1841 whereby the government allowed individuals to assert their claims to government land before it was offered for sale. It was an "every man for himself" kind of mentality and historically there were many early disputes as to who had a legal claim to a piece of land.

We do not know of any specific land disputes that occurred in the Hopkins area, but there certainly was a displacement of native peoples previously using the land for hunting, fishing and living. There was an uneasy truce and mistrust between the natives and the squatters, but plenty of cordial interaction, too. The Hopkins area has some stories passed down from the early white settlers such as this from Daniel Dow:

In 1850 when I first came to Minnesota, I took a claim at Lake Harriet near where the pavilion now [1914] stands. The ruins of the old Steven's Mission were on my claim. It had been built in 1834. I did not keep this claim long, though I built a log cabin there and kept bachelor's hall, but soon took a claim where my present house stands in Hopkins. I built a cabin here but boarded with a widow and her children. All the food we had was game, pork and buckwheat cakes. The buckwheat they had brought from their home and it was all ground in the coffee mill then sifted through a horsehair sieve before it could be used. There were seven in the family to grind for, so it kept one person grinding all the time.

I was supposed to live alone in my cabin but hardly ever spent a night without the companionship of some Sioux Indians who were hunting around there. I gladly received them as they were friendly, and their company was much better than none. One winter they came in such numbers that at night the floor was entirely covered by their sleeping forms. Early in the morning, they would go out and all day hunt the deer, with which the woods abounded. It was very cold and the slain deer froze immediately. They stacked them up, making a huge pile. Suddenly all the Indians left. One morning shortly after I was working in the clearing around my cabin, when I saw a line of squaws which I think was a block long, coming over the trail which led from Shakopee to Hopkins. The squaws went to the pile of

deer. Each took one on her back and silently trudged away over the trail toward Shakopee. Some of the squaws were so small that the frozen carcass had to be adjusted by another squaw or it would drag on the ground. They were two weeks removing this pile of deer and had to walk twenty-eight miles with each one before they got home with it.

From other pioneer stories, we know the native people living nearby were very curious about these newcomers and would often observe them and sometimes walk into a cabin unannounced. We also know they would ask for or take food because they were hungry.

The white settlers were afraid of what the Indians might do. There is a story handed down in the Miller family about some Sioux who approached the young curly haired Frank Miller while his family was away and painted his face with berry juice. Daniel Dow, who was working for the Miller family at the time, spoke to them and they left without incident, but Frank always felt they were going to kidnap him.

The Sioux and Ojibway nations were observed by the whites as having occasional forays into each other's territory to seek vengeance or create bedlam. "A midnight march, surprise, slaughter, burning and retreat, with scalps of slain foes as trophies" were observed. The Harley Hopkins family witnessed some of the battle preparations. Chester L. Hopkins, son of Harley H. Hopkins, told this story to the editors of *Old Rail Fence Corners* published in 1914:

"When I was a little boy we had a grindstone in our yard which was used by us and our few scattered neighbors. One night we were awakened by hearing the grindstone going, and father went to the door to see who was using it. A party of forty Sioux braves on their ponies were standing around, while some of the braves ground their knives which each in his turn put in his belt. It was a bright moonlight night and we could see them as plainly as if it was day. The Indians were in full war paint and feathers and after their task was accomplished, rode one after the other over the hill where they stood out like black silhouettes, and finally disappeared. They were probably going to a war dance."

The Ojibway launched a final surprise attack against the Sioux at Shakopee on May 27, 1858, which became known as the "Battle of Shakopee." The Sioux repelled the attackers after five hours of fighting. "The retreating Chippawas came up the old trail towards Lake Mille Lacs stopping overnight at the furniture factory grounds [at Minnetonka Mills] and had a war dance where Burwell School is now," stated Sarah Faribault in *Old Rail Fence Corners*. The earliest Hopkins area white settlers lived along this trail and must have experienced some of the terror of that night.

White settlers could not make legal settlement on the land until it was surveyed and brought to market. It appears the land titles in the Hopkins area in Minnetonka Township were available to be proved in October 1855, because that is when virtually all the land in the area was legally purchased from the government.

By 1855, Minnetonka Mills was quite a bustling place. It had a sawmill and furniture factory. Timber was cut at different points on Lake Minnetonka and rafted down the lake to the mill. By 1857, the Mills' furniture factory was turning out 300 bedsteads and 2000 chairs per week. By some accounts, 100 people were employed at the Mills. At least two of Hopkins' early settlers had strong ties to Minnetonka Mills in its earliest years. John P. Miller built a hotel there in 1857 that was run by William Harrington, a cousin to Simon Stevens. The Widow Gordon is believed to have cooked at Harrington's Hotel.

However, it wasn't until 1858, the year Minnesota became a state, that Minnetonka Town in Township 117 North, Range 22 West was officially established. This 36-square mile legal entity had larger boundaries than the present City of Minnetonka, which is approximately 28 square miles today. Portions of what was later to become Hopkins were carved out of this township. The easterly portions of Hopkins were originally in Minneapolis Township, the dividing line being approximately Highway 169 today.

The map of 1860 (see beginning of chapter) shows a platted town area on Minnehaha Creek where the Minnetonka Mill site was located. The sawmill built in 1852 burned in 1854 and was replaced by another sawmill with a furniture factory in 1855. By 1860, however, neither the sawmill nor the factory were in existence and many people had moved elsewhere. The census for Minnetonka Township showed 17 unoccupied company cottages in the fall of 1860. The Minnetonka town site rallied after the Civil War when Tom Perkins built a flourmill on the site of the old sawmill in 1869, but that, too, had closed by 1885.

The 1860 map is one of the earliest plat maps of Min-

netonka Township. West Minneapolis (now named Hopkins) was created out of sections 13, 24 and 25 in Minnetonka Township, and 19 and 20 in Minneapolis Township in 1893. Later, more of Minnetonka Township was annexed to Hopkins. But in 1860, only a few of the original landowners in the Hopkins area are shown on the map, namely: J. Osborn in Sect. 24, S.L. Woodard in Sect. 19, J.P. Miller in both 23 and 24, Mary Gordon in Sect. 25, and F. Peiheck (should be Pesek or Peshek) on the southeast side of Peiheck (Pesek) Lake, later known as Shady Oak Lake.

As can be seen on the 1860 map, four trails lead to the Minnetonka Mill area, in addition to a road north of the mill that is an east-west route to Fort Ridgley. Those living in the Hopkins area had several paths they could access. An east-west road connecting Excelsior to Lake Calhoun labeled "to Glencoe" is the closest road. It is reported that Harley H. Hopkins, later founder of Hopkins Station, was influential in securing the Glencoe road during the Territorial period. The actual bill for the Territorial Road from Minneapolis to Glencoe was signed in 1856 by the Minnesota Legislature and states that "Thomas W. Pierce, Edwin Hedderly and John H. Stevens were appointed commissioners to locate and mark out a Territorial road from Minneapolis to Glencoe via Lake Calhoun near Bass Lake (so called,) to John P. Miller's and thence by the way of Excelsior to Glencoe." Connecting to this Glencoe Road are two main north-south roads: one from the Minnetonka Mill area heading toward Shakopee, the other leaving the Mill area heading in a southeasterly direction to connect with roads leading to Murphy's Ferry and Fort Snelling on the Minnesota River.

It was on these early trails that the first white settlers made their way to Hopkins.

Early Settlers
Yankee Settlers
The earliest white settlers in Hopkins were native-born New Englanders, predominantly of Scotch-Irish descent, who came west as the frontier opened up hoping to cultivate the land. Much of New England town life was transferred to the various communities these serious and energetic Yankees established.

Mary (Draper) Gordon, a widow, was the first known white settler in Hopkins. In 1852, with her five sons, she settled on 160 acres in Section 25 in Minnetonka Township, south of Excelsior Boulevard and west of Hwy 169. George Andrews took a place just west of her at about the same time. George Andrews sold his land to John P. Miller in 1853 and moved farther out into Minnetonka Township.

Mary Gordon was one of the many white settlers who settled on land in the hopes of acquiring the land once it was surveyed and became legally available. Mary Gordon filed on her land in Hopkins on October 5, 1855. Her brother, Rufus E. Draper, purchased the quarter section of land north of hers in Section 25 on the same day. According to an affidavit given by Rufus E. Draper, Mary settled on her land the 7th of July 1855. She received the official land patent from the government on April 2, 1857.

Mary Gordon's family represents the many native-born New Englanders who headed west with the opportunities that abounded and kept heading west with the frontier. She stayed in the Hopkins area for less than 8 years.

Mary Draper was born in New York, the daughter of Joshua Draper and Betsey Vaughn. She married Wheeler Gordon about 1830 in Indiana. They resided for some time in Columbia, Sauk County, Wisconsin Territory where Mary's father helped establish the Biron Mill near Mineral Point. Mary Gordon had five children, her husband died in 1847 and she came to Minnesota with her father and brothers who were lumbermen and millers. In 1850, she and her children were living with the Drapers in St. Anthony before she moved to Minnetonka Township. Joshua Draper and Mary Gerdus [Gordon] were among ten who organized the First Baptist Church

Catherine (Didie) Miller and John P. Miller

of St. Anthony in 1850, and were also charter members of the First Baptist Church of Minneapolis in 1853.

If Mary Gordon came to Minnetonka Township as early as 1852 as Col. John Stevens stated in 1895 in his book *History of Minneapolis and Hennepin County*, this would be around the same time a saw mill was being established by Simon Stevens (John Stevens' brother), Calvin Tuttle and James Shaver in the Minnetonka Mills area. Knowing Mary Gordon's brothers and father were in the lumber business, she very likely moved to this area as part of the group affiliated with this sawmill that operated in Minnetonka Township north of her claim. Avery Stubbs noted that she is believed to have worked as a cook at the Harrington Hotel in Minnetonka Town.

Mary Gordon most likely left the area because of the demise of the mill. By 1860, Mary Gordon had moved farther west. She lived near one of her sons in Gordon Township (named after J.M. Gordon) in Todd Co, Minnesota. Several of her sons moved even farther west to the States of Washington and California.

John P. Miller is reputed to be the first white man to farm in Hopkins and the first person to build a frame home here. If Mary Gordon represents the many settlers who stayed only a short time in the area, John Miller represents the opposite; he lived in Hopkins over 40 years and some of his descendants are still in the area.

John P. Miller was one of the pioneers of Hennepin County. He was born in Berks County, Pennsylvania in 1809, but from his boyhood, he lived in Bucyrus, Ohio. He married Rachel Parks and had a child, Eliza Ann. After his wife died in 1837, he married Catharine Didie, also a native of Pennsylvania. They had three more chil-

One develops a feeling of great respect, admiration, even awe for the fortitude and determination exhibited by the pioneer families of this area. Most of the things we take for granted today and accept as a part of our every day living stem from the humble beginnings and toil of the pioneer group. One historian has remarked that without the immigrants of this period, the North would probably have lost the Civil War. We owe these people far more than most of us realize.

—Hugh Firmage, Former Hopkins Teacher

dren: Charles, Lucretia, and Frank (said to be the third white child born in St. Paul) and adopted a daughter, Edith Lovejoy.

In 1848, John P. Miller moved to Rockford, Illinois. In April 1849, Mr. Miller came to St. Paul, Minnesota Territory with a party of settlers that included John H. Stevens, the first white settler of Minneapolis and writer of several history books. Miller kept a boarding house and helped build the first hall in which the Legislature assembled. Daniel Steele was living with the John P. Miller family in the 1850 census. Both were listed as carpenters. Minnesota Territorial Governor Alexander Ramsey was living a few houses away.

Miller was the second or third to build on land that is now Minneapolis, the first being Colonel John Stevens, who erected the first house west of the Mississippi. Miller, a friend of Stevens' from the East, helped build Stevens' house, located then near the present Hennepin Avenue Bridge. (The John Stevens house has been preserved and was moved to Minnehaha Park where it can still be seen today.)

Colonel John H. Stevens tells the story of John P. Miller settling in Minneapolis in his 1890 book, *Personal Recollections of Minnesota and its People and Early History of Minneapolis:*

"…Colonel Francis Lee of the Sixth infantry was commander of Fort Snelling at the time. He reluctantly gave John P. Miller… a permit to occupy one hundred and sixty acres, which was subsequently known as Atwater's Addition to Minneapolis. Mr. Miller took possession of this land in August 1851… He had a partner with him in the claim, a Mr. Daniel Steele, who remained for over a year and then sold out his interest in the claim to Mr. Miller. They built a comfortable dwelling-house, barn, and stables, and broke up some eighty acres of land. For a year or two, Mr. Miller was the most extensive farmer in the colony. He remained on his claim some three years, when in consequence of uncertainty of obtaining a title to the land, he sold out for a very fair price to his neighbor, Edward Murphy. The latter soon sold to Judge Atwater, who pre-empted it in April, 1855…The Indian lands having been opened for settlers, Mr. Miller made a claim in the neighborhood of Minnetonka Mills, from which time to the present day he has been one of the most prominent farmers and citizens of the county…"

John P. Miller was in a party of nine men who trudged on horseback over roadless countryside to reach Lake Minnetonka in September, 1852. They used Simon Stevens' claim shanty at Minnetonka Mills as a base of

Engraving of the John P. Miller residence from the *Illustrated Atlas of Minnesota* published by A.T. Andreas, Chicago, IL, 1874.

operation and their journey was documented by editor Col. John P. Owens in *The Minnesotian*, a St. Paul newspaper. While on this excursion, Miller and Dr. Ames went fishing on Minnehaha Creek and immediately caught enough fish to feed 12 men, then fished for another twenty minutes and brought in more bass—40 pounds of fish altogether.

Miller first settled in Section 26 in Minnetonka Township (later to become Hopkins) in 1853. He built a log hut on the former Andrews property south of the current Excelsior Boulevard (Co Rd. 3) and in line with Ninth Avenue South. Around 1900, this was the site of the Red Wing Sewer Pipe Factory. Daniel Dow, another early pioneer, helped the Miller family move to their new home and spent his first winter in the Hopkins area living with the Millers.

After losing this property on a mortgage claim, Miller bought some property a short distance to the north. He erected a second log hut in 1860 facing south on what is now Mainstreet and 18th Avenue in Hopkins. He eventually erected a fine frame house—the first ever in Hopkins—a steel engraving of which was published in the 1874 *Illustrated Atlas of Minnesota*.

Catharine Didie Miller has the distinction of being one of a few women who made it into the old history books, her friend, Col. John H. Stevens writing this about her in 1895:

There are few, indeed, of the present generation, who have any conception of the trials and experiences of their parents, if they chanced to be among the pioneers of any of the Western territories from 1840 to 1860. Many of the present generation imagine that they have, or are, passing through many hardships... but had they been pioneers in the States of Ohio, Illinois, Wisconsin, and then in Minnesota, they would realize how bright and easy has been their voyage in the "Golden West". One of those who has passed through the experiences of pioneer life is Mrs. Miller... much beloved and honored, by those who knew her, and many hearts were saddened when she had reached her journey's end. Peacefully and quietly she passed away, March 30th, 1892, and a journey, replete with trials and vicissitudes was o'er.

Many of John and Catherine Miller's descendants were community leaders. Frank Miller married Nellie Maloney and their son, Archie Miller, was a notable politician. Archie Miller graduated from Hopkins High School in 1907 and from the Minnesota College of Law in 1918. He

was Hopkins' Justice of the Peace from 1916-1918, clerk recorder 1926-1931, board of education clerk from 1920-1931, State Senator beginning in 1931 serving rural Hennepin County and assumed the role of Lieutenant Governor of Minnesota on 6 May 1943 due to Governor Stassen's call to active duty in the Navy during World War II.

Frank Miller's grandsons, Jerre and Robert, have the distinction of being the only two brothers to serve consecutive terms as Hopkins' Mayors—Jerre Miller served from 1975 to 1981 and Robert (Bob) Miller from 1981 to 1985. Frank Miller had an interesting life, experiencing the Indian troubles and the Civil War. As a youth, he had run away to enlist in the Civil War, but was caught and brought home before he got into the Army. He met a most ignoble death in August 1930 when he was struck by a motorcycle while walking along Excelsior Avenue between 17th and 18th Avenues. He was a few months short of being 80 years old.

John P. Miller's son Charles, eight years older than Frank, enlisted to fight in the Civil War in 1861 and was the father of Will Miller and the grandfather of Grace, Keith, Dorothy, Jean and Betty Miller. A third John Miller son, Harry, was killed during World War I. Daughter Lucretia Miller married John R. Jackson and lived in the Mayview area. An adopted daughter, Edith Lovejoy, married Frank Perkins, son of a prominent doctor. Daughter Eliza had died about 1853.

Daniel E. Dow came to St. Anthony from Waterville, Maine in late 1850 or 1851. At age twenty-one, he purchased Nicollet Island in what was to become Minneapolis, for two guns, plus the previous owner threw in six steel traps and two frying pans. He lived on Nicollet Island for over a year, supporting himself by trapping pigeons and selling them to the cook at a lumber mill for seventy-five cents a dozen. He could catch eight or nine dozen pigeons a day. Dow sold Nicollet Island for a pair of oxen and a breaking plow. He also was a blacksmith for about two years, then Dow took a claim on the east side of Lake Calhoun where he most likely met his future wife, Belinda Morse (Morris) Hamilton. The Leathers family also lived on the east shore of Lake Calhoun. Mrs. Leathers was a sister to Belinda Hamilton and also moved to Hopkins.

Around 1853 Dow spent about a year working for John P. Miller who at that time was establishing his home in the Hopkins area. Dow acquired 80 acres in 1853 where the Minneapolis Threshing Machine Company plant was later built. He built a log cabin near 9th

Daniel E. Dow cir. 1890.

Avenue and 2nd St. S. and boarded with a widow and her children. In 1855, he married Belinda Hamilton who had also acquired 80 acres in the vicinity. At first Dow did not have any money to purchase a door for his cabin, so his wife sewed rags together to make a rag drop to keep the cold out all winter. After living in this cabin for a few years, the Dows built a house at 1002 First Street South.

Belinda Hamilton had been married to Charles Hamilton and had three children. Charles was a sheriff in Des Moines County, Iowa and he died either before they left Iowa or en route to Minnesota. Their children were John (born in 1848), Martha ("Mattie" born in 1851) and Charles A. (born in 1853). John enlisted in the Civil War when he was 16 and died in 1866 as a young man. Mattie married Mr. Fricks and died fairly young, in 1885. Charles married Hattie Waterman and had two sons, Austin and Archie. Charles ran a livery in Hopkins around 1888 and lived at 46-9th Avenue South in Hopkins.

Belinda Hamilton's land was between 5th and 13th Avenues from the railroad right-of-ways to Excelsior Avenue. After she married Daniel Dow, their combined 160 acres became a successful farm, plus they had extra

The interior of the Dow House Cir 1897. L-R back: Lewellyn E. (Dolly) Dow, Belinda Hamilton Dow, Daniel E. Dow, Lillian Wood Dow. Front: Hazel M. Dow, Lewellyn D. Dow.

land to sell. In 1871, the Minneapolis and St. Louis Railroad purchased a right-of-way through the Dow's property. In 1880, the Dows sold some land for the branch line of the railroad going to Minnetonka Mills and also to the Minneapolis, Lyndale and Minnetonka Railway that was later to become the streetcar line to Lake Minnetonka. The Minneapolis Threshing Machine Company was built on some of the Dow's land in 1887. These land sales resulted in enough money to build a fifteen-room house, completed in 1894, that was a local Hopkins landmark until the mid-1960s.

The Dow house had a ballroom on the third floor, the front room was finished in cherry wood, the library was in maple, the dining room was ash with oak paneling and the morning room had silk walls. The stairway walls were faced with embossed leather. There was a galvanized metal bathtub enclosed in wood. There was an ice box that was iced from outside. The house was located on the site of the present day Post Office at 9th and First Street South. The Dow house was used as the town library in its final years.

Daniel and Belinda Dow had three children. Alice, born in 1856, died in 1874 of tuberculosis. Alvin (1858-1888) also had a short life. Lewellyn E. (Dolly, 1864-1941) inherited the family home and married Lillian Wood of Excelsior. In about 1874, a traveling peddler called at the Dow home. He was a widower with a daughter about four years old. Belinda Dow offered to provide a home for the girl whose name was Minnie C. Meyst. She was adopted and raised by the Dows, married William Feudner and lived out her life in Hopkins. She passed away in 1938.

Daniel Dow was active in the real estate business after the coming of the M.T.M. factory. He sold lots to M.T.M. employees and the businesses that came with them. He built a grocery store on the southeast corner of 7th and Excelsior Avenues for his son, Dolly. Later he built a saloon for Dolly on the corner of 11th and Excelsior Avenues known as "Glueck's corner; this bar was Archies for many years and it is now Decoys. Daniel Dow served as the mayor of West Minneapolis for one year in 1898. Belinda Hamilton Dow died during that same year, on November 15, 1898. At that time Luzerne Lawton, the school principal, was living in the old Dow home at 1002 First St. S. Because of ill health, he resigned and then died shortly thereafter. Daniel Dow married Lawton's widow, Edith, sometime in 1899. Daniel E. Dow died in 1919.

The L.E. Dow grocery store built cir. 1887 was located at 7th and Excelsior Avenue, razed in 1938.

Lewellyn (Dolly) Dow lived in the big Dow home after his father died. He and Lillian had three children: Hazel M. Dow (1888-1913), Lewellyn A. Dow (1892-1912) and Ruby Dow (1894-unk.) who married Edwin C. Larson in 1916 in Duluth. Lewellyn was not as successful as his father. He operated various saloons in Hopkins and Minneapolis. He sold shoes out of his car for a while and rented out boats on Bush Lake where he lived in his later life. By 1935 he was experiencing adverse times. There had been no maintenance on the Dow home after Daniel died. Taxes were in arrears. Lewellyn Dow suggested that the Village of Hopkins take over the house and property. On August 29, 1935, the Village acquired the property for $4,300. About twenty years later, in 1954, Lewellyn died in poverty in a miserable cabin at the age of 90.

Charles and Sarah A. (Sizer) Bassett came from New York with their children and settled on an 80-acre claim next to and east of Belinda Hamilton's claim in May 1854. Their property was from 9th Street to the Poor Farm Road (now Washington Avenue). The Harley Hopkins farm lay just east of the present Washington Avenue, the dividing line between the Bassett and Hopkins farms. Whether the Charles Bassett family came before or after the Hopkins family, we don't know, but they were neighbors. Charles Bassett settled in a log cabin, but within a few years, he built a frame house for his growing family, which eventually included ten children.

Three of the Bassett's children died at an early age, including daughter Elizabeth, who died at age 16 after being kicked by a horse. One of the daughters, Clara, married William Oltman who ran a furniture store and undertaking parlor on Excelsior Avenue in downtown Hopkins for many years. The youngest Basset child, Myrtle, became Mrs. William Parsonage, of 3515 First Avenue South, Minneapolis. She told stories about her family to the Hopkins Historical Society archivist when she was 74 years old. Myrtle was the most unexpected child of the Bassetts. She was born when her mother was over 50 years old and her father over 60. The doctor had thought that Mrs. Bassett was ill and later called the fine baby girl "a very healthy looking tumor."

Mrs. Parsonage remembered many of her old neighbors, including the Dow, the Miller and the Hopkins families. She recalled dances held in the halls around

George and Amelia Burnes.

the countryside at the Dow, Campbell or Eidam homes. Mr. Dow was the regular chauffeur for the ride to the Eidam's Store on the Mills Road. Mrs. Charles Bassett loved to dance, although she had been brought up in a strict environment where dancing was forbidden. Once, after having arrived home after a vigorous session of dancing, Mrs. Bassett suddenly remembered that they had forgotten the baby at the home where the dance was held. The baby was brought home the next day and all was well.

During the frightening time following the New Ulm massacre, the Bassetts stayed at the Harley Hopkins house. Many settlers went to stay at Minneapolis hotels, including the Hopkins family.

Charles Bassett lived to be 85; he died in Hopkins April 11,1902. Sarah Bassett died at age 76 on December 17, 1911.

George M. Burnes came from Taunton, Massachusetts in 1855 with his wife Amelia Cameron Burnes and five children. Burnes purchased an ox team and wagon and brought his family to Minnetonka Mills where they first settled in a settler's cabin a short distance west of the Minnetonka Town Hall (located on Minnetonka Blvd. and Baker Rd). Mr. Burnes operated a blacksmith shop there. In the spring of 1856, they moved to a claim shanty where the main building of the Hennepin County Poor Farm later stood. In 1857, Burnes purchased 80 acres from the government on Minnetonka Blvd. In 1861, he bought the north half of the Bassett farm. A grand home was built by the Burnes family on this large farm in 1862. The Burnes family lived continuously in this home for 70 years until it was torn down

Dr. Catherine Burnes (seated) and Diana Burnes Campbell.

equip and run a general repair shop on his farm. He had a famous herd of cattle, and purchased the first steam thresher in the State of Minnesota. When this thresher was first tried on the farm in 1868, the neighbors all stayed away because they were sure it would blow up. George Burnes met an untimely death in 1870 while working with a threshing machine.

Most famous of the Burnes' children was Dr. Catherine A. Burnes, the first practicing physician in Hopkins and the first woman physician licensed by the State of Minnesota to practice medicine in 1886. "Doc Kate" would always dress in black from head to foot and is reputed to have driven a black buggy pulled by a black horse. She was born in 1849 in Massachusetts, attended the first school in Hopkins built by her father and other early pioneers. At age 18, she began her career as a teacher in Minneapolis and later taught in what is now Bloomington and Eden Prairie. In 1879, she became one of the first women graduates of the University of Minnesota. She enrolled in the Minneapolis College of Physicians and Surgeons to train as a doctor. This college was private and did not offer medical degrees, but upon completion of the course work and training, the graduates were referred to the University of Minnesota for examination. Having passed her boards, Doc Kate returned to Hopkins and practiced here for over 25 years. Always active in civic affairs, she was a headstrong individualist who believed that gender was never an obstacle to succeeding in life's challenges and was, like her father, ahead of her time.

A son, George Burnes, Jr., was village treasurer and long-time treasurer of school district No 19 (Hopkins). Daughter Diana Burnes married Samuel Campbell who started the first grocery store near Hopkins Station.

The first real blacksmith shop in Minnetonka Mills was owned by George Burnes about 1855. It was demolished about 1975 over protests of Minnetonka historian Dana Frear, who was actually crying over the thought of destroying it. Avery Stubbs reports that the bulldozer won out; he thought it was demolished to make way for the Dairy Queen stand.

Harley Holmes Hopkins was born in 1823 in Foster Center (Providence), Rhode Island. He came to the Minnesota Territory in 1854 with his wife, Eliza A. Randall Hopkins, son Chester and daughter Florinda and several other families. In this group were Zadock Spaulding, Curtis Phillips, Syles A. Seamans, George Bennett, Albert Hopkins, and Boen Briggs and their families. Five of the families decided to settle in the

in 1939. This home was the site of many social, political and intellectual gatherings of the early pioneers. In later years the Burnes' homestead was known as the Campbell farm and Anne Campbell Borland, granddaughter of Mr. and Mrs. George Burnes, lived on the old place for many years.

George Burnes was very active in the early politics of the state. His home was the meeting place for the group that founded Minnetonka Township and he was elected the first township treasurer. He donated land for the first school in Hopkins in 1862. A piano was brought to the Burnes house in 1868 and musical evenings there became events to be remembered. One group that met regularly in the Burnes home was the Minneapolis Athenaeum Club, which founded and organized the Minneapolis Public Library, George Burnes being one of the founding members. Visiting celebrities in Minneapolis were often entertained at the Burnes house as it was one of the largest in the area. There were seven bedrooms upstairs and a large dining room, living room, two bedrooms and a kitchen and pantry downstairs.

The mechanical ingenuity of Mr. Burnes led him to

This steel engraving of Harley H. Hopkins, the man after whom the town of Hopkins was named, has become the historical symbol for Hopkins.

vicinity of Lake Minnewashta and Lake Minnetonka on heavily wooded property. Harley Hopkins and Boen Briggs preempted the southwest and southeast quarter, respectively, of Section 19 in Minnetonka Township where it was not so heavily wooded. Each of the two friends constructed a shanty near the center of his claim. Harley's claim shanty, built in 1854, was on Van Buren Avenue a few rods south of Excelsior Boulevard, Briggs' site was a few rods north of the later residence of Lester Boyce on Maple Hill Road in Interlachen Addition.

Harley's 160 acres were between Washington and Harrison Avenues and between 2nd Streets North and South. In 1861, Harley built a 15-room frame house at approximately 213 Excelsior Avenue East, the site of the present Super Valu North Annex, north of Excelsior Avenue and east of Highway 169. The stone for this home's foundation was brought by ox cart from St. Paul. The town of Hopkins officially took its name from Harley Hopkins 36 years after he died.

Harley H. Hopkins descends from a noted patriot and Rhode Island politician, Stephen Hopkins, one of the signers of the Declaration of Independence. Harley possessed an adventurer's spirit, for in 1849 he went to California, via the Isthmus of Panama, in search of gold. Not striking it rich, he returned to Rhode Island and made his way to Minnesota traveling from St. Louis to

St. Paul by steamboat. Not as well known as Harley is his brother Albert H. Hopkins, who lived in Hopkins for a short while around 1859 before settling permanently in Excelsior (where he had first settled). Albert deserves to be remembered as the man who installed the first engines in the once-renowned steamers on Lake Minnetonka.

In 1871, Harley Hopkins negotiated a deal with the Minneapolis and St. Louis Railroad, who wanted to buy some of his land. Instead of selling the land outright, Harley donated the land with the stipulations that he and his wife would receive free transportation on the railroad and that a railway station bearing the name "Hopkins" be established on the property. Failure to comply would mean the land would revert back to Harley or his heirs. Harley became claim agent and station manager. The Hopkins Post Office was initially set up in the Hopkins Station. Harley was appointed the first postmaster by President Rutherford B. Hayes in 1873. Later, the post office operated from the Hopkins' home. The desk that served as the first Hopkins post office is still owned by a descendant of Harley and Eliza Hopkins.

The Hopkins' hospitality was famous and their home was a favorite stopover for people traveling between Minneapolis and Lake Minnetonka. During the Indian troubles in the 1860s, the Hopkins home provided shelter for white settlers from the Minnetonka area and points west. The household usually included four or

Eliza Hopkins.

Tombstone of Harley and Eliza Hopkins at Lakewood Cemetery in Minneapolis.

five boarders, teachers or railroad workers. The Hopkins family also raised Anna McKenzie from a baby. Anna's mother had died in a log cabin by Minnehaha Creek and her father could not take care of her, so the Hopkins family took her in and raised her.

Harley Hopkins served on the Hennepin County Board of Commissioners (1865-1868), was Hennepin County Sheriff (1869-1870) and from 1872-1882 he worked for the Minneapolis and St. Louis Railroad in addition to being postmaster. Harley died in 1882, and President James A. Garfield appointed Harley's daughter Florinda to succeed him. At this time, the post office was moved back into the Hopkins depot.

When Anna McKenzie married Frank Wade, Mr. and Mrs. Hopkins furnished them with two housekeeping rooms in their big house at 213 Excelsior Avenue. There the three Wade children (Alexina (Ali), Henry and Arthur) were born. The Wades lived in this home for many years. Alexina and Henry were still living there in 1946 when bulldozers and wreckers moved into the yard to tear down the house that had just been sold to Red Owl. In the 1860s, 70s and 80s, this house was home, boarding house, free hotel, community center, first aid station, lying-in hospital, dance hall, post office and banquet hall for the whole countryside. In it Alexina Wade saw five persons die of tuberculosis, one of them her father.

The following is from J.L. Markham guest-writing the Cedric Adams' Column in the *Minneapolis Star* of February 24, 1956:

MISS WADE is at her delightful best when calling up the pioneer yarns she heard from the lips of Grandma Hopkins. Grandma glanced out the window one after-

This photo of the Harley H. Hopkins home (far right) was taken following the 1925 tornado that hit southeast Hopkins and destroyed Justus Lumber (across the street) and parts of the M.T.M. plant.

noon and reeled at the sight of eight Indians approaching her stoop. She grabbed two freshly baked apple pies and her long butcher knife, greeted them at the door with a confident smile. She began cutting and serving the wedges to the confounded red-skins. Their belligerence was dissolved in seconds. In minutes they were motioning for seconds on the pie! Luckily there was enough pie for another go-around. And so the brave lady was able to wave the Indian lads away, all but one, after filling them up to here with her pie. This fellow insisted, via signs and grunts, that there must be one more pie left. But Mrs. Hopkins induced him in good time to git along with his pals and peddle his papers…A strange couple appeared, desperate for a roof over their heads. Mr. H. suggested they build a room onto the Hopkins hut and stay right there. That they did… A Negro chap turned up, stranded, and was taken in and raised up to 18 years. He felt he should make his own way then and departed, with the hugs and blessings of his white benefactors and a gift of $500 besides! So it went, at the Hopkins home, during those rugged pioneer years. Hospitality, charity, compassion and the good neighbor spirit ruled the daily life of all who lived under the Hopkins roof.

Chester L. Hopkins (1847-1920) was the first President of the Village of West Minneapolis.

Chester Hopkins, the son of Harley and Eliza, had been living in North Minneapolis working for the railroad, but after his mother died, about 1889, he moved back to West Minneapolis and built an 11-room house just east of where his parents had lived. This home had a novelty at the time—a bathroom. Lester Boyce came to admire the bathroom being built, so Chester invited him to come up on any Saturday night he wanted to have a bath. Grandpa Boyce took him up on his offer and on many Saturday nights thereafter, he could be seen walking the tracks to the Hopkins home with his parcel of clean clothes and toiletries ready for his bath.

Chester was the first President of the Council of the Village of West Minneapolis. His former home on Excelsior Ave. E., also was destroyed about 1946 to make way for the Red Owl Company but it was apparently taken apart and pieces were used in other homes.

Bohemian Settlers

At the same time the native-born easterners were settling in western Hennepin County, some foreign-born Bohemian immigrants were also settling here. They were fleeing the rule of the Austrian Empire who controlled their homeland, now part of Czechoslovakia.

The first Bohemians settled near Shady Oak Lake in 1853, wrote home about the abundant land here and were soon joined by others. A tightly knit ethnic Czech community was established in Minnetonka Township and north Eden Prairie. There was a break in immigration during the Civil War, but after the war ended, more Bohemians came to join their friends and relatives. In the mid-1890s, there was a third wave of Bohemian immigrants who primarily came to work in the Minneapolis Threshing Machine (M.T.M.) factory.

Francis Pesek (Peshek) and **Joseph Prib** (possibly spelled Przib) settled on the south edge of Shady Oak Lake in 1853. Shady Oak Lake was called Pesek Lake for a while. Joseph Prib lived only a short time and was buried on what was later called Chastek hill on the southeast corner of the lake. Francis Pesek liked what he found here so well that he wrote back to his relatives and friends in Bohemia, describing the area as a wonderful farming area with lots of trees for wood and a climate similar to the homeland. He spoke of America as a land of opportunity where men could make as much as a dollar a month plus room and board. As a result, a number of individuals and families came to this area the following year, thus beginning the Bohemian Settlement

William S. Smetana Pharmacy store front, 916 Excelsior Avenue.

that has a long and rich history in the Hopkins, Eden Prairie and Minnetonka communities.

Some of the early Bohemian settlers who came prior to the Civil War were: the Joseph **Smetana** family, Joseph and Frank **Bren**, Joseph and John **Makousky**, Joseph **Empanger** and family, John **Chastek**, Joseph **Holasek**, Philip **Dominick** and their families and in 1860, the Joseph **Schmeidel** family joined the group. After the Civil War, in 1868, these Bohemian families joined the colony: Winslow **Dvorak**, **Petrak**, **Feltl**, **Kokesh**, **Souba**, **Kuchera** and **Picha** families.

The Bohemian settlement from the first was self sufficient because most of the settlers were skilled craftsmen, tailors, carpenters, stone masons, cobblers, cabinet makers and the like. A tight-knit community developed and for several generations the Czechoslovakian language would be heard around the Hopkins community. Up until about 1925, a store wouldn't open its doors without having a Bohemian clerk on duty and there were many Czech-owned businesses in Hopkins.

Most Czechs who came to work for the factory lived in company homes in an area north of the Minneapolis and St. Louis Railroad tracks and west of 11th Avenue. This area of Hopkins became known as "barefoot valley" for the Czech women were industrious and frugal; being very poor, they wore shoes only on Sundays and on special occasions.

The Bohemian immigrants prized education highly and worked hard for what they accomplished; many of

their offspring achieved great success in the many fields they tackled and contributed greatly to the success of Hopkins. A count of Bohemian surnames showed 171 distinct names in the Hopkins area. Books could be written about the many early Bohemian settlers, but here we highlight only a few.

Joseph Smetana was born in Bohemia in 1838. He came to Hopkins in 1855 and rented land, which became the site of the Hennepin County Home, known as the Poor Farm. Joseph Smetana later bought 80 acres overlooking Shady Oak Lake. A settler's first task was to clear the land of trees. When Smetana was asked why the Bohemian families had chosen this heavily wooded land, he answered that the Czechs never had enough wood in Bohemia, where only the wealthy had access to what little timber there was, so he looked at the wood as an asset, not a detriment.

John Joseph Feltl, his wife Josephine Dvorak, and their eight-year-old daughter Anna and five-month-old son John Joseph Jr. left Bohemia in 1867. The voyage to America took seven weeks. The Feltl family took a train from Philadelphia, Pennsylvania to St. Cloud, Minnesota, where they traveled down the Mississippi River on a hand-propelled flatboat to Minneapolis, landing approximately where the flour mills were located. John Sr. became ill from three days of rain and could not watch the family's trunk, which was stolen. They arrived in Minneapolis with nothing except the clothes on their backs and one gun. When the citizens of Minneapolis saw the mother with the baby in her arms, they passed the hat and collected two dollars and fifty cents for the family.

The Feltl family reached Hopkins by oxen and wagon owned by Joseph Empanger who already had settled in Minnetonka Township. They stayed with various Bohemian families until some land became available in Section 36 of Minnetonka Township. At the land auction, John Joseph

John Joseph Feltl, Jr.

Feltl did not understand English enough to know what he was bidding. He assumed the upward bidding was by 25 cents on the entire 80 acres, but it actually was an increase of 25 cents on each acre. As a result, the price of the land was bid up to $17.25 per acre, an exorbitant price when the going price of land in Minnetonka Township was $1.25 per acre. Records show the actual price of the land was $10.50 per acre. In any event, the Feltls were taken advantage of, which was an unfortunate common occurrence where foreigners were concerned.

The original Feltl "home" was in a hole in the ground covered with a hay roof located in what is now the old part of St. Margaret's Cemetery. The gun—the only item not stolen on their river trip—was sold for three dollars and fifty cents to buy boards to build a small one-room house. While cutting hay, their tiny home burned down. Times became harder still and the family's diet that winter consisted mainly of frozen potatoes. Many of the early Czech settlers endured similar difficulties and hardships faced by the Feltl family.

Most amazing of all was that the Feltl family not only endured, but it prospered. The little baby boy, John Joseph Feltl, Jr., never expected to survive the journey to America, lived on the home place for 95 years. He and John Empanger are considered the fathers of the raspberry industry in Hopkins.

Jan M. Chastek was born in Brandejs, beyond Orlice, in what is now Czechoslovakia in 1837. As a 17 year old, he came to America with his parents in 1854. After a ship journey of 7 weeks and 2 days, the family traveled by train from New York City to Buffalo, Detroit, Chicago (a little village) and then to Racine, Wisconsin, where a good number of Bohemians lived. He and his father chopped wood for a living in Caledonia where they heard about Minnesota—that it had an abundance of unoccupied acreage and that it would be a good place to farm.

Below are some excerpts from Jan M. Chastek's story, published in 1905 in Amerikan Norodni, Chicago, Illinois, translated from the Czech by Betty Uherka:

There were six of us families and when we came to St. Paul, two of the younger immigrants of our group went to seek out a farmer. The following day then they returned from their mission with joyful, happy faces and with good news! We immediately ventured on to seek this new opportunity. We drove 18 miles southwest from St. Paul, and all that we could see along the way looked hopeful, for we were traveling in beautiful country!

In Minneapolis, which we bypassed along the way— at that time had only one store and one blacksmith shop. In East Minneapolis one street was completed at the present time. Portions of the Mississippi bridge had been taken down so we got across by way of a scow. After such a scenic trip we got to the assigned place and settled onto government property. This territory was in reality a wasteland—that is, wet lands, brush and ponds. There were many animals, mostly large deer and waterfowl. We had to share occupancy together with the Indians, as they were still in their rightful dwellings.

There was not a lack of meat, as there were many wild animals. Pheasants, ducks, deer, mushrooms and other wild life. This wild meat was not one of our favorite kinds of meat, but there were other concerns of greater difficulty. As far as any property—we did not have any. Instead, we brought with us a debt of $24.00. But because of the fact that we brought with us motivation and willingness to work—that is where our hope and wealth was.

I was really quite young and my father was quite old for the extremely hard work that was awaiting us. But because of these conditions, we especially put forth much effort so that we could accomplish a livelihood.

Our very first type of home was a shack made of sod, branches and brush as an attempt to protect us from the Indians. All who moved in tried to have enough soil so as to be able to grow enough crops so as to supply food for the coming year.

We planted some potatoes and corn, and each one of us waited longingly as to how the crops will turn out. How happy we were when the corn was a foot high, and later a foot and a quarter. But how extreme was our painful disappointment and our hopes when one morning we discovered that our entire field of corn was trampled down and eaten up. Two of the oxen were responsible for this from one of the settlers who had been here just a year before us. They belonged to Frank Pesek. He came from Caledonia, Wisconsin. We were all devastated over the destruction of our hopeful crop, but fortunately not for long. Not having had sufficient knowledge in regards to growing crops—we had planted the corn extremely thick and close together. The corn came up as rather weak plants as a result, but in the end it turned out that we had a much larger and abundant crop than one of the previous immigrants whose corn seemed to be more promising from the beginning of the season.

So we gradually attempted to farm, or rather struggle to make a living for six years. In the autumn of the *first year the price for the land was to be paid. We had 80 acres. We had to pay $1.25 an acre and money just was not available. We had to go to the bank and borrow. The bank loaned the money, but charged us 36% interest, which had to be paid quarterly. In order to come up with the money for the interest, we had to find a job and jobs [on] farms were about 8 miles from where we lived. I went to work with my brother-in-law—Holasek, and at the same time, my father tried to do as much work as he could at our home… On Mondays we would leave for our jobs and would return on Saturdays—not for needed rest, but rather to help out an elderly father with work on our place. It was a bitter existence. Finally conditions became, with time, somewhat improved, but in the meantime my father passed away on this place in 1862.*

To add to the difficulties, disturbing news began to arrive from the south that a Civil War was beginning. We had thousands of notions to enlist in the army as many familiar people did, but I could not forsake my aged mother in the most difficult times. Besides that, I had purchased property in the neighborhood of the Glen Lake area. It was approximately 160 acres. In spite of how I felt about wars—the draft came into effect and everyone had to register, regardless of whatever responsibilities they felt that they had. It was in the year 1864. Many tried to escape from the draft, but I and my friends Joseph Smetana and Frank Bren enlisted before we were drafted, even though all three of us had our mothers that we needed to take care of.

On the 14th day of August I was assigned to Cavalry in Hatchers Battalion for two years. Besides all this turmoil from the year 1861, the Indians from the northern states, and they even having gotten assistance from the south, were threatening even our area so at that point our family decided hastily to head for Minneapolis.

Jan Chastek was assigned to a battalion to guard the boundary line between the Indians and the settlers. He tells of how cold it was for the horses and men. His orders changed to send him to where a battle was being fought in the south but while waiting for the steamships for transport, his orders were again changed. He was assigned to Fort Ripley and spent a most severe winter with the temperature dropping to as low as 42 degrees below zero. He was discharged in May after the war was over.

During the time that I served under the stars and stripes, someone was taking care of my mother. This

immigrant was not able to be drafted, due to having lost his three fingers on his right hand at a sawmill. My property was rented for one year. The second year my brother-in-law managed it, as he also had some property in the area. Therefore my property was tended to during my time of service, with the exception of 16 acres. I gladly and willingly got busy with the work, along with whatever my mother tried to do, in spite of her age….

Before long, stood a log house—our home on this acreage in the Glen Lake area, and we also built other additions—necessary buildings for farming. My mother began getting somewhat lonesome; as I would be working outdoors much of the time, and even I began to admit that it is time that I should be getting married.

I did find a girlfriend, whose name was Anna Pribylova from Racine, Wisconsin. That is where my parents settled. The wedding was held in Racine on the holiday of St. Joseph in 1868. But when I brought my bride with me, to my property, no way did she like any of it. It is a wonder that she did not run away, as she was so extremely lonesome in this isolation! But when our family was born, the lonesomeness ended. Times became better. In a few years a railroad was built somewhat [near our place] from Minneapolis to St. Louis. It was projected to come right past our home, but the nearby lake made it not possible, so it was built one-half mile further.

The nearest train was 3 miles to Hopkins. The owner of that land, Mr. Hopkins, gave the necessary land for the railroad—free of charge—but with the conditions that he will always be able to ride on the train free. Thus the small town of Hopkins began to grow, and grow quite rapidly. A factory was built for manufacturing farm machinery (M.T.M.Co.) yet his development did not prosper as much as he would have liked at this time. At the present time Hopkins has 2 schools, a High School, some stores, saloons, a fine Masonic Temple, and Headquarters for Odd Fellows, and an Opera Hall and other fine buildings.

With the progress such as it was of a growing town, the value and cost of any property or lots elevated in price. A place to build can cost anywhere from $200 to as high as $1,000. In fact the development and progress of this town even had a great effect on the surrounding area, so that at the present time the cost of an acre is from $50 to as high as $100.

In the surrounding area there are quite a few

immigrants who are farming, as an approximate guess, about 150 families. The times and conditions have greatly changed from the time that I spent in service and returned back to live with my mother and how they have changed from when we first lived in the wilderness!

Today our property has great improvements in comparison to the previous years. We now have the necessary buildings, also cattle, grain and granaries, and needed equipment for agriculture. So much has become a reality. The buildings are protected from the north with [a] wooded hill, and there is a nearby fishing lake. Because of the fact that the land is rather near a town, it thus increases the value of the property…

In this Homestead, dwells my proud family, but it is beginning to scatter. I now look upon this soil on which I spent a large part of my life in labor and drudgery, with joy, as I realize what all has transpired.

With my guide beside me, together having raised a family successfully, and having had many unfortunate experiences, it all has been a good education, with freedom throughout it all, we all are now happy in this vast land of America, the land of freedom and opportunity. I am very grateful for it all, that peacefully I was able to overcome adversity, and now, without fear, I can look back upon it all, after having been given much strength, with a sense of accomplishment.

Frank J. Kokesh was born of immigrant parents on April 16, 1870 in Minnetonka Township. In 1892, he enlisted in the U.S. Army for three years. As a soldier in Company D, 22nd Infantry Regiment, he was stationed at Fort Keogh, Montana. He was discharged with the rank of Sergeant. (The army uniform that Frank wore can be seen at the Hopkins Historical Society.) Frank was employed at the Minneapolis Threshing Machine Company before he went into the hardware business in 1903.

Kokesh Hardware had a reputation as one of the most completely stocked hardware stores in this part of the state. It was a Hopkins institution that sat on the corner of 10th and Excelsior Avenues for well over 60 years. In 1958, the Kokesh building was moved off its foundation onto 10th Avenue, business continued in the middle of the street at the old building while a new hardware store was built. "Kokesh" continued into the third generation of owners. It became a successful sporting goods, golf and athletic store in 1966, eventually locating at Shady Oak Road and County Road 3.

Scandinavian Settlers

Skilled machinists from Scandinavia, mostly from Sweden and Denmark, also moved into the Hopkins area, establishing and running the great M.T.M. factory, as well as the town itself. While most Scandinavians did

Frank Kokesh Hardware store interior, 1904.

not face the wilderness encountered by their Yankee and Czech predecessors, one Scandinavian who did help tame the wilderness was Andrew Olson.

Andrew A. Olson was born in Kristianstad, Sweden in 1844. Christine Johnson also was from the same town. When she first came to Minnesota, she worked in a boarding house in Minneapolis and then for a Mr. Henke in his house near Lake Calhoun. Andrew and Christine were married in 1867 and came to Hopkins in 1869, where they both worked on the John P. Miller farm. Their first child, Hattie, was born in the Miller's home in 1869. In 1874, the Olsons purchased 40 acres from Ignac Souba for $600 on the north edge of present-day Hopkins, an area now occupied by the Chapel View Nursing Home and the Alice Smith School. When negotiating the deal to buy their land, the banker stated that he would let them work the land and then foreclose on them. This infuriated a stranger named Schultz, who had overheard the conversation, so he bought the land and held the $600 mortgage for the Olson family instead. This began a lifelong friendship between Olson and Schultz.

With the help of his wife and his eldest daughter, Olson cleared the land, always carrying a gun for protection against the wolves prevalent in the area. Olson's farm was successful and in 1891 he built a new home, having sold much of his land to real estate companies for $1,000 an acre. The Olson's home was known as a haven for homeless wanderers, where a meal and a bed were offered, especially to Swedish immigrants. Christine Olson was a midwife, bringing into the world many of the children born in Hopkins before 1900. She would heat pails of hot water and sterilize sheets in the oven of the kitchen stove. She was interested in Swedish Hospital in Minneapolis and supplied its first silverware. Her grandson worked as a surgeon there. Andrew Olson was the founder of Gethsemane Church. He got ten families together and they built a church with the idea that if the church fell through, the building would make a good dance hall.

Paul Swenson was born in Koge, Denmark, March

The Andrew Olson family in front of their home on Minnetonka Mills Road near 7th Avenue North, built 1887-1888.

24, 1848. He was noted for his mechanical and organizational skill with the MacDonald Threshing Machine Company of Fond du Lac, Wisconsin. The company moved to Hopkins in 1887. This was the beginning of the Minneapolis Threshing Machine Company and Paul Swenson became superintendent of the plant. Although he was barely five feet tall, Swenson became the most powerful man in Hopkins.

During his years in Hopkins, Paul Swenson was the first treasurer of the village council, served 15 years as president (mayor) of Hopkins during four different periods, was first vice president of the State bank of Hopkins (today the Norwest-Wells Fargo Bank) and then was the bank's president. He was a member of several fraternal organizations and was instrumental in building various churches and public buildings in Hopkins.

With all of Paul Swenson's power, he was a benefactor to many people in Hopkins. One such person was Charles Blomquist, who worked at the Minneapolis Threshing Company for a short time. Swenson sug-

Paul Swenson 1848-1927.

gested to Blomquist that he purchase the bankrupt Lyons Mercantile Company. Blomquist put in a bid. A few days prior to the opening of the bids, Swenson informed Blomquist that his bid was too low and encouraged him to find a partner to raise the bid. Blomquist found a partner and the company was purchased. The result was the founding of the Anderson and Blomquist Grocery. Swenson's ability to learn the amounts of supposedly sealed bids was indication of the uncanny amount of power Swenson held.

Swenson died July 28, 1927 and left instructions that his funeral rites be conducted in the fire apparatus room of the City Hall under the direction of the I.O.O.F. and Knights of Columbus lodges. His funeral was arranged by a committee comprised of Drs. Blake and Moore, Gus Japs, Frank Sefcik and S.S. Smith, a Minneapolis attorney. Burial was in the highest point available in Grandview Cemetery at the time.

Alfred Johnson was born in Sweden and brought his skills as a "smithy" to America. He arrived in Minneapolis and set up a blacksmith shop there in 1888. When he was told he could find work in Hopkins, he moved to the east end of Hopkins and continued his trade. The firing of the anvil was something that was done during the days of the blacksmith era. To celebrate the Fourth of July, the smithy would take two blacksmith anvils, place one in a normal position, spread black powder over its surface, then place the second anvil on top of it, bottom side up. A firebrand was applied, resulting in an enormous explosion.

Andrew Justus was born in 1866. At the age of 15 he left Sweden alone and came to America. He worked for the C. A. Smith Lumber Company in Minneapolis. In 1893 he moved to West Minneapolis and started its first lumber business with two other partners on land between Excelsior Avenue East and the M. & St. Louis Railway tracks east of Washington Avenue. Less than three months later, on June 30, the panic of 1893 threatened to put a quick end to a fledgling business. But Andrew Justus' dream of a better life carried him through and four years later, he was able to buy out his partners.

"Every Time a Square Deal" was the Justus Lumber trademark. The company grew with the growing town. Andrew Justus put in long hard days piling and loading lumber, hitching and caring for his team of horses and

The Alfred Johnson Blacksmith Shop located on the north side of Excelsior Avenue at Tyler Avenue.

doing whatever was needed to build his business. The lumber company remained at its original location for 78 years, from 1893 to 1971 and was run by three generations of Justus men. In 1971, the business moved to its present location at Eleventh Avenue South and Excelsior Boulevard (County Road 3).

Christian Tosteson was the creative force behind the Minneapolis Threshing Machine Company, the backbone of Hopkins for many years. He was the mechanical genius behind the threshing machine separator, one of the most important inventions of its day. It is said he turned down the job of being superintendent of the factory and recommended Paul Swenson instead. He was remembered as an exceptionally fine person, kind to everyone and genuinely interested in helping others. He started the Methodist church in Hopkins and urged the Johnson brothers to open a meat market, which thrived on the main street of Hopkins for many years, later changing to Hovander's and then Tait's grocery stores. He was also instrumental in getting the Anderson Brothers to open a dry goods store in Hopkins.

Levi Longfellow came from Machias, Maine, to St. Anthony, Minnesota, in 1852 when he was 9 years old. His father, Jacob Longfellow, was a lumberman. Levi Longfellow was the creative force that created the town of Hopkins, but he never lived in Hopkins.

Levi Longfellow was President of Longfellow Brothers Company, Commission Merchants, fruit and produce, located at 6th St. and 1st Ave. N., in Minneapolis, established in 1870. He put together the deal that brought the Minneapolis Threshing Machine Company to Hopkins.

Longfellow acquired the Dow properties (160 acres) in December 1886. He then offered 40 acres to the M.T.M. Company at no cost if on January 1, 1888 they had a brick factory building operating with at least 100 employees. The company succeeded in meeting the deadline. Longfellow was the largest stockholder of the new M.T.M. Company, owning about 50% more than John McDonald, the organizer of the company. He was also the Treasurer of the company.

Immediately after the factory was built, Longfellow platted "West Minneapolis First Division." The West Minneapolis Land Co., of which Longfellow was a member, platted "West Minneapolis Center." With the influx of workers at the M.T.M., Longfellow was busy selling lots for homes and businesses.

Levi Longfellow became State Commander of the Grand Army of the Republic (G.A.R.) in 1906, was an

original Trustee for Asbury Hospital in Minneapolis, was a member of the Board of Trustees of the Minneapolis Soldiers Home and a Charter member of Hennepin Avenue Methodist Church. He donated land for the Methodist church in Hopkins. Longfellow lived at 1806 La Salle Avenue, Minneapolis. He had two daughters, Beatrice and Grace, and a son, Newton. He died at age 83 on February 26, 1926.

Railroads and Streetcars

John P. Miller...at the ripe age of 85...lived to see from his front door the smoke of five steam locomotives upon five different lines or railways and [was] able to walk to the three railway stations within a mile of his home." [J.P. Miller lived until July 1894.]

—"Minnetonka Mills Early History" from the *History of Hennepin County*, by Atwater and Stevens, 1895

The first railroad to run through Minnetonka Township was the St. Paul, Minneapolis and Manitoba (later the **Great Northern**), which ran through Minnetonka Mills to Spring Park on the north shore of Lake Minnetonka beginning in 1867. This train connected to James J. Hill's Hotel Lafayette on Minnetonka Beach and started the legendary tourist industry on the lake, which had its heyday in the 1880s and early 1890s.

The second railroad through our area was built in 1869 by the Minnesota Valley Railroad Company, which was a line from Minneapolis to Merriam through Hopkins. This later became part of the Chicago and Northwestern Railroad.

The most important railway for our area was the **Minneapolis and St. Louis Railroad (M.&St.L.)**, which began buying land from property owners for a railway right-of-way through Hopkins in 1870. Their goal was to attain an independent outlet to the south and the east from Minneapolis to haul flour and lumber from the Minnesota heartland to the eastern and foreign markets. On June 23, 1870, the *Minneapolis Tribune* reported 50 men had started building the line. We can only imagine the excitement of our earliest pioneers when on November 25, 1871 the inaugural steam engine chuffed out of Minneapolis and traveled through Hopkins on its way to Carver and Sioux City Junction. Soon thereafter, trains were running through Hopkins all the way to St. Louis, Missouri on a regular schedule.

The Hopkins Band and a Milwaukee Railroad steam train loaded with threshing rigs at the M.T.M. factory, about 1900.

The first railroad station was built in 1872 or 1873 by the M.&St.L. on land acquired from Harley H. Hopkins with the stipulation that it be named "Hopkins."

Around 1880, more land was acquired for the Pacific Division of the M.&St.L. connecting to Lake Minnetonka and beyond to South Dakota. This line made a sharp turn to the northwest a short distance past the Hopkins depot. (This line today is the walking path that runs north of Maetzold field.) When completed as far as Excelsior, the M.&St.L. began conducting excursions from Minneapolis to Lake Minnetonka and Lake Waconia, Hopkins being a stop along the way. On one of the

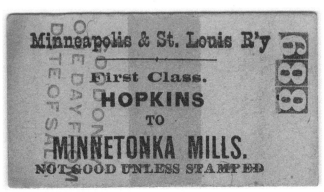

M.&St.L. ticket from Hopkins to Minnetonka Mills, April 1, 1893.

first trips, a nearly empty excursion train collided with another train from Minnetonka City just after the track curved. The head-on collision occurred in Souba's field between Fifth and Fifteenth Avenues north. The engineers and firemen from both trains jumped free but they were unable to rescue the only passenger, a young Hopkins Station telegraph operator, Miss Minnie Reeve, who was scalded by the hot water from the steam engine and died later at the Harley H. Hopkins residence.

The M.&St.L. was the first standard-gauge railroad to serve the southern Lake Minnetonka region. The people in Excelsior were excited at the coming of the train. Two large hotels were erected to serve the elegant tourists from as far away as Chicago or St. Louis who now had a way to access the legendary Lake Minnetonka. The Minnetonka Lake Park Hotel (later called the Lake Park and owned by the M.&St.L.) and the Hotel St. Louis were the first grand hotels built on the southern part of Lake Minnetonka. The coming of the "Louie" railroad made it possible for south Lake Minnetonka to develop even more than the northern part.

The M.&St.L. did a grand passenger business through Hopkins to Lake Minnetonka beginning in the 1880s but competing railways took their share of the business.

TIME IS MONEY

West Minneapolis, the great residence and manufacturing suburb of Minneapolis, is the largest railroad center West of Chicago, being the junction of seven great lines covering the entire West and Northwest. Over forty passenger trains alone daily. Distance only three miles from the city limits, and fifteen minutes ride from the city depots, with a ten cent fare. The direct and only route to far-famed Lake Minnetonka, the greatest watering place of the Northwest, the terminus of the city Motor Line.

Minneapolis Threshing Co. Works, Minneapolis Smelting Co. Works, West Minneapolis Roller Mill Co. Works, North West Wood and Iron Co. Works, with other contemplated manufactories, employing one thousand men. This suburb is unsurpassed in beauty of landscape and natural scenery, in the garden lands between the city and the lake, and easier and pleasanter of access than Lake or Thirtieth Streets in the city, where lots are sold for $2,000 and $2,500 each. Lots in West Minneapolis for sale from $300.00 to $600.00 each, on easy terms. "A stitch in time saves nine." Buy early. BARTLETT & PARKER, 221 Bank of Minneapolis Building, Minneapolis, Minn.

—from *Map of West Minneapolis and Surrounding Country*, 1888.

The Great Northern had built a Wayzata station in 1879 and was doing a brisk business on the north shore of Lake Minnetonka. It dropped a line down through Hopkins called the Hutchinson Division (named after Hutchinson Junction in St. Louis Park) to compete with the M.&St.L. on the south shore of the lake. It built along the abandoned right-of-way of the "motor line" to Excelsior and continued on to St. Bonifacious and Hutchinson. This is the railroad track that enters Hopkins from the northeast behind the Supervalu North Annex (formerly Red Owl) building and intersects with all the other railroad lines in a tangled interchange at Excelsior Avenue east and Highway 169.

The original "motor line" was a narrow gauge (3 foot) steam powered railway that ran from Lake Harriet to Excelsior from July 20, 1882 until the line was abandoned in August 1886. The "motor line" came through the southern edge of Interlachen Park and crossed the Milwaukee & M.&St.L. tracks at Hopkins, then traveled via 2nd Street South of Hopkins through the Glen Lake area to Excelsior.

The **Chicago, Milwaukee and St. Paul and Pacific Railroad (C.M.&St.P.)** (also known as the Milwaukee Road) constructed a 28-mile line from South Min-

neapolis to Benton Junction (now Cologne, Minnesota) in 1880 that came through Hopkins, paralleling the M.&St.L. but split off and veered south through Shady Oak Lake while the M.&St.L. went north of the lake. Shady Oak Lake used to be one lake until the Milwaukee Railroad built two trestles across it that divided it into three lakes. One of the trestles sank to the bottom of the lake and had to be rebuilt. In 1889, the C.M.&St.P. built a 7.84-mile spur from Hopkins to Deephaven, virtually to the doors of the four-story Hotel St. Louis.

The depression of 1893 put a crimp on the tourist business, as did the railroad expansion throughout the country, which made it possible for other vacation spots to develop. About the turn of the century, the Great Northern quit Lake Minnetonka's south shore and extended its line from Spring Park along the northern side to St. Bonifacious. Upon completion of this line, the Great Northern abandoned their line between Hopkins and St. Bonifacious. This abandoned Great Northern line became the streetcar route in 1905. The Hotel St. Louis was torn down in 1905 and

Map of Minnetonka Township of 1874 shows two railways in the area—the St. Paul & Pacific (later The Great Northern) running through Minnetonka Mills area on its way to Wayzata and beyond and the M.& St.L. running through Hopkins on its way to the Minnesota River Valley and Sioux City Iowa. Andreas, *Illustrated Atlas of the State of Minnesota*, Chicago, IL, 1874.

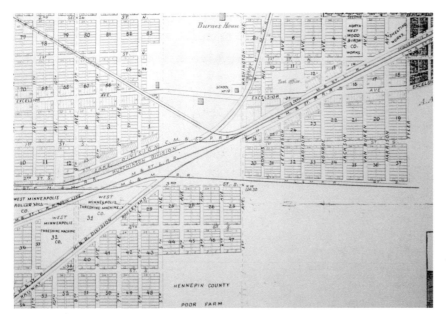

Most of the major train lines through Hopkins were in place by 1888. From the *Map of West Minneapolis and Surrounding Country*, A. Hageboeck, lithographer, Minneapolis, Minnesota.

people TO the lake, while the yellow "streetcar boats" carried throngs ON the lake. The streetcar boats were named after the main routes of the electric railroad. One of the boats was named the "Hopkins."

The Lake Park Hotel was razed and by 1926, the streetcar boats had ceased to run as part of the trolley's fleet. Six years later, the trolley service was discontinued west of Hopkins and the Minnetonka streetcar lines were scrapped.

The era of hotels, commuter trains, interurban cars and lake steamers ended and in its place came private homes on Lake Minnetonka and blacktopped highways. Passenger service eventually ended but the M.&St.L. continued to serve Hopkins until the 1960s in an even greater role—that of shipping its freight.

with its demise, the Milwaukee Road ceased running into Deephaven.

Meanwhile the Lake Park hotel was operating at a deficit and the M.&St.L.'s equity in that business was purchased by the Minneapolis & St. Paul Suburban Railway under the leadership of Thomas Lowry. The trolley line also leased the short Tonka Bay branch so that its cars could reach the hotel. At the same time, the electric road built its own tracks from Hopkins to Manitou Junction, partly using the Great Northern's right-of-way along County Road 3 south of downtown Hopkins. It leased the Milwaukee's line to Deephaven, bought a fleet of boats, constructed several more and for two decades the yellow trolleys brought a multitude of

Of far greater importance to the development of Hopkins than the transportation of settlers or tourists is the economic opportunity that the railroads provided. It was sheer genius that the great Minneapolis Threshing Machine Company, major maker of farm machinery in an emerging farm economy, located west of the mill city in 1887 and by 1889 found itself neatly tucked in a wedge of land between the M.&St.L. and C.M.&St.P. railroads, with close access to the Great Northern. Location, indeed!

Throughout the years, various feeder lines were built directly to the docks of the many manufacturing businesses in Hopkins, which accounts for the tangle of rail lines in the industrial parts of town.

The streetcar boat the Hopkins, operating on Lake Minnetonka.

A postcard showing the interior of the Minnetonka Fast Electric Car, Twin Cities lines (left) and a vertical depiction of the car (right). Photo compliments of Dean Empanger.

In the 1960s, three railroads were still running through Hopkins—the M.&St.L., the Milwaukee and the Great Northern. The Chicago and Northwestern bought the M.&St.L. in the 1960s. On June 21, 1980 the last train ran on the former M.&St.L tracks. Today, the only railroad that comes through Hopkins using the former Milwaukee tracks now owned by the Canadian Pacific is the Twin Cities and Western, which has trackage rights on these tracks.

The Depots. Hopkins has had several railroad depots. The original M.&St.L. depot that Harley Hopkins knew was replaced by a new red brick depot about 1903. This is now the Depot Coffee House. It is located close to where the original Hopkins depot sat, but is set back from Excelsior Avenue more than the original one.

On January 8, 1912, a Great Northern Railway Station was opened at Hopkins with James A. Tobin as the first agent. This station was located north of Excelsior Boulevard approximately where Highway 169 is now. A second Great Northern Depot was built at 2nd Street South and 9th Avenue south. This neat white building was loaded onto a flatcar and moved in 1966 to the north side of Cedar Lake to be used as a work building for the railroad.

The only depot in Hopkins that is still used by the

A train carrying sugar beets headed to Chaska to be refined into table sugar. Photo taken by the Hopkins depot November 6, 1946.

The M.&St.L. Railroad Depot in Hopkins, now the Depot Coffee House.

Throughout the 1870's, the rails advanced—often along Indian trails and buffalo paths—into the wheat-lands and forests. Railroads opened the interior of Minnesota to farming; new settlers, aided by the colonization projects of the railroads, poured in; land values increased. Carloads of wheat were hauled eastward while machinery and farming implements moved westward over the rails in an ever-increasing flow. Towns and cities got their start from the railroad and grew up along the right-of-way.

—"Minnesota's Railroads, Their Part in the Development of the State," by the Association of American Railroads, Washington, D.C.

The Milwaukee Railroad Depot now owned by the Canadian Pacific is still in use in Hopkins. This building dates back to about 1925. The original C.M.&St.P. depot was severely damaged in the 1925 tornado that destroyed Justus Lumber nearby.

Burlington Northern trains were the last to use the former Great Northern spur track to Hopkins. Photo taken circa 1970.

railroad is the Milwaukee Depot, south of Excelsior Avenue and west of Highway 169. It is a work building used by the Canadian Pacific Railroad, the only railroad remaining in 2002.

Streetcars. In 1897, work began on Hopkins' first streetcar line. Known as the "Walker Line," regular service began on June 16, 1899. T.B. Walker, a lumberman, built a streetcar line that came through St. Louis Park along Lake Street, traveled on Monk Avenue in a southwesterly direction to its terminus in Hopkins at the "Bushnell Station" at about 6th Street and 1st Street North (where Tremont Plaza Hotel is today). It couldn't go any farther because the Great Northern railroad would not give them permission to cross their tracks. Walker's "Black Maria" line consisted of two cars that had long benches but no seats as such. Walker's service made possible a general exodus out of Hopkins to Minneapolis on Saturday nights. Hopkins residents would go to see shows at the Dewey and Bijou on Washington Avenue in Minneapolis and to use the banks, which were open until 9:00 p.m. On the return trip, the car was often so overloaded that the men would have to get out and shove the car up the grade at Oak Hill.

In the fall of 1905, the Twin City Rapid Transit Company started streetcar service between Minneapolis and Hopkins. Passengers were initially unloaded at

the M.T.M. plant, but on June 17, 1906, a spur track was completed that ran up to Ninth and Excelsior Avenues. By 1912, Hopkins residents could take advantage of four inter-urban lines. City-to-city fare was ten cents, which was collected in two fares of five cents each, allowing passengers to transfer at either end of the line to any local streetcar they wanted. The 390 miles of standard gauge track ran from south Stillwater on the St. Croix River to Tonka Bay at Lake Minnetonka. The excursion cars out to Lake Minnetonka went quite a bit faster after crossing the trestle in Hopkins, often hitting speeds of 60 mph.

In the early 1900s, streetcars ran 31 round-trips a day from Minneapolis to Excelsior beginning at 4:03 a.m. and ending at 11:03 p.m. In addition, there were 8 round-trips a day from Minneapolis to Deephaven, with 10 on Sundays. Thus, Hopkins' residents had 39 round-trips available each day, with more on Sundays. From Hennepin Avenue at Washington in Minneapolis to Excelsior it was 18 miles and the trip took 42 minutes. One statistic showed 92,000 passengers per summer were transported to Lake Minnetonka on the streetcars. Hopkins experienced a major loss when the streetcars were discontinued.

By 1932, competition from private autos and buses was too much for the streetcars and all the rails west of

The T.B. Walker streetcar.

Streetcar heading east toward Minneapolis at 9th Avenue South in Hopkins. The railway trestle can be seen in the background. There was no streetcar "depot" in Hopkins except for this small shelter next to the Great Northern Depot. Photo from "Twin Cities Lines—The 1940s," Aaron Isaacs, editor, MN Transportation Museum.

Hopkins were removed. The end of the line and turnaround became 9th and Excelsior Avenues in Hopkins. Service to Hopkins continued until the end of July, 1951, when because of lack of business, it was decided that cars would "loop" at Brookside station in Edina, not in Hopkins. Streetcars soon faded from the scene. There have been many regrets about the loss of streetcar transportation through the years, but Hennepin County has been purchasing abandoned railroad beds since at least the early 1980s to be used as a commuter rail transportation corridor in the future.

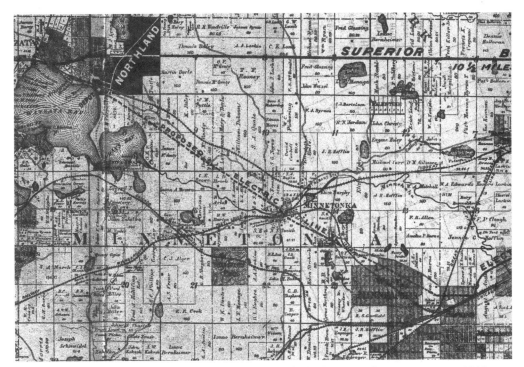

Early land speculators had many big ideas, only some of which came to fruition. Here in a 1901 advertisement for "Northland" (which never worked out), is a proposed electric line through Hopkins, which was never built, following the route of Minnetonka Mills Road.

Meanwhile, many of the abandoned railroad beds have been turned into the Hennepin County Regional Trail System that provide walking and biking opportunities for many of Hopkins' citizens.

The Elevated Streetcar viaduct south of downtown Hopkins. Two big trestles were built to go over the tracks near Ninth Avenue South.

"[This photo is] a view looking west toward a bridge crossing the main lines of the M.&St.L. and the C.M.& St.P. railroads in south Hopkins. The bridge was built by the Twin City Rapid Transit Company for use by the Excelsior line, the Deephaven line and the Como-Hopkins line. The year of the photo may have been in the late teens or early nineteen-twenties. The building shown at the left is one of the several occupied by the Minneapolis Threshing Machine Company and succeeding owners. The camera was located at about Fifth Avenue South. There may have been, even at that time, a road crossing the railroad tracks at that point and leading south to the area then called Peaceful Valley. The water tank seen in the background was a part of the water system servicing both the city and the manufacturing plant.

[This photo] is of particular interest to me. In those days, I lived on Excelsior Avenue where the Red Owl plant is now located. From our home, we could see the bridge and the cars as they passed over it. In 1915, I started to regularly commute to work in Minneapolis and the streetcars provided a clean and reliable way to travel. For me to reach the car stop at Third Avenue, it was necessary to traverse a path through an open field now the site of the plant of Super Valu Stores Inc. I learned that if I saw an east-bound car on the bridge at about the location of the car in the picture there was ample time for me to catch it.

Therefore, each weekday morning for about eight years as I left home I would look toward the bridge to determine whether I could walk leisurely to the car stop or whether I must run. I believe that I never failed to catch the streetcar but there were seldom many seconds to spare."

—Henry H. Wade

Published in the *Hopkins Review* November 21, 1979.
Henry Wade lived in the former Harley H. Hopkins
house until the mid-1940s.

From "West Minneapolis" to "Hopkins"

In the southwest quarter of Section 19 of Minnetonka Township, lived the pioneer Harley H. Hopkins. In 1871, Harley gave some land to the M.&St.L. Railroad with the stipulation that the station be named "Hopkins Station." Soon, a post office was set up in this station that also bore the name "Hopkins" and Harley H. Hopkins was appointed postmaster.

About fifteen years later, in 1887, the Minneapolis Threshing Machine Company built a factory about a mile west of the Hopkins depot. The company formed the West Minneapolis Land Company and proceeded to purchase the west one-half of the Harley Hopkins farm except for the site of the Hopkins home. (Harley H. Hopkins had died in 1882.) The land company platted the entire 160 acres into the "West Minneapolis Center" subdivision.

Within a couple of years, with the factory in operation, a land boom erupted. Only six years after the founding of the Minneapolis Threshing Machine Company, a petition to incorporate the Village of West Minneapolis stated there were 1,105 persons living in the Village on October 12, 1893. The petition also listed ten subdivisions that had already been filed with the County Auditor of Hennepin County; eight of the subdivisions included the name "West Minneapolis" in their title.

Upon presentation of the petition in 1893, the county auditor appointed several men to post the notice of election to approve the incorporation: "said election to take place November 18, 1893 at Olson Hall, situated over the post office at **Bushnell, Minn.**, and being on the 3rd floor of the brick building on the corner of Excelsior and Ninth Avenues."

Some explanation of the word "Bushnell" is in order. Up to this point in history, the Hopkins post office had been located in the eastern part of the community near the M.&St.L. railway depot, also known as the Hopkins Depot. However, on July 21, 1892, the M.T.M. Company managed to get another post office approved nearer to its headquarters. It was named after an M.T.M. and West Minneapolis Land Company official, John B. Bushnell, but operated out of a store on the corner of Excelsior Ave. and 9th run by a man named John D. Helps. Helps is listed in the 1893-94 Minneapolis City Directory as president and treasurer of the West Minneapolis Supply Company, with his residence in West Minneapolis, and also as the Postmaster of the Bushnell Post Office. For a period of three years, until August 15,

J.F. Koblas, Helmer Olson, Vaelao Talton, Stephen Paolik, Edward Hollister, Wm Lauer, M.H. Edom, Chas. F. Haish, A.C. Anderson, John Petsack, Frank Wachuta, H.H. Frank, Otto Holmberg, P.O. Swanson, C.J. Anderson, Jos. Miller, H. Anderson, M. Olson, H. Hanson, Charles Clauson, Frank Sackrison, Fred Souba, James Fillipi, Andrew A. Olson, Fred A. Lack, Andrew Nelson, John Kirjunrjpti, J. Matson, August J. Person, T.A. Johnson, E.A. Close, J. Fogelberg, C. Bassett, Hans Swenson, W. Bettshart, Jos. Hamack, Frank Levenrose, H.A.C. Thompson, C. Tostenson.

Signers of the Petition to incorporate the Village of West Minneapolis, October 12, 1893. (From the newspaper so the spelling of some of the names is probably wrong.)

1895, there were two post offices: Hopkins in the east and Bushnell in the west. During this indecisive time, the community voted to take the name "**West Minneapolis.**" The incorporation of the Village of West Minneapolis became effective at 3:00 p.m. on the afternoon of November 27, 1893.

The confusion of post office names soon resolved itself. In 1894, Edward Eidam was appointed postmaster. He relocated the Hopkins post office to his store in the 700 block of Excelsior Avenue, thus pleasing the M.T.M. Company officials. Soon after, the Bushnell post office was merged with the Hopkins post office.

Most people came to refer to the town as "Hopkins" not knowing nor recognizing that the official governmental unit was called "West Minneapolis." Even

Letter addressed to the Bushnell Post Office, early 1890s.

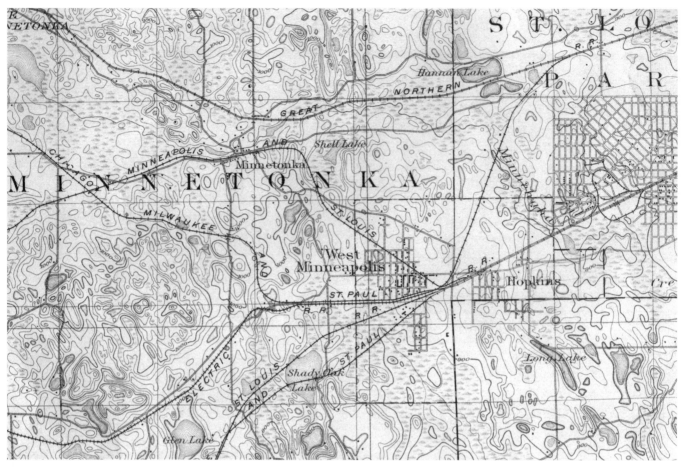

Both West Minneapolis and Hopkins are shown on this 1916 map from the *Geologic Atlas of the U.S., Minneapolis-St. Paul Folio,* by Frederick W. Sardeson, Washington, D.C.

mapmakers listed two areas, both Hopkins and West Minneapolis.

One can imagine the nightmare for a village clerk who had to file papers with the "West Minneapolis" title while everyone else referred to the area as "Hopkins." In 1928, after 35 years of ambiguity, Archie H. Miller, West Minneapolis Village Clerk, drew up a resolution to change the name of the village to "Hopkins." The Village Council promptly adopted the resolution and on August 16, 1928, the Village began to carry the name that old pioneer Harley H. Hopkins had insisted upon— Hopkins.

The First Village Government

The first West Minneapolis village council meeting was held on December 19, 1893. The only business transacted was a motion instructing the President of the Council, Chester L. Hopkins, to employ Captain Cross as village attorney to do what was necessary to establish a village government. Besides Chester Hopkins, the first village council also included Fred Souba, Andrew A.

Olson and William Hosp as trustees and E.A. Close as recorder.

Two months later, on February 20, 1894, the village council adopted Ordinances 1-14, covering such problems as misdemeanors, breaches of the peace, disorderly conduct, drunkenness and nudity. Disorderly houses and prostitution were covered in one ordinance. Others dealt with vagrancy, gambling, outhouses, slaughterhouses, nude bathing, discharge of firearms and fast driving. (Horses, mules or other animals were restricted to 8 miles per hour.) Fishing and hunting were forbidden on Sunday. The need to control some of these problems may have been the reason for the incorporation of the village.

In the summer of 1895, an ordinance to regulate and license auctioneers, peddlers, billiards, pool, bowling and saloons was adopted.

The growing population soon began to change the town from having rural to city problems. In April 1901, the council adopted an ordinance establishing a system of house numbers, the system that still sets our city apart from the numbering system that governs the rest of the Metro area. In August of 1901, a city water system was approved, along with authorization to issue $15,000 in bonds to pay for the system. In 1903 authorization was given to the Northwestern Telephone Exchange Company to install a telephone system in town. By that time, dogs had become a problem. An ordinance providing for licensing dogs—$1.50 for male and $3.00 for female—and for appointment of a "dog killer" to catch and dispose of dogs not conforming to the ordinance was adopted in May 1904.

In 1905, the council approved an ordinance authorizing the Minneapolis and St. Paul Suburban Railway Company to operate street railway lines within the village, with the fare established at 5 cents per ride. A week later authorization was granted the Tri-State Telephone and Telegraph Company to operate a second telephone system in the village. The Tri-State system would provide for communication with Minneapolis and the rest of the world. The Northwestern system was a local system.

Also in May 1905, the council ordered the sale of bonds totaling $12,000 for the purpose of building and equipping a municipal gas works. That action established a coal fueled plant that furnished the town with heating and lighting gas until 1930 when the system was sold to the Minneapolis Gas Company, at which time Hopkins was connected to the larger system and the coal system was abandoned.

The village was off to a great start. Members of the village council often had lengthy tenures in the early years. Chester Hopkins was president (mayor) for two terms, William Hosp was a trustee for 12 years, E.A. Close was recorder for 27 years and Fred Souba was mayor for five years. Many men, once elected to the council, spent many years on it, such as Louis Lundquist who spent 11 years as treasurer, Emil Peterson, who was a trustee for 13 years; Dr. G.W. Moore was mayor for 12 years, setting a record only superceded by Paul Swenson who spent 15 years as mayor.

What "Hopkins" Had About 1900

Although West Minneapolis was a small community when it was incorporated as a village in 1893, it grew rapidly around the turn of the century. By 1910, there were 533 families and 468 dwellings. The commercial area was growing rapidly.

It would be impossible to mention all the merchants located in the village over time; there were too many

Hopkins actually obtained its first street lights before the turn of the century. (Two kerosene lamps were installed in 1897, one at the M.& St.L. railroad depot, the other near the Methodist church on ninth Avenue South.)

After much needling in 1899 by Editor H.L. Hollister of the Hopkins News, village fathers added three sputtering coal oil lamps at Seventh, Eighth and Ninth, and burdened Constable Al Cooper with the task of turning them on and off, which probably makes Constable Al the community's first lamplighter.

Shortly after the 20th century was ushered in, the village went all out and installed a new fangled pressure gasoline light system...

businesses that came and went without leaving a record. A few businesses were established about the turn of the century and they are still operating today. These will be further discussed in the next chapter.

The newspapers can give us some insight about what was located in the village at the beginning of the 20th century. *The Hopkins News* published every Saturday by Harold L. Hollister, carried advertisements for the following businesses on March 3, 1900:

P.O. Swanson, General Merchandise

J.J. Koçourek Hardware

Marsh's Drug Store

North Star Provision Co.

J.F. Koblas, prop. Meats, fish, butter, eggs

E.H. Eidam Store, general merchandise

Anderson Brothers Dry Goods

W.A. Smith Contractor and Builder
    (leave orders at Smetana Drug)

J.Y. Kern, Manufacturer of Union Label Cigars

West Minneapolis Fuel Co (wood and coal),
    E.A. Close, Proprietor

Gordon and Son Bicycles

Wm. S. Smetana Prescription Druggist

Oscar Quist Shoes

Chas. Boehm Wood Sawing

PANORAMIC VIEW OF HOPKINS TAKEN FROM STREET CAR BRIDGE.

This masterful panoramic view of Hopkins was taken from the streetcar bridge and published in the July 26, 1906 Hopkins News. The octagonal building in the center was the gas works building.

Anton A. Olson, The Grocer (everything first class)

Hotel Hollister, rates $1.00 per day,
   Edward Hollister, Proprietor

EXCELSIOR AVENUE, LOOKING EAST.

Mr. and Mrs. C.A. Bacon inside their Bacon drug store, southeast corner of 8th and Excelsior Avenue.

M.E. Nelson, Barber

Lewis Peterson, Restaurant

R.J. Mather Barber Shop

Depew Transfer Co., Trunks 50 cents to the City

Charles Hamilton, first class Livery Barn

D.E. Dow selling house for $4,000
   2 1/2 miles from Hopkins

Mrs. Truman's Millinery, first class Dressmaking

Additional items of interest from this newspaper:

- "Misses Lind and Lillygren will be absent from their millinery store for two weeks."
- "A total abstinence society will meet in the I.O.O.F. hall."
- Arbor day was observed with the planting of trees near the school.
- There was a separate news column for "The Thresher Works."

The Hopkins News of May 7, 1903 contained advertisements for many firms not listed three years earlier:

Albert F. Anders, New Livery Stable

S.E. Svec, Staple and Fancy Groceries

Jos. Hamack, Clothing Store
   (featuring suits priced from $7-16)

J. Truman and Beckman Shoes (for women)

P.J. Vonderloh, Hardware

A.B. Peterson, Contractor and Builder

Western Lumber Co.

E.S. Brown, Barber

C.A. Bacon Drugs

Mrs. C. Wasserziehr, Mandolin and Guitar Teacher, 627 1st Ave S.

Prof. Ernest Fleck, Teacher of band, orchestra, violin and stringed instruments

John Shonka, new line of Spring Goods

Anderson & Blomquist, General Merchandise

Hollister and Smetana Real Estate

J.R. Scales, Barber

Nels S. Wolff, Painter and Paper Hanger

C.M. Reed, House Painter

Dr. John Watson, Physician

Chas Swedberg, Watches

Curtis and Smith, Laundry

James Blake, Physician, Marsh Building

Dr. A.B. Sweet, Physician

There was a railroad timetable in this newspaper and the news that the Hennepin County Commissioners had agreed to "open the cross road leading to the Boulevard from Hopkins." Mr. Fred Souba was present and commented, "It is one of the best improvements that could be made."

The Hopkins News of July 26, 1906 was a special issue featuring Hopkins and had many large ads in addition to good photographs of the town. Note that the term "Hopkins" was used exclusively in this article; one would not know that the town's name was "West Minneapolis." Here are some additional establishments mentioned in this issue:

First National Bank

Smetana's Pharmacy and Ice Cream Parlor

J.O. Harrison, Hardware and Stoves

Swedberg & Shaughnesey, Photographic Studio

Moran Boiler Co

William Strobeck Furniture Dealer and Undertaking

B.C. Decker, Barber Shop

Brown's Barber Shop (union shop)

Hopkins Steam Laundry

The Columbia Saloon, wine, liquors and cigars Birkhofer Beer always on tap (J.J. Kopesky) "come in and be treated right"

Ad for Swedburg & Co., "Up To Date Jewelers and Photographers."

Swedburg & Co., 809 Excelsior Avenue about 1912-16.

Wm. Oltman, Sewing Machines, Funeral Director and Undertaking

J. Erickson's Billiard and Pool Room, in I.O.O.F. Block

J.M. Hogan's Barber Shop, in Odd Fellows Block Corner Excelsior & 9th. Friday is ladies Day, 10 Baths for $1.75, shower and tub baths

The August Hentschel and Charles Blomquist grocery store, 810 Excelsior Avenue, about 1907-1914.

Kocourek & Bren Hardware

Sorensen & Wallace, Caterers, Hopkins Bakery, board by day or week

John Klopp, Blacksmith and Carriage Worker

W.J. Miller & Co, Dress Goods

Ziegler & Neubhauer, successors to J.F. Koblas, "all kinds of meats"

Harold L. Hollister, Real Estate Fire Insurance, Tornado Insurance

Eidam and O'Leary, light and heavy hauling

Louis Lundquist, manufacturer of cement sidewalks

Twin City Nursery, Jos. G. Hofflin, Salesman

Justus Lumber

Miller's Dry Goods

G.W. Moore, M.D.

Dr. W.S. Lindsley, dentist

Hopkins News, newspaper office

Commercial Hotel, formerly Hollister House (photo of building)

Hopkins Feed Mill, Docken Brothers

The Moran Boiler Co., west side of Washington Avenue, just north of railroad tracks.

The July 26, 1906 newspaper also prominently displayed the following information about the village:

WHAT HOPKINS HAS: Seven grocery stores, two dry goods stores, two meat markets, one newspaper, two paint stores, one millinery store, two shoe stores, two jewelry stores, one photograph gallery, two drug stores, two confectionery stores, nine saloons, three livery barns, one wood and coal yard, two concrete block factories, two furniture stores, three barber shops, one steam laundry, one bank, three hardware stores, one lumber yard, one bicycle and auto repair shop, one feed mill, three restaurants, four hotels, one real estate office, one telephone exchange, gas works owned by the village, waterworks owned by the village, several miles of cement walks, five churches, three schools, threshing machine factory, boiler shops, paint factory, two clothing stores, two tailor shops.

RAILROADS: Great Northern Branch from Minneapolis; all branches of Minneapolis & St. Louis; Western Division of C.M. & St. Paul; Minnetonka electric road; Deep Haven electric road; Hopkins, St. Louis Park and Minneapolis to Hennepin Avenue.

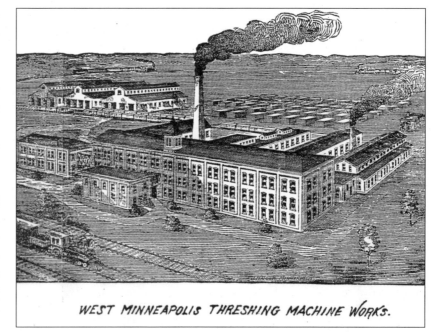

WEST MINNEAPOLIS THRESHING MACHINE WORKS.

WHAT WE HAVE NOT: No tumble down houses. No streets lined with loafers. No empty houses. No millionaires. No idle capital.

OTHER INSTITUTIONS: Hennepin County Poor Farm. Jail. Fire Department. Several large poultry ranches. Many fruit farms. Truck gardeners. Dairymen.

WHAT WE WANT: More factories. More residents. More houses to rent. More patch farmers.

The *Hopkins News* editor promoted Hopkins to various groups, giving us a unique glimpse of what life was like in Hopkins at the turn of the century:

RETIRED FARMERS: There are a good many farmers, perhaps thousands in Minnesota, who have spent the best years of their life at hard labor on the old homestead, but with the declining years and the children grown up and gone from home, they do not feel able to continue the toilsome labor that was their lot in younger years. They desire a change. Some place near the city, where perchance their children could come home oftener, sometimes a home near the University where the young folks are finishing their education... A city

WHEN IN HOPKINS STOP AT THE

Commercial Hotel

Formerly **Hollister House**

L. N. Savaria
Proprietor

Transient
Trade
A
Specialty

Direct Car Line to TWIN CITIES and FAIR GROUNDS.

Panoramic view of Hopkins looking north along 9th Avenue South about 1903.

flat is no place for the sturdy sons and daughters of the free country. Father likes to keep a horse and raise his own vegetables. Mother enjoys putting up fruit from her own garden and the fresh milk from the family cow. A few chickens, the vines on the porch, the flower beds. It all goes to make the home cheerful. Well, but where can a person have all these conveniences and at the same time be within a few minutes ride of the big city? At Hopkins… To all retired farmers and those who want a comfortable place to live with the advantage of both country and city life we would try and direct your steps this way. It is the best suburban town in Minnesota today.

LABOR: Persons seeking a location naturally want to know what the opportunities are for finding employment. Even a capitalist does not wish to invest where there is no demand for labor. Property would soon go down in price. Not so at Hopkins. The great workshops of the Minneapolis Threshing Machine Co. employ nearly one thousand men and their business is steadily increasing. But this is not the only place where a person can find employment as there are smaller industries and besides the street railway have a large crew of men at work near here extending and improving the roadbeds of their lines… Carpenters, brick layers, plumbers, plasterers, gardeners. There is no one out of work here from necessity nor has there been for some years with the exception of a short shut down at the factory for repairs… Some desirable business lots are yet for sale at *the price of from \$500 to \$1,500 for 50 foot front by 130 to the alley on Excelsior Ave., the principal business thoroughfare.*

THE MUNICIPAL GAS PLANT

One of the improvements that [was] added to Hopkins and which is greatly appreciated by consumers as well as the general public, is the municipal gas plant. This plant is what is known as the "Tenney process," something altogether different in the way of gas manufacture, superior in quality of lighting, maintenance, less expensive, and cost of installation less in comparison with other plants. Since this plant has been put in operation, there have been visiting delegations from many towns and cities whose inspection of the plant proved to their entire satisfaction that the "Tenney process" was what they were looking for in the way of lighting. The ingredients that are used in the manufacture of this gas [are] crude oil, coal and water. There are two miles of mains laid on the principal street and although the lamps are two blocks apart on the outskirts of the village, the illuminating power of the incandescent lamps are sufficient for pedestrians to see their way the darkest nights…

—*Hopkins News* July 26, 1906

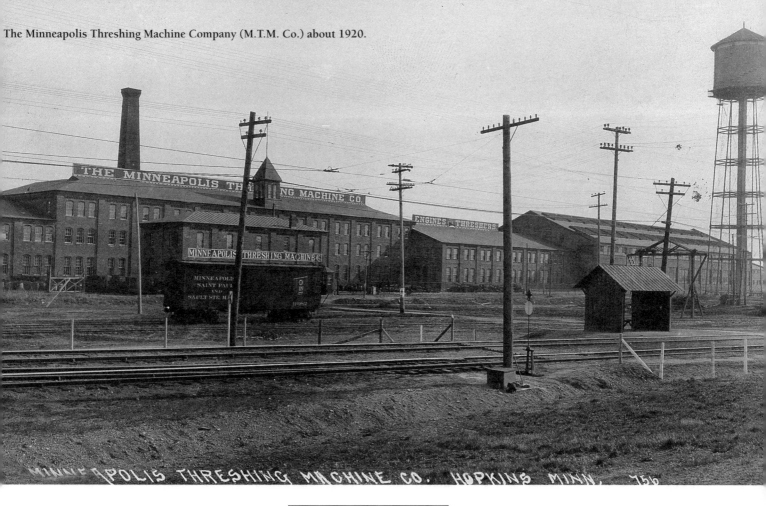

The Minneapolis Threshing Machine Company (M.T.M. Co.) about 1920.

CHAPTER 3

Hopkins at Work

The primary work for the early Hopkins residents was an age-old one: agriculture. The Czech settlers were subsistence farmers and the Yankees also cleared and cultivated the land to feed their families and maybe earn some extra cash through the sale of crops. Homemade butter, eggs, wool, some grain, loads of cordwood sold to the Minneapolis and St. Louis Railroad after 1871 and wild cranberries provided a little cash.

The settlers' first task was to clear the land of trees, which were cut and then split into rails, used to fence small clearings and to keep wild animals out of the crops. They were content to till the land and gather together with others of similar heritage to rear their children and have an abundant life in an agrarian society.

Then came the railroads. Between 1871 and 1881, three railroads were built through the area, opening its potential for heavy industrialized business. In 1887 the

Minneapolis Threshing Machine (M.T.M.) Company began building its plant along two main railroads, assured of easy supply of raw materials and equally easy distribution of the finished threshing machines. An 1881 book on the History of Hennepin County stated: "There are no stores or public buildings at Hopkins." That was about to change.

Situated astride the vast grain growing areas of the Midwest, the little Hopkins factory was destined to supply farmers with the machines that would free them from the back-breaking labor of separating grain from straw. It was inevitable that such a business would thrive and draw into the area mechanically minded workers from Europe to work in the factory and independent minded shopkeepers to supply the needs of the factory workers. The census of 1890 is not available, but by 1900, West Minneapolis had a population of 1,648; this almost doubled by 1910 to 3,022.

The Minneapolis Threshing Machine Company

The Minneapolis Threshing Machine Company (M.T.M. Co.) began as a wagon and bob sleigh manufacturing company in Racine, Wisconsin. It was moved to Fond Du Lac, Wisconsin, and the firm changed its name to McDonald Threshing Machine Company. It produced a wooden separator run by horse power.

From 1887 to 1945, you could just about say that Hopkins was the factory and the factory was Hopkins. The factory was the life of the town, no question about it. It's the reason that any other business in Hopkins existed. You either worked at M.T.M. or your business was set up for those who did.

—Clint Blomquist, *Sun-Sailor*, April 2, 1984

In 1887, the owner John S. McDonald decided to expand his firm and head west to an area near St. Anthony, Minnesota, called Minnetonka Township. He connected with some investors, Levi Longfellow of Minneapolis among them, and proceeded to build a plant on 40 acres of land formerly owned by Daniel Dow.

The plant was renamed the "Minneapolis" Threshing Machine Company because Minneapolis was the largest nearby community. It most likely moved to West Minneapolis because of the availability of trains to ship goods and bring in workers.

McDonald sent his woodworking shop foreman from the Fond Du Lac plant to supervise the construction of the new plant. During the winter of 1887-1888, there were no houses for John Owen Harrison and his family, so they lived in the factory that was under construction.

The factory was soon finished and the new company quickly established itself as a leader in the then-expanding threshing machine industry. Immigrants from Scandinavia and Bohemia soon made up the work force of the plant. By 1889, the firm was producing the first steam traction engines.

In 1893, M.T.M. sent a threshing machine and a steam engine to the World's Columbian Exposition in Chicago. The nickel-plated machinery drew great attention and received several medals.

A severe depression also began in 1893 and farmers stopped buying machinery. The effect on M.T.M. and West Minneapolis was devastating. Families had no money for fuel to heat their homes. Some chopped their furniture to burn in the stove. By 1895, the M.T.M. workweek was just three days long. Eventually it was cut to two days, but the management was able to keep it

Lineup of steam engines at M.T.M.

M.T.M. Shop area, early 1900s.

open. When the depression ended and the demand for machinery increased, M.T.M. was still in business and able to produce steam engines and threshing machines.

Always an innovator in the farm machinery business, M.T.M. developed and marketed the first cylinder corn sheller. It continued to expand in the early 20th century, employing up to 800 people and having a payroll in excess of $40,000 a month. Company records show it was generating $2,000,000 in sales annually in 1903. West Minneapolis and its citizens became dependent on the factory for survival.

As was typical of many one-industry towns, the factory needed all the workers it could get so management made sure no other competitive businesses located in the town. They could do this because many M.T.M. managers were also elected to the village council. A typical scenario would be like this: a company would propose to move to the village, the village council would refuse to build a road to access the factory, so the business would locate elsewhere.

The one major exception appears to be the Red Wing Sewer Pipe Company factory, which was built in 1908 near M.T.M. A branch of a company based in Red Wing, Minnesota, it made sewer pipe sold primarily to munic-

ipalities, and at its peak was shipping ten to twelve railroad cars of sewer pipe out of Hopkins daily.

Working conditions at M.T.M. were probably about average for any factory of the period. The work was hard and the wages low. Charles Beckman, who with his father put in over 100 years with the firm, began work

Irving Horner and Hans Smith loading a kiln at M.T.M.

M.T.M. Warehouse about 1926.

grain separator being shipped from West Minneapolis by train to get to the grain fields of the Dakotas.

M.T.M. continued to build steam engines until 1926. They then switched to machinery powered by other fuels.

A new era began in April 1929, when M.T.M. merged with the Minneapolis Steel and Machinery Company (founded 1902) and the Moline Plow Company of Moline, Illinois (founded 1870). The new company, Minneapolis Moline Power Implement Company, had combined assets of 33 million dollars and was the fifth largest manufacturer of farm machinery in the United States.

The 1930s should have been the golden age for Minneapolis Moline. Company president W.C. McFarlane told the *Hennepin County Review* on March 20, 1930 that more than 1,300 workers were on the payroll. A night shift had been added to make up for inventory destroyed when a warehouse in St. Louis Park burned down. McFarlane was confident about the future. He told the Review, "In the farm implement industry, the outlook for business never looked better to me."

He could not have been more wrong. The great depression hit and by late 1930, there were severe cutbacks at the factory. By early fall, 1931, the workforce at Minneapolis Moline dropped to two or three hundred workers. By June 1932, Minneapolis Moline employed

in 1891 at age 13. He was employed as a sweeper/trucker, moving parts from one department to another, and worked 10 hours a day for 80 cents.

John Milbert, who started at the foundry when he was 15 in 1889, had a more demanding and dangerous job. He had to climb a vertical ladder, carrying on his back a hod full of pig iron, scrap iron and coke, which he dumped into the top of the furnace—for an hourly wage of 10 cents. Later, a ramp was built so the men could push the material to the top of the furnace in a wheelbarrow. Finally, the job was made "easy" when management installed a windlass to get the materials to the top of the furnace.

For years, M.T.M. was run by Paul Swenson, who was also mayor of West Minneapolis. One of Swenson's superintendents was Henry Moore, who was also the city's first fire chief. Swenson and his superintendents ran what was thought of as a benevolent dictatorship. With his overall control of the community's employment and village council, Swenson enjoyed unquestioned authority.

Work at the plant was by no means steady. It shut down for six months, beginning at Thanksgiving. The employees often took odd jobs to feed their families. Paul Stepanek, who started at M.T.M. in 1916, recalls he would do threshing work in the Dakotas to earn money. Once he crawled into the blower of an M.T.M.

M.T.M. Core Room, year unknown.

Minneapolis Moline Hopkins Plant looking northwest to southeast, 1951.

only about 35 people. Through government programs of Roosevelt's "New Deal" the U.S. economy slowly strengthened and Minneapolis Moline was able to begin slowly hiring in April 1935.

By 1937, the worst was over, but the work force was no longer willing to take orders from any benevolent dictator. In 1938, the workers went on a sit-down strike to protest the firing of John Biby, who had refused to take an order from a foreman, contending his seniority rights were being ignored. All plant operations were halted within an hour of the strike's beginning. About 400 workers began the sit-down strike action in four-hour shifts. The plant remained closed for five weeks. On February 4, 1939, the strike ended with the appointment of an outside arbitrator and Biby was found to be insubordinate by the arbitrator and given a 90-day disciplinary lay-off.

America began a belated strengthening of its armed forces in 1939 to face the threat posed by the Axis powers. Minneapolis Moline became a major defense industry provider prior to and during World War II. Using its engineering skills employed for agriculture to the benefit of the military, it developed one of the first all-terrain vehicles. Women were hired to work in production for the first time.

Minneapolis Moline turned out war supplies in record-setting numbers during World War II, winning War Department citations for both quantity and quality of materials assembled.

Following World War II, Minneapolis Moline returned to the production of farm implements. They continued their innovative leadership in this field. Bon D. Grussing was the head of the firm's award winning public relations department. He and his assistant, John Rusinko, were responsible for developing promotional material uniting the farmer's use of Minneapolis Moline machinery with environmentally sound agricultural practices.

Both men made the farm products manufactured by Minneapolis Moline exciting by staging dramatic expositions featuring their corporation's equipment. In 1951 the firm was honored by the Public Relations Society of America for "meritorious public relations performance in the field of agriculture."

A Russian delegation visited the Hopkins plant of Minneapolis Moline in the early 1950s to see first-hand how farm implements were manufactured in the U.S. The unannounced visit caught many Minneapolis Moline workers by surprise when Aleksandr Ehevski, assistant to the Soviet minister of agriculture implement production, Fedorovich Bogach, head of a tractor and machinery pool in the Ukraine and a delegation of officials from the U.S. State Department, toured the facilities. Ken Wakershauser of the *Hennepin County Review* reported the Soviet tour of Hopkins was an "unforgettable" experience.

Dedicated to preserving the environment, Minneapolis Moline's John Rusinko produced a conservation movie entitled "To Conserve Our Heritage." Considered the finest conservation movie shot in America to that time, it was awarded the George Washington honor medal by the Freedom Foundation at Valley Forge, the 1954 award of the Film Council festival and the national honor award of the Izaak Walton League. It marked the first time the Izaak Walton League had ever presented an award to an industry. Years ahead of its time, the Minneapolis Moline movie showed the devastation caused by pollution, silt-laden streams, soil-eroded fields, foolish and selfish timber destruction. The film also lifted the audience with breath-taking scenes of fresh water, soil holding practices, proper forestry practices and lush green fields.

Minneapolis Moline also had a library of other famous conservation movies. They included "A Saga of the Soil," "Progress for Plenty," "Birds of the Prairie," "Waterfowl in Spring," "This Heritage is Ours," 'The Soil is Good," "Rivers and the Soil" and "Progress for Plenty." While the movies might not have been as famous they were certainly well watched. According to the *Minneapolis Tribune*, more than 100,000,000 people had viewed them around the world. The Hopkins Historical Society has copies of many of these 16mm films in its collection.

The agricultural economy began to slow down in the mid-50s. The *Minneapolis Tribune* in 1956 reported that staff reductions were being made at Minneapolis Moline. Three key executives resigned according to W.C. MacFarlane, Vice Chairman of the Board of Directors, "out of economic necessity." The article also announced that 25 clerical positions had been eliminated as well. It closed its foundry operation also.

In January 1963, Minneapolis Moline became a subsidiary of the White Motor Company. 350 workers transferred, about 450 lost their jobs and about 350 workers remained. By 1980, White Motor had filed for bankruptcy. In addition, White Motor Company was involved in a scandal in which alleged mismanagement of the employee's pension fund left many retired lifelong

This historic tractor built in 1918 was known as the Model "D" Universal. Equipped with electric starting motor, electric lights, battery and electric speed control of the engine, it was used in Nebraska from 1918 until 1953, when it was purchased by W.L. Pringle, Vice President and Director of Marketing, Minneapolis Moline, Inc. for use at state and county fairs. In 1957, it was moved to Hopkins and used in parades, including the 1958 Minnesota Centennial. It was placed on exhibition at the Smithsonian institution on July 13, 1962.

Berry pickers on the John Feltl farm in the 1920s or 30s.

Minneapolis Moline employees with no retirement fund. The economic hardship created by the pension fund collapse drew the attention of the Minnesota Congressional delegation and subsequently the U.S. Congress passed and the President signed the Employment Retirement Income Security Act (ERISA), which established rules and regulations concerning the management of pension funds in America.

In 1985 Allied Products Company (APCO) purchased White Farm Equipment and by 1986, demolition began on the vacated Minneapolis Moline buildings in Hopkins. The only buildings left in town that were owned by Minneapolis Moline/White Motor are the Napco/Venturian building at Excelsior Boulevard and 17th Avenue South, which was built in 1951 as a parts department and a smaller building also used for parts, now owned by the Dodge dealership on 17th Avenue North and Highway 7.

Agriculture / Raspberries

Agriculture played an important role in the history of Hopkins. Early farmers discovered the land southwest of West Minneapolis in Minnetonka Township was ideal for growing raspberries. The farmers credited with bringing raspberries to Hopkins are Joe and John Empanger. They received several plants as a gift from

George Pratt in the spring of 1880. Pratt's farm was located near the intersection of Wooddale Avenue and Excelsior Boulevard in St. Louis Park.

The Empangers initially planted the Philadelphia Raspberry bush on their farm and through the years made significant contributions to the development of better varieties. The Empangers never were commercial growers of raspberries but beginning in the 1880s, other Czechs farmers who lived near Shady Oak Lake in Min-

Lavonne Borgman and Johanna Schmit with raspberries at Chastek's cir. 1950.

netonka began growing raspberries and it became a big commercial industry for the area. They found they could get into raspberry farming without as large an investment as other lines of farming.

Minnesota's hard winters often caused serious damage to the delicate raspberry bushes. In 1886, John Feltl developed the concept of plowing a furrow along a row of raspberry plants and covering the entire plant with rich, black earth for winter storage. Feltl's banking practice was soon widely adopted by other raspberry farmers.

Hopkins children often worked in the raspberry fields. They would get up at 4:00 AM, walk to the raspberry farms where they worked all day before quitting

The Chastek work crew posing with the berries about 1950.

at 6:00 PM. Alvina Young (later Mrs. Gorden Noleen) recalled walking 5 miles from her home to pick berries at the Lenander and Dominick farms. She would pick about four crates per day. There were 24 boxes of raspberries in a crate. She was paid 48 cents per crate.

By the 1920s, growing raspberries had become a big business for Hopkins area farmers. It is estimated that at one time the Hopkins area had over 800 acres planted in raspberries! Most were used for fresh market consumption. In 1922, the Feltls hauled 248 cases of raspberries to Commission Row in Minneapolis. The cases brought payment of $1000—an astronomical amount of money in 1922. From the late 1920s through the war years,

Hopkins dominated the raspberry scene in Minnesota and for that matter, the nation. It became known as the "Raspberry Capital of the World." But berry growing was hard work.

During the horse and buggy era, the farmers would have to leave home at 2 o'clock a.m. to be at the farmer's market in Minneapolis at 6 o'clock when it opened. The only day they did not pick berries was Saturday because the market was closed on Sunday. Saturday was the day to hoe the potatoes, carrots, cucumber and melon plants and set out the young berry plants that were needed for the future raspberry crop. It took three years to grow plants to a productive state. The plants had to be nurtured to survive the winter and tied to poles to withstand wind; the berries had to be picked, crated and hauled to market. As Dr. Frank Kucera stated in his memoirs, "I often wondered when the buyers complained about the price of $10.00 per crate of 24 pints to a crate if they knew how much work it took to produce these berries... I believe the farmers were entitled to that price every time, but I know that many times they got much less."

By 1913, farmers were marketing their berries through cooperative associations rather than in the central Minneapolis market. This way, they could tend to the finer details of cultivation and leave behind marketing worries. The Hopkins area growers used the Excelsior Fruit

Clint Chastek beer truck with raspberry and celery display, 1947.

Growers Cooperative, which served towns located principally on the M.&St.L. and Chicago, Milwaukee, St. Paul and Pacific Railroads.

The Depression struck hard in the 1930s and many Hopkins raspberry farmers went out of business. A sweltering heat wave in 1931 was followed by a drought. Hennepin County farmers lost nearly $3,000,000 in income. Since raspberries were a delicious fruit and not a necessary staple, consumers felt they couldn't spend their money on such luxuries. Many of the truck farmers switched to staples such as tomatoes, corn, green peppers and cauliflower. Some raspberries continued to be grown though, for in 1934 the total production was listed as 125,000 crates, which were shipped from town in 86 railroad freight cars.

Throughout the 1950s and 1960s, some raspberries continued to be grown in the Hopkins area, but the number of patches continued to dwindle. Hopkins' reputation as the raspberry capital of the world was lamented in the Columbus, Kansas *Daily Advocate* of August 12, 1983 with a quote from Clint Blomquist, Curator of the Hopkins Historical Society: "We'd ship raspberries out by the freight carload, and we had to import people for 40 or 50 miles away in season to pick berries… now there are no berry patches…Well, there's one… but the lady who runs it is in her 80s, and her daughter says that when she dies, the berry patch dies with her."

The Berry Box Factory

The raspberry farmers needed boxes and crates to safely ship their product to market. That need resulted in a bustling box industry in Hopkins. The Hopkins Fruit Package Company, known as 'the "berry box factory," was located in the McDonald Building on the north side of Excelsior Avenue (now Mainstreet) between 5th and 7th Avenues. The company was sold to R.A. Wright of Excelsior who owned the Wright Fruit Package Company. The company moved its headquarters to Hopkins.

The Wright Fruit Package Company did business in 26 states and Canada. The wood used to manufacture the crates came from a special sawmill in Cumberland, Wisconsin. Business became so good for a period of time that Wright

operated two manufacturing plants in Hopkins, as well as his plant in Excelsior.

At times demand for the boxes would outpace production. Mike Brecka recalled that the Hopkins Police had to be called to the factory to control desperate customers who were stealing the crates instead of buying them. Wright died in the early 1930s. The postmaster, William Perbix bought the company from the estate. Eventually the berry box industry declined along with the agribusiness it served.

Bren Berry Box Factory

It was a hot summer day in 1936 when the crop was failing that two brothers, Theodore (Ted) and Edwin Bren, decided to start a business making boxes and crates for local raspberry farmers. They used the old barn with white trim on Shady Oak Road that had been built by their grandfather, Joseph Bren, just after the Civil War. Joseph had been granted the land in lieu of payment for service in the Union Army. In 1938, the little family-run factory in the barn produced between 50,000 to 60,000 raspberry crates. Many Hopkins youth were employed at the factory and remember receiving cuts from the staples that held the simple boxes together.

By 1971, the lathe that used to turn out thousands of berry boxes was put to use making veneer for emery boards. On another hot day in 1971, the old Bren Berry Box factory burned to the ground. The heat from the fire was so intense it blistered the paint on a fireman's car

The Wright Berry Box Factory, 621-623 Excelsior Ave, 1920.

Hopkins' first store – The S.C. Campbell Store was built in the 1880s and burned down about 1903. Location: south side of Excelsior Avenue just west of the railroad crossing across from the current Super Valu North Annex (formerly Red Owl).

There were numerous other grocers in Hopkins through the years doing a tremendous amount of business on the main street and they all seemed to be related. Grocery delivery was common. A homeowner would give a delivery order as the delivery vehicle came by. They could expect their items the next day. After telephones became common, grocery orders would be phoned in to the store for delivery.

Alfred and August Johnson came to the U.S. in 1887 and founded the **Johnson Brothers Meat Market** in 1893. Before refrigeration came in the 1930s, Elmer Johnson remembers delivering meat twice a day to the south part of town where all the boarding houses were; meat was also delivered once a day to the north side of town and every-other day to the east end.

parked 40 yards away. This was the end of the berry box industry in Hopkins. Some of the berry boxes can still be seen at the Hopkins Historical Society. They were made by simple machines. Ted Bren remembered his grandfather "lumberjacked" his own wood for the berry crates and hand-sawed slats to a thickness of 1/8 inch for boxes in the old days.

The Grocery Town

With the growth of the threshing machine factory and the community, there developed a demand for goods. Hopkins' first store was opened in the 1880s by Sam Campbell, whose wife was Diana Burnes. Built at approximately 210 Excelsior Avenue East, Campbell's store eliminated the need for residents to walk to Minneapolis or St. Anthony to purchase needed goods or commodities. The Campbell store was the home of the Hopkins post office from 1891-1894. It burned down in 1903 when a boxcar on the M.&St.L. Railroad caught fire and ignited the store also.

The second known store was Eidam's store. Ed Eidam moved his store from Minnetonka Mills to Hopkins, locating at 712 Excelsior Avenue to be nearer to the M.T.M. factory than the other store. Eidam's Store also served as the Hopkins post office prior to 1900. A second generation, Lou Eidam and his wife, still operated Eidam's store in the early 1930s.

Waldo Hovander came to Hopkins in 1888 at the age of two years with his father. He began working at the Johnson Brothers Meat Market when he was 13 years old. He married into the Johnson family and he and his brother Herman purchased the meat market and ran it under the name **Hovander Brothers** beginning in 1925 and then as **Hovander Foods** from 1947 to 1971. Hovander's moved to a big new store at 30 9th Avenue North in 1956. This was purchased by Bob Tait in 1971. **Tait's Market** continued the tradition of civic leadership

The Johnson Brothers Meat Market at 910 Excelsior Avenue. Herman and Waldo Hovander are behind the counter, 1914.

Hovander's Grocery in Hopkins at 30-9th Avenue N.

and fine foods until it was purchased in 2001 by **Driskill's** based out of the Glen Lake area of Minnetonka. Today, Driskill's is the only full-service grocery store in Hopkins.

Arthur Plankers became the manager of the first Red Owl corporate store in Hopkins in 1926. In 1935, he resigned from Red Owl and opened his own supermarket two doors away on Excelsior Avenue called **Plankers Red and White Store**. He had a statewide reputation as a buyer of produce. This store closed in 1955. Plankers was one of the founders of the Hopkins Raspberry Festival.

When Minneapolis Moline started to sell less farm equipment due to a declining agricultural economy after World War II, it also lost its clout with the Hopkins Village Council. Other industries were finally allowed to locate in Hopkins. The January 14, 1946 newspaper reported that three major food distribution centers were being built in Hopkins—National Tea, Red Owl and Winston and Newell Company (soon to be known as Super Valu). In addition, the Superior Separator Company moved to Hopkins. The Hopkins Civic and Commerce Association estimated that these four businesses alone would bring 1500 new jobs to the area.

The **National Tea Company** opened an office and warehouse on 30 acres of land purchased from Lester Boyce, pioneer Hopkins settler, northeast of the corner of Blake Road and Excelsior Avenue East. The **Red Owl Company** opened a warehouse, bakery and supermarket on Excelsior Avenue East near Washington Avenue, on the site of the two heritage Harley H. Hopkins' homes. The **Country Club** Stores Warehouse was

also located in Hopkins on 5th Avenue South in an old Minneapolis Moline storage building. It burned to the ground in a spectacular fire on a windy spring day in 1965. Food-related businesses, such as Powell's Candy Company and Merchants Refrigeration, a cold storage facility, also called Hopkins home.

Thus, the grocery distribution industry became a major force in Hopkins. It has been estimated that 85% of the food sold in the Metropolitan area in 1986 was shipped through Hopkins. This legacy continues today with the huge presence of Supervalu, one of the nation's leading food distribution companies. **Rainbow Foods** is also located in Hopkins, at 8000 Excelsior Avenue, in the former Powell Candy Company.

In September 1952, **Super Valu Stores, Inc.** opened in Hopkins between Monroe and Jefferson Avenues on 16 acres of land. For many years, Supervalu's corporate office was above the warehouse on Jefferson Avenue South in Hopkins; in 1980, it moved to Eden Prairie.

Locally familiar were the National and Red Owl Food Store emblems.

A.E. Sackrison's grocery delivery truck of 1920.

May 3, 1948 Red Owl Stores Inc. officially opened its new facility in Hopkins. Cedric Adams, famous newspaperman and WCCO radio personality was the emcee.

The Winston Newell Company warehouse in Hopkins advertised the Super Valu brand prior to 1953.

Supervalu's North Regional Offices are in Hopkins and the 579,000 square feet Minneapolis Distribution Center warehouse, the equivalent of 11 football fields, takes up a huge portion of south Hopkins real estate. The Perishables Building, on 5th Street South was remodeled in 2001. This added another 313,000 square feet of warehouse space to the Supervalu campus, where approximately 62,400 truckloads of merchandise are received annually.

Supervalu acquired Red Owl in 1989, which included the original Red Owl warehouse building north of Excelsior Avenue. The Northern Region of Supervalu employs more than 2,000 people at its distribution centers in Hopkins, Des Moines, Iowa, and Bismarck and Fargo, North Dakota.

Supervalu traces its beginnings back to 1870, when its predecessors, B.S. Bull, Newell & Harrison wholesale grocers, provided fresh produce to the Minneapolis community. It became "SuperValu Stores, Inc." around the time it moved to Hopkins and continued to acquire food wholesalers around the country. Today, SUPERVALU INC. (corporate name changed in 1992) is one of the largest food wholesaler in America, covering 37 states.

The state-of-the-art Supervalu campus in Hopkins, completed in 2001, has some innovative features in distribution technology. An entire wing of the dry grocery warehouse is designed for "cross dock" operations, in which full pallets of goods move directly from vendor trucks to delivery trucks without ever being warehoused. This efficient system reduces handling, labor and storage costs, thus keeping food prices down. And in case you are wondering, in the huge dry grocery warehouse there are 126 truck dock doors to serve inbound/outbound traffic; it is open 24 hours a day and has 38-foot high ceilings.

Pederson Dairy had a large milk delivery business, as this fleet of vehicles demonstrates.

Dairies

The Campbell farm, formerly the Burnes farm, located where Campbell Drive is now in Hobby Acres was where Hopkins residents got their milk. Every evening after milking time, you would see streams of people walking with their containers from north Hopkins to get fresh milk. Small containers of milk cost 3 cents and large pails were 10 cents. All were filled and the parade of people would head for home.

Farther to the east, by Monk (now Blake) Road and Second Street North, was Jasperson's Dairy. Mr. Jasperson did mostly home deliveries. He was a familiar figure, swaying from side to side as he completed his route every morning.

Pederson's Dairy was located just south of the Yellowstone Trail (Excelsior Avenue) across from the Hennepin County Poor farm. This was the last dairy to close, having been taken by Hennepin County when County Road 18 (now an even bigger #169) was built. Morril Pederson made most of the commercial stops by servicing the restaurants and retail stores in the area.

Ice and Fuel

Before home refrigeration, there also was the ice man. Clarence Ream delivered ice in Hopkins. The signs in the windows on his route had a card that would be turned to "25," "50," or "75 pounds." Most of the average iceboxes took 50 pounds. Then he would cut the chunk needed from a huge 200-pound ice hunk in the delivery truck, covered with canvas to slow the melting. At one time, the ice came from Shady Oak Lake, which was crystal clear. The ice was harvested in the winter by Krautkremer's Ice and Fuel located on Seventh Avenue South.

In the wintertime, the same drivers were kept busy delivering fuel oil to those who could afford an oil burner—a step up from the wood and coal stoves used by many residents to keep their houses warm.

Other Industries

Other industries were associated with Hopkins during its history. The second largest factory in town was the **Red Wing Sewer Pipe Company**, built in 1908 along what is now Excelsior Boulevard (Hennepin County Road 3). The plant produced an enormous amount of sewer pipe, which was shipped to developing communities in Minnesota, the Dakotas and Montana.

The Red Wing Sewer Pipe Company kept 16 furnaces operating 24 hours a day making clay sewer pipe. The firm shipped 12 railroad cars of pipe per day from its Hopkins plant in 1919. By 1924, hard times forced the company to close its 33-acre factory. It remained closed until 1930 when the National Bricklite Company

The Red Wing Sewer Pipe Company before 1909.

What is now the Hopkins Tech Center was Minneapolis Moline in 1956.

bought it. But that firm also quickly failed and the plant was abandoned.

Mayon Plastic Products company has been at the corner of County Road 73 (17th Ave.) and Highway 7 since about 1946 when it was established by Ray Johnson and M.C. Nelson. It manufactures plastic tubing for medical and industrial purposes. Its parent company, Kennedy Mayonnaise salad dressing, was originally in Minneapolis. For many years, a large mayonnaise salad dressing bottle graced the building.

In 1962, **Napco Industries** bought the Janney-Semple-Hill Hardware Company distribution building at 1111-1199 County Road 3 (now Excelsior Boulevard) in Hopkins, built by Minneapolis Moline in 1951. This building at the time was one of the largest completely contained manufacturing buildings in the Twin Cities, with 340,000 square feet, railroad sidings, track loading docks, etc. Napco was one of the leading automotive parts manufacturer and supplier of service parts and components for commercial and military vehicles. Now called the Hopkins Tech Center, the building is owned by **Venturian** Holdings L.L.C. and houses about 26 tenants including Venturian, Napco International, Clima-A-Tech Industries, Drew-Pearson Marketing Inc, In-Line Corp and Hennepin Technical College.

Napco built the red brick building to the east of it in 1963, which has been occupied by various companies affiliated with Napco such as Dana Corp (moved out in 1981), Spicer Heavy Axle and Electrocraft (once a wholly-owned subsidiary of Napco, but sold in 1980). Venturian currently owns both buildings but sold the remainder of Napco in October 2001. A remnant of the industrial past is a large brick smokestack that previously said "Moline," but was changed to "Napco."

Honeywell Inc./Alliant Techsystems Inc.

One of the largest and most visible high-tech companies

to ever be located in Hopkins was Honeywell, Inc. In 1953, Honeywell's first corporate research center moved into the former main building of the Hennepin County Poor Farm and stayed there for about twenty years. Honeywell's Ordnance Division moved to Hopkins in 1956, renting only a portion of the building originally built by the Terminal Warehouse Company at 600 NE Second Street. The Ordnance Division products came to include the MK46 torpedo, large and small caliber ammunition, controls for aiming tank guns and smart weapons. Initially, engineers, draftsmen and technicians shared the building with warehoused goods; at one time, this was 65,000 bags of sugar.

As the Ordnance Division expanded, they took over more and more of the building, which was enlarged several times in the 1960s. Parking lots were added and eventually Honeywell purchased the building in 1980. The growth in Hopkins' more upscale neighborhoods in the 1950s and 1960s parallels the growth of Honeywell and other smaller technology oriented companies that moved to Hopkins during this time.

After the Vietnam War and thus U.S. Defense Department contracts had ended, Honeywell began to downsize. On October 1, 1990, Honeywell divested their military products units and the former Ordnance Division became an independent corporation named Alliant Techsystems Inc., which manufactured conventional munitions, space and strategic systems and defense systems.

With this spin-off of Honeywell, Hopkins became the scene of one of the more colorful results of the Vietnam War—the antiwar demonstration. The "Honeywell Project" was a protest group formed in 1968 to protest Honeywell's manufacture of cluster bombs used by the U.S.A. during the Vietnam War. Peaceful antiwar demonstrations (sit-ins) resulted in numerous arrests of protestors from 1982 to 1989 at Honeywell. Sit-ins resumed at Alliant in 1996 to protest its manufacturing of land mines and other war items; numerous arrests of protestors for trespassing occurred in the late 1990's.

The Hopkins authorities had various responses over time, from massive, temporary, arrests to no arrests so the protestors would not have the sought-after media forum. Alliant Techsystems moved out of Hopkins in the fall of 2001, thus relieving the cost and personnel

Harry Leathers and his automobile named the "Hopkins."

Dahlberg Brothers Ford Motors and was located on the northeast corner of 11th and Excelsior Avenue.

Harry's mother was Franklin Morris, sister of Mrs. Daniel Dow. Franklin had married Harry Leathers, an inventor of sorts, who did quite well financially, but the family did not reap the benefits of the wealth he accrued because he moved to the west and left the family to shift for themselves. When the Dows built their large brick house, Franklin Leathers got the wooden house at the end of 10th Avenue facing First Street, where she raised her two sons, Harry Jr. and George, by running a boarding house.

In the 1930s, Oscar Dahlberg of Dahlberg Ford, Earl Girard of Girard Motors and Harold Grossman of Suburban Chevrolet cooperated in an unusual radio advertising campaign to attract customers to Hopkins. Advertising together for a

burdens to Hopkins' police and legal departments. Alliant is now located in Edina and Plymouth.

Good use was made of one of the former Honeywell parking lots. It became a neighborhood of single-family homes called Parkside.

Hopkins has always tried to nurture its high-tech companies. Several new industrial parks have been developed, including the handsome Cornerstone Business Park on 11th Avenue South that went up in 1996 at a cost of $6 million and houses the Lathrop Paint corporate headquarters, L.A. Loving, Shippers Supply, Inc. and others. The former M.B. Hagen Little League field on 11th Avenue South now boasts the $1.2 million Diamond Laboratories warehouse and office facilities.

The Automobile Industry

Harry Leathers Jr. of Hopkins is said to have built the first automobile to drive on Hennepin Avenue about 1895. Harry, born about 1875, and his brother George were skilled mechanics. They owned a bicycle and motor repair shop on Excelsior Avenue, in the Leathers Building, on Excelsior Avenue in the middle of the block between 10th and 11th Avenues. Upstairs in this building was the first telephone exchange and a dental office occupied by Dr. Ed Smetana.

George was killed at a young age when his motorcycle was hit by a streetcar on the Minnetonka Mills road. Harry married Freda Swanson about the time he went into the automobile business, which was the first Ford Automobile agency in Hopkins. It later became

Low Overhead Deal–Hopkins is impressed with its booming car industry (perhaps "ecstatic" is a better word). Big business is imperative for any community, and when that business is ethically and profitably run, the rewards are obvious. The future is likely to find even greater car sales activity on Excelsior Avenue, until the glittering thoroughfare is one long mass of chrome. Hopkins will likely give in to this envelopment, for it not only needs its cars, it likes them.

—*Select Twin Cities Magazine*, September, 1962

The first Ford agency in Hopkins.

My First Car–I remember way back in 1933 when I bought my first car, a second-hand 1931 Ford Model A sedan from Ed Stoops a salesman for Dahlberg Ford Agency in Hopkins. The previous owner of this car traded it in on a new 1934 V8 Ford with a stick shift, the newest and last word in Fords.

Because the company I worked for in downtown Minneapolis was moving to the St. Paul midway district, I had either to move to St. Paul or to buy a car and remain living in Hopkins. Friday I bought the car, but I didn't know how to drive it. Mr. Stoops took me for my only lesson the same evening after suppertime. We drove in St. Louis Park, which then had a lot of open country and many gravel roads and not much traffic. My driver's license cost 35 cents and all I had to do was complete a form at the bank and the license was mailed directly to me—no written test or road test as required today.

The following evening I took Frank Shimota, my mother, Mrs. Eugenie Mahoney and my brother Jim for a ride—and also a few thrills.

On Monday morning, an uncle who worked in Minneapolis rode along for my first trip into downtown Minneapolis. I drove Excelsior Boulevard (Highway 7 was not built then) to Hennepin Avenue, then to Hennepin and Sixth Street, where I stalled the car on the streetcar tracks as I was making a turn left. I got it started again and dropped my uncle off on First Avenue N. By this time I was a nervous wreck and, needless to say, not worth much on my job all day knowing I would again have to drive back to Hopkins at the end of the working day.

Tuesday the company moved to St. Paul and I drove across Lake Street, stopping 10 feet back for streetcar passengers to board or get off. I picked up five fellow coworkers along Lake Street who also got some thrills riding with me, especially when I was driving between the streetcar and the railing on the Lake Street bridge.

The silence in the car then was deafening. They nicknamed me Barney Oldfield but stuck by me the 10 years I drove to and from St. Paul.

I learned to drive a car in a hurry back in 1933!

—by Vivian Mahoney Blomquist,
Hopkins Review, August 29, 1979

"low overhead" deal, once the customers got to Hopkins, the friendly competition began. Large prominently displayed signs, new and used car lots featuring multicolored plastic flags and automobiles sporting huge price tags on their windshields took over Excelsior Avenue.

By 1962, two more auto dealers had joined the group: Town's Edge Oldsmobile owned by Jack Walser and Countryside Rambler owned by Wally McCarthy. At this time, Hopkins' auto dealers sold more automobiles per capita than were sold anywhere else in the area, and some zealous citizens claimed that should be broadened to include the upper Midwest or even the country. The claims stem from the fact that new car sales in Hopkins were $1200 per capita in 1962, contrasted with $200 per capita for Minneapolis. The other good thing was that 80% of the car buyers came from outside of Hopkins.

Along the 16-block-long main street, in 1962 there were 6 major car dealer showrooms and 12 car sales lots. This was probably the peak for auto sales in Hopkins, which started to dwindle in the 1970s because modern, indoor car showrooms and huge auto dealership "strips" started to be built along the major freeways in newer suburbs.

Hopkins still has a strong automobile focus, although now it has smaller auto parts and service deal-

The familiar dachshund, irreverently known as the "wiener dog" advertised the "low overhead deal" for Suburban Chevrolet in the 1963 Hopkins phone book.

The Suburban Chevrolet showroom at 1106 Excelsior Avenue in 1956 advertised the "low overhead deal."

erships, and general repair and body shops, with a few smaller new and used car sales lots. A look in a recent Hopkins telephone book yielded over 25 automobile parts or service businesses in the vicinity of downtown Hopkins, many located along the "new" Excelsior Boulevard, formerly named 2nd Street South or County Road 3, where there is even a trendy new concept—an automobile service mall.

Bars and Restaurants

Hopkins was a hardworking factory town and has always had the reputation of being a hard-partying town, too. Mention Hopkins to many people and the first thing they say is "Bursch's" if they don't mention the raspberry festival. Whether known as saloons, taverns, bars, restaurants, nightclubs, cafes or now sports bars, Hopkins has always had plenty of them. (The "Snake Pit" was

this editor's personal favorite nickname for a bar.)

Robert L. Ripley featured Hopkins in his famous "Believe It or Not" syndication of bygone years. Hopkins had more saloons and more churches per capita than any other city of the same population.

Servicemen on leave or furlough during World War II could start at Shady Oak Road and walk through Hopkins to Blake Road, and if they had one drink in each establishment, they'd spend about $2.50 in 1940s dollars and this would be their itinerary:

The **Nitebawk Cafe** at Shady Oak Road; then walking down Excelsior Avenue – **Milbert's Grocery & Bar** at 1209; **Glueck's Corner** at 11th; **Ray & Tony's** at 906; **Jeg's Corner** at 9th & Main; **Matt's Cafe** just opposite Jeg's at 9th & Main; deviate south on 9th one-quarter block to **Long's Bar**; back to 819 – **Blue Ribbon Bar**; 908 Bar at 814; **Lil's Cafe** at 715; **Bursch's Cafe & Bar** at 706; **Hugo Zill's Tavern** (in the former Schutz Livery Building at 711 Excelsior Ave.) and then all the way out to East Hopkins to **Ronnie's Cafe** at Excelsior Boulevard and Blake Road.

Total consumption would be way too much but a lot of friends could be seen throughout the evening.

The bar and restaurant scene in Hopkins has really changed since the 1940s. Today, if you were to take this same route, you would consume a lot of fast food, oriental foods, pizza, subs, coffee and tea, in addition to having alcoholic beverages at the more upscale sports bars and restaurants now in Hopkins. Mainstreet is still

Ad for Archies, from the 1956 telephone book.

For 48 years Bursch's was Hopkins' most famous dining establishment. This is a 1956 photo of the restaurant at 706 Excelsior Ave. In 1959 it moved around the corner to 17-8th Avenue S.

The Columbia saloon, 622 Excelsior Avenue W about 1900.

Justus Lumber Co. in 1893.

a great place to meet friends and business acquaintances or take the family out to eat. Throughout the 1990s, the City of Hopkins has put a lot of effort into the redevelopment of Mainstreet establishments. The new Hopkins arts area has attracted high quality restaurants, many of which are in buildings that formerly were old-time saloons. Mixing the new with the old is one of the things that Hopkins does best.

Long-Term Family Owned Businesses

Justus Lumber is the oldest business in Hopkins. Founded by a 26-year old Swedish immigrant in 1893, the business has just recently (2001) been sold by the Justus family to Scherer Bros. Lumber Company.

Andrew Justus moved to West Minneapolis in 1893 and founded the community's first lumber business. His partners were Enoch Broberg and John Swanson. Less than three months after he invested a $325.00 family

Justus Lumber Company in 1956, located south of Excelsior Avenue approximately where Highway 169 is today.

inheritance on the company, the panic of 1893 hit. Andrew's dream of a better life carried him through the crisis, and after four years of hard work, he was able to buy out his partners. Located on part of the former Harley H. Hopkins farm, in the area between Excelsior Avenue east and the M.&St.L. Railway, east of Washington Avenue for 78 years (from 1893-1971), Justus Lumber was strategically located to receive and sell building supplies for the growing community.

In 1925, a devastating tornado ripped through eastern Hopkins and Justus Lumber Company was virtually demolished. Undaunted, Andrew Justus built the business back up, and continued to fulfill his promise of "every time a square deal" to his customers.

Andrew Justus' son, Andy, joined the business in 1932 and his youngest son, Cavour, came aboard three years later. In 1943, Justus Lumber celebrated its 50th anniversary. A banquet marking the occasion was attended by all of the company's employees and their families as well as a number of civic leaders, including the mayor of Hopkins. Nearly 6 years later, in 1949, Andrew Justus passed away at the age of 82, content with the knowledge that the company he founded was in capable hands.

In 1950, sons Andy and Cavour renovated and expanded the 57-year-old Justus Lumber building at Excelsior and Washington. In 1967, Cavour decided to pursue other interests and sold his shares back to the company. Two years later, Justus Lumber welcomed its third generation of Justus men as Andy's son, Jim, joined the growing company. The expansion of County Road 18 into Highway 169 forced Justus Lumber to move to its current location at 11th Avenue South and Excelsior Boulevard (Co Rd 3) in 1971. Peter Throdahl, the son of Andrew's daughter, June, joined the Justus team in 1989.

Peter Throdahl had worked for his grandfather's company for 32 years when he became president of the Justus division of Scherer Bros. Lumber in August 2001. Agreeing to stay for 32 months with the new company to orchestrate the transition, Throdahl plans on taking his grandfather's desk with him when he leaves. The company is left in good hands. Scherer Bros. manufactures some of its own window and door products, a specialty of the Justus Lumber Company.

Mashek Cleaners and Tailors, the oldest family-run business in Hopkins, is about 88 years old and is run by the third and fourth generations of the Mashek family. John Mashek came to Hopkins from Bohemia in 1910 and opened a tailor shop in 1914 at 808 Excelsior Avenue. In those days, men's suits were made by hand and John probably made $50-$70 per week. John's son Jerry Sr. took over his father's business in 1944, doing mostly alterations. They bought their first dry cleaning machine in 1970 and it lasted 7 years. Gerald C. (Jerry Jr.) remembers this vividly because it broke down the day his father retired and headed for Florida and he had to replace it with one that cost $20,000. About 1930 the business moved to the south side of Excelsior Avenue between 10th and 11th and is now located at 916 Mainstreet.

Koss Paint was started by John Koss who worked at a Minneapolis linseed oil plant before taking a job with the M.T.M. in their paint shop where he painted steam engines. When the plant shut down for the winter, or on days off, he and Frank Shimota would paint houses in addition to cutting cordwood for extra income. They used horses and wagons for hauling tools and ladders. John Koss built a house on 7th Avenue and began to store paint and supplies in his home. In 1912, he built a paint store on the north side of Mainstreet which was only open from 7-9:00 p.m. because he worked at M.T.M. during the day. In the early days, paint was very simple–there was oil-based paint, varnish and calcimine, a dusty powder.

In 1920, John Koss bought a truck so he could paint homes farther away from the shop. He painted many of the fine homes in Minnetonka, Minneapolis, Edina and Bloomington. In 1940, the Koss Paint shop at 720-722

Koss Paint ad from the 1956 Hopkins Telephone Book.

Mainstreet was built. John Koss was joined in the business by his son Frank and daughter-in-law Esther, who ran the wallpaper end of the business. Frank supplemented his income, especially in the slow winter months, by running an insurance agency out of the same building. John Koss retired in 1950 and passed away in 1959. Esther's son, Jim took over the business and enlarged the company from selling retail to also selling wholesale to lumber yards and other paint stores. The company has a reputation for excellent paint matching and servicing special orders. Koss Paint now has five divisions, but is no longer at their long-time location on Mainstreet. That block is being vacated and will be demolished in 2002 to make way for a new development.

Pokorny Company, 65 Seventh Avenue South, is also an old family-run business. Henry Pokorny Sr. worked with Bill Bren in his hardware store fixing cars. In those days the hardware stores also handled plumbing and sheet metal work, so that is how Henry learned an additional trade. In 1922, Henry began his own plumbing business at 54 Sixth Avenue South, working out of the garage of his home.

After World War II, when son, Henry Jr., got out of the service, a home on the corner near his father's place came up for sale. An insurance policy had luckily matured, so Henry Jr. had the $2,000 it would take to purchase this property. With his brother, John Roger Pokorny, Henry Jr. built the Pokorny Plumbing building

Strobeck Electric and Undertaking store interior 1004 Excelsior Avenue.

at 65 Seventh Ave S. Henry Sr, Henry, Jr. and John Roger ran the business together as Pokorny Company, Plumbing, Heating and Air Conditioning for many years. Henry Sr. passed away in 1964. Henry Jr. retired in 1987, turning over his part of the business to his sons Paul and Larry. John Roger still works part-time with his son Steve in a spin-off business of plumbing only.

Washburn-McReavy, Stobeck-Johnson Chapel funeral home has a long history in both Hopkins and Minnesota. The current owner, Washburn-McReavy, is the oldest independent family-owned business in the State of Minnesota. That family business was established in 1857, one year before Minnesota became a state and is now a fourth-generation business with 10 chapels throughout the Twin Cities metropolitan area. In 1978, Washburn-McReavy purchased the Strobeck Johnson Chapel, a long-time Hopkins funeral home.

William Strobeck worked for the Oltman Funeral Home located at 7th and Excelsior Avenues and trained at the University of Minnesota. In 1907, Strobeck opened his own undertaking business, which he operated with various co-owners and side businesses until 1958 when Arthur E. Johnson and his nephew Ronald W. Johnson became owners.

For a while around 1910, William and his brother Oscar Strobeck operated under the name "Strobeck Brothers Furniture and Undertaking." They were located at 1004 Excelsior Avenue when they were known as Strobeck Electrical and Undertaking. Jerry Martinson was co-owner with Strobeck and sold out to Larry Hauge during World War II. In the 1940s, the mortuary was located on 10th Avenue South where Fowler's Craft Shop was for many years. In 1951, Hauge bought the former Souba residence west of St. Joseph's Church and made it into Strobeck-Hauge funeral home. This is its location today. For 36 years the Johnsons ran the funeral home under the name Strobeck-Johnson, a Hopkins institution that has the same telephone number it had in 1944. However, prices are certainly higher now. In 1944, a funeral cost about $255.

Doctors and Other Professionals

Until the 1960s, Hopkins was still a small town. If a doctor set up practice in town, chances are the doctor was also a well-known and respected civic leader. Many lawyers, dentists, pastors, bankers, newspaper editors and store owners had the same respect and admiration of the community. But it is the old-time doctors that really capture our imagination as we write this book and we want to remember here some of Hopkins' earliest doctors.

Dr. Catherine Burnes was the first doctor to serve the Hopkins area. She began her work in 1886 and served Hopkins until 1917. Catherine Burnes was the daughter of pioneer George M. Burnes. She was remembered for always wearing a black fedora, a long black coat, a skirt, carrying her little black satchel, and having a ten-dollar bill pinned to her coat. "Doc Kate" lived to be 83 years of age.

The next doctor was **Dr. Albert B. Sweet** who was born in 1847 in Walden, Vermont. He was a soldier in the Civil War with Company F 4th Minnesota Voluntary Infantry accompanying General Sherman on his march. Albert Sweet studied medicine at the University of Minnesota, came to Hopkins in 1892 and retired in 1922. The Sweets had two children: Harry and Lottie. Dr. Sweet lived to be 95 and died at the Veteran's Hospital.

Dr. George Wilbur Moore was born in Moore's Hills, Indiana in 1870 and graduated from Central High School in Minneapolis. He was enrolled in Bellevue Medical School for one and half years. He returned to Minneapolis and entered the University of Minnesota medical school where he got his medical degree in 1892. He came to Hopkins in 1895.

He was an active leader in functions that pertained to the growth and development of Hopkins. He was first elected mayor in 1908 and served as Hopkins' chief executive intermittently until 1936.

Dr. Moore's first marriage was to Charlotte Bell in 1893 and they had two sons: Richard Watts and John Wilbur. In 1904 Charlotte died. Following her in death was John Wilbur who died in 1918. He was one of the first to enlist in World War I. The Hopkins V.F.W. Post is named in his honor.

In 1906, Dr. Moore married Emily Yeager of St. Paul and they had two children. The first child died at age five and the second in infancy.

As an outdoorsman he loved his hunting and fishing. There were times when the Moores would entertain and their guests were served a whole duck for dinner. He was noted for his lack of outerwear and in the dead of winter, he could be seen walking the streets in his shirt sleeves. Many people did not know he wore doeskin underwear under his shirt, made from the deer that he shot.

Richard Koss remembers Dr. Moore as the "sugar doctor" who always brought along candy on housecalls dreaded by sick children. Moore also loved to talk baseball at the local barber shop for hours on end; when his waiting room got full, someone would come and fetch him at the barber shop to come see his patients.

Dr. Moore was feted on his 64th birthday at a homecoming event sponsored by the Civic and Commerce

Dr. George W. Moore, Mayor of Hopkins 1908, 1915-21, 1932-35.

club. This was held at the Fairgrounds, where he was lauded by Senator Archie H. Miller. Again in 1939 when he retired from his active practice, a gathering was held that included Mrs. Margaret Moore McHale, not a relative but the first baby he brought into the world. There was mention of many other babies he delivered including M.B. Hagen.

Dr. James Blake was born in Ontario, Canada in 1872. Upon finishing grammar school at age 16, he came to the United States. He went to Mankato Normal where he graduated from a four-year course in two years in 1892. He then went on to graduate from the University of Minnesota medical school in 1901.

Dr. Blake came to Hopkins and started his practice in 1902. His first office was in the John Koss building and later moved to the Oddfellows Building on the northeast corner of 9th and Excelsior. In 1928, he built his own clinic at 15 Ninth Avenue South.

He married Catherine Agnes McDonald in Mankato in 1904. This union bore four sons and two daughters: Donald, James, Allan, Paul, Mary and Jeanette. Three of the sons pursued medical careers, James and Allan practiced in Hopkins and Paul was a neurosurgeon. Mary and Jeanette both became nurses.

Drs. Moore and Blake were not what one would call good businessmen, but they were kindhearted. Many stories are told about how they went through their accounts receivable and threw out many more than they

Dr. James Blake Sr.

would keep because they knew the lack of money of many of their patients.

Mrs. Blake became a powerful force in public health and nursing movements. She also was very active in the Red Cross. In the mid-1920's she formed the Agnes Blake Study Club for the betterment of Hopkins. She rose to the presidency of the Auxiliary of the Minnesota Medical Association in 1931 and in 1932 to the presidency of the National Auxiliary of the American Medical Association.

A testimonial banquet sponsored by the George R. Wolff Post was a highlight in Dr. Blake's career. In 1951, he was one of eighteen doctors to receive the State Medical Association Fifty-Year Award.

The dreaded diseases of that time were diphtheria, small pox, typhoid fever and consumption (tuberculosis or T.B.)

Dr. Frank Kucera followed Dr. Blake in coming to Hopkins. He was a graduate of the University of Minnesota medical school. In 1921 he came to Hopkins where he practiced above the Thor Skottegard Bakery, midway between 8th and 9th Streets on the north side of Excelsior Avenue. Later his office moved upstairs in the Leathers Building and then to the Nels

Wolff Paint and Wallpaper store between 10th and 11th Streets on the north side of Excelsior Avenue. When Dr. Kucera announced his retirement in 1976, nearly all of the ladies in Hopkins were resigned to the fact that the end had come, for Dr. Kucera's wife, Alma, was a yeoman worker for the ladies of Hopkins.

A copy of Dr. Kucera's memoirs is on file at the Hopkins Historical Society. Dr. Kucera was a long-time school board member. While on the board, Dr. Kucera insisted on chest X-rays for all teachers to ensure they did not have T.B. One teacher had been treated for T.B. but insisted she was not in the infectious stage. The school board required her to produce a physician's statement indicating she tested negative, which she could not do, so she was fired. She died shortly thereafter. Dr. Kucera arranged with the Glen Lake Sanitarium to do the Von Pirquet test on the entire school population. Hopkins school children had 78% positive reaction, while Excelsior had 28%. They assumed this teacher had infected many students.

Drs. Drill, Picha and many others followed in the town of Hopkins, and the town was also graced with fine dentists—Drs. Ed Smetana, Madden, McHale, Malerich and his son A.H. Malerich, Jr.

Martin B. Hagen, Entrepreneur, was born in 1893 and went by the nickname "Punchy" most of his life. He was a Hopkins boy who became probably the biggest entrepreneur in the city's history. In about 1915, he rented a space about six feet wide between what is now Bud's Music and Hoagies Restaurant. He had a roof put over the area, a floor, a door and window in front, and a door in back and Punchy Hagen was in business.

The interior of the Martin B. Hagen laundry shop at 822 Excelsior Avenue W.

Ad for M.B. Hagen Realty Co. from
the 1956 Hopkins Telephone book.

Three young entrepreneurs: Einar Jorgensen, Martin B. Hagen and Roy Kelley.

Hagen operated a shoeshine stand and also started a laundry with his brother Ralph (known as "Putie Pants") who helped with pickup and delivery. He acquired a pedestal, placed it in the front window and set a phonograph on it. The first phonograph he sold was on a day when he met Lou Eidam on the street. He told Lou he would like to sell him the phonograph but Lou said he did not have any money. Punchy then said he would trade but Lou said he had nothing to trade. Punchy then told Lou that he had the span of mules behind his store. That is the story of the first phonograph "sold" in Hopkins.

After his shoeshine stand and laundry business, M.B. Hagen expanded into appliances, insurance and real estate and moved to 902 Excelsior Avenue. When Punchy sold a home, he generally included in the transaction an electric refrigerator and range. At one time, he was the biggest Westinghouse appliance dealer in the northwest.

Punchy later moved to 1013 Excelsior. One day John and Fran Brecka were admiring a refrigerator through the window. Punchy went outside and said, "Why don't you buy the refrigerator for Fran?" John said, "I ain't got no money." Punchy said that was all right, he would deliver it the next day and they could pay him each month whatever they could. The next day, the Breckas had a new refrigerator!

Punchy's son Don and son-in-law, Herb Mason, continued the business and developed such top salesmen as Eugene Riley, Frenchy Faucher, Don Pobuda and others.

A big event each year was when Punchy Hagen entertained the Rotary Club at his home on Lake Minnetonka. Another big event was when he entertained the Raspberry Festival queen candidates and dignitaries at his home.

Antiques, Restaurants, Theater and Art

It's taken about two decades of renovation and renewal, but Mainstreet Hopkins has taken on a whole new character, replacing car dealerships and saloons with a movie theater and arts center, coffee shops, family restaurants and antique and specialty shops.

Businesses are thriving on the 16-block stretch of Mainstreet thanks to some innovative financing perks for business owners and the removal of the pedestrian mall installed with good intentions in the 1970s but deemed a failure that ultimately hurt business.

"Hopkins has taken on a new look and gone from bars and cars to antiques and restaurants."

—Ed Hanlon, long-time Hopkins realtor

A trip down Mainstreet today will remind you of what a Midwestern Main Street used to look like, yet it is strangely modern, too. Renovated facades and signs, topped off with the addition of a beautiful brick clock tower and plaza, windowed storefronts, neat sidewalks, all add to the variety and charm that is now Downtown Hopkins.

With its long history and great location, it is no wonder that Hopkins has recently become an antique dealer's dream. There are currently over a dozen antique shops in town, a business in which the more shops there are, the better business is for them all. Many of the

Michaelangelo's Trattoria, 802 Mainstreet, has street appeal with an outdoor seating area and murals on its façade.

Chez Francoise, 1023 Mainstreet, is an eclectic gift shop located next door to the Boston Garden Restaurant, a favorite family dining spot.

R. Ralston Collectibles, Antiques and Art, 1719 Mainstreet, is one of the many new antique shops in Hopkins.

A beautiful exterior remodeling job was done on an old Hopkins building at 9th Avenue and Mainstreet, now Mary Frances Antiques.

The entire northeast corner of Mainstreet and 8th Avenue has been remodeled to house Glenrose Floral and other gift and antique shops. Formerly the Hopkins City Hall and Fire Station were located on this corner.

shops are based on the mall concept whereby different dealers rent space from the owners and take turns tending the store. Having so many shops in town, particularly within walking distance of each other, is causing Hopkins to become a destination for those who value good quality antiques and collectibles. In addition, Hopkins also has several thrift and gift shops that can add interest to the hunt.

When Suburban Chevrolet moved from Mainstreet Hopkins to Eden Prairie in 1994, the city got a chance to bring back a movie theater, which Hopkins had not had since 1985 and to do something even more ambitious—develop a community art center.

The city bought the property between 11th and 12th

Avenues on either side of Mainstreet and solicited private developers for the movie theater and a restaurant. The new Hopkins Theater opened in the winter of 1997 as a six-screen second-run movie house. Ample parking was provided by a city-owned two-story parking garage erected on 11th Avenue South. The Big Ten Restaurant, with a sports bar theme, opened on the southwest corner of 11th and Mainstreet next to the theater. Several coffee shops (Monkabean, Pekoe and Java) opened in the vicinity.

The Hopkins Center for the Arts was a joint project among the City of Hopkins, the Hopkins Area Art Association (HAAA), the Hopkins School District and the Child's Play Theatre Company, now known as Stages

Before its most recent transformation, Mainstreet Hopkins had an abundance of auto dealerships, gas stations and bars. This photo was taken about 1956 from 12th Avenue looking east. Today, Hopkins Center for the Arts is on the north (left) side of Mainstreet and the Hopkins Theater and Big Ten Restaurant are on the south (right).

The stunning Hopkins Center for the Arts is now the anchor for the lively Hopkins art, theater and music scene. Photo compliments of the City of Hopkins.

Theatre. The $4.25 million art center had its ground breaking on April 23, 1997, and grand opening on November 9 with over 3,000 attending the open house. The 35,900-square-foot building houses a 723-seat auditorium and offices for Stages Theatre, a dance studio, a smaller performance space, an art gallery and art classrooms for the Hopkins School District. The large two-story glass lobby area spanning an entire city block provides a giant "wow" factor. The well-lit lobby has an art gallery and display space along its walls and its hospitality extends to the street where in the evening the art work and ambience can be enjoyed by people strolling along its spacious front sidewalk.

In April 1997, Glenrose Floral also began construction of a retail and office complex three blocks west of the Art Center at 8th Avenue and Mainstreet. This modernized the entire block north of Mainstreet between 7th and 8th.

Since 1997, several more revitalization projects have occurred in or near Downtown Hopkins. Hopkins is once again a nice place to spend an evening—eating out and going to a movie or a play. It's also a great place to spend time in the daytime, exploring the many antique and specialty shops that have added a new focus to Hopkins.

Stages Theatre Company 2002-2003 Season

Harriet's Halloween Candy *Based on the book by Nancy Carlson*

Lord of the Flies *Based on the book by William Golding*

A Christmas Carol *Based on the book by Charles Dickens*

And a Child Shall Lead Them: Brown vs. Board of Education *A World Premier*

Dreams of a Bird Woman: The Sacagawea Story *A World Premier*

Joseph and the Amazing Technicolor Dreamcoat *A Musical*

Dot and Tot of Merryland *Based on the book by L. Frank Baum*

The Dow family and house when the house was new, about mid-1890s.

CHAPTER 4

Neighborhoods and Housing

This chapter, like Hopkins, has a little bit of everything. It would be impossible to chronicle the growth of the Hopkins neighborhoods with any kind of completeness. We will highlight here some of the more historically significant or interesting dwellings and try to describe some of the growth in neighborhoods that make up Hopkins today.

The first homes were simple settlers' cottages hand-built out of logs. Wood frame farm homes were built after saw mills started to produce boards. Several of the earliest frame homes in Hopkins were built big to accommodate travelers in addition to friends and relatives—the Miller, Burnes, Dow and Hopkins homes were noted for their hospitality to travelers and served as both hotel and home in the early days.

The Dow House

When pioneers Daniel E. Dow and Belinda Hamilton married, their combined farm was over 160 acres. They sold some of their land to developers of the M.T.M. factory in 1887 and sold additional land for home sites. The land sales resulted in enough money to build a fifteen-room mansion of the highest quality. The Dow house was built between 1888 and 1894. It included a third-floor ballroom and a bathtub, a novelty at the time. The house was the center of social life of the early community of Hopkins and it was considered quite an honor to be invited to a party at this stately home.

The Dow House was the crown jewel of Hopkins' houses, a landmark that stood between 9th and 10th Avenues South at Second Street South until it was torn

Hopkins in 1979, more than anything else, is a city that defies description as a "suburb." ... There are almost seven thousand dwelling units of all types. They span the complete range from publicly assisted housing (for families and elderly) to mansions, with all types of homes, patio homes and apartments in between... Literally hundreds of businesses and industries operate within Hopkins.... As a consequence, Hopkins gets a healthy influx of people during the day as people arrive to work and shop.... Hopkins in 1979 remains what it has been for a long, long time—growing, changing, producing and serving. It provides the advantages of small-city living in a metropolitan setting—and that is becoming rare in our world. We're four square miles with a little bit of everything."

—Bill Craig, Hopkins City Manager,
Hopkins Review, March, 1979

down by the City of Hopkins in April of 1965. The Village of Hopkins purchased the Dow house from Daniel and Belinda's son, Lewellyn (Dolly) Dow, in 1935 when he had come upon hard times and could not pay the

taxes. It was used by the M.T.M. Company for a few years and as a community center during the depression. On October 11, 1938, as the village was getting ready to use the building as a community center, a fire broke out in the Dow mansion caused by a workman setting it afire while removing paint with a blowtorch. The third floor was destroyed. A simpler roof was built to replace the former elaborate gabled and dormered roof. The porches were removed to prevent someone from falling through and getting injured.

In 1948, the City Library moved into the building. Several generations of Hopkins residents remember when "going to the library" also meant exploring the nooks and crannies of this big old Victorian beauty. It served as a library until 1963, when the heavy weight of the books made the city decide it was structurally unsafe to use as a library anymore.

The city determined it would cost $20,000 to fix up the old structure to a reasonable semblance of its original state. In a poll, 65% of the public wanted to save the building. The City Council put out pleas for the public to find a feasible plan to use the building, but none materialized. The Dow house sat empty until 1965 while the city determined what to do. Meanwhile, they were spending taxpayers' money on a vacant building.

The Dow House and parkland property in 1945. There was a rock garden and picnic shelter in addition to the city's water tower. It was truly the focal point of the town.

The City-owned Dow House in early 1938 still had porches attached and an elaborately gabled roof.

Discussions in the early 1960s about whether or not to save the Dow house captures the dilemma citizens and city leaders inevitably face—to restore coveted landmarks at an exorbitant cost, or allow the landmarks to be destroyed in order to make way for improvements that will help modernize and be cost effective for the city. In Hopkins, this same issue has arisen time and again. The old Opera Hall has been successfully rehabilitated, the old South Junior High has been redesigned and reused and there are other success stories, too, but for the Dow house, an era came to a close when the City Council voted in early February, 1965, to auction off the fire places, save a few interesting architectural pieces and tear the building down.

The end came in April 1965 when a contractor tore down the Dow house with little fanfare and "with the greatest of ease" because of the decrepit condition of the structure. Some of the architectural features of the Dow house were saved. The "DOW" leaded glass window graces a wall of the Hopkins Historical Society and a small section of the ornate stairway banister greets visitors to the Society's museum. The 9-foot high fireplace mantelpiece was loaned to Franz Hall to be used in the restoration of his old home at 557 Dayton Avenue, St. Paul.

The city sold the property for $125,000 to the U.S. Government in 1966 to build a new Hopkins post office. Today the post office, 910 First Street South, sits on the site of the former Dow house.

The Dow house was just one of many grand old homes now gone. Many simple dwellings such as worker homes are also gone. Some survive in photos, while others do not even have photographs to bring them back to memory. Some turn of the century homes survive but they have been remodeled to such an extent their early owners would hardly recognize them.

The First Neighborhoods

The major problem facing the M.T.M. factory was housing for their workers and families. The need gave birth to the West Minneapolis Land Company on July 20, 1887 started by four Minneapolis businessmen whose purpose for incorporating was for "the building of tenements." They began their work on July 21, 1887, when the Harley Hopkins family sold the company 80 acres of their farm. Within two months, the plat of "West Minneapolis Center" covered all the land from what is now County Road 18 to Tyler Avenue and from 2nd Street North to Second Street South. After building a few homes to house employees of the threshing machine factory, the West Minneapolis Land Company filed for bankruptcy during the depression of 1893.

The Beehive

The two-story tenement called the "beehive" was one of the first structures built by the West Minneapolis Land Company about 1887 to create much needed living quarters for workers. It was located on the north side of Excelsior Avenue and the west corner of Van Buren. It served as the first home for hundreds if not thousands of early settlers that moved to West Minneapolis seek-

I moved to the "beehive" during the summer of 1908 or 1909. It was an old run down building then, much in need of repairs and paint.… The beehive had about 12 rooms on each floor. There were 8 bedrooms in the central part that did not have any windows. There were transoms over each door that could be tipped in or out to get air from the adjoining room… The building had no plumbing, electricity or central heating. I lived upstairs and that meant pumping water from a well outside and carrying it up stairs in a pail. In the winter time we would have to take a tea kettle of boiling water down to the pump and pour it down in the pump to thaw it out and to prime it, if no one else had used it just before you…

—Florence (Stenzel) Portner, 1978

The only known photo of the beehive was in the background of a photo taken of Earl Heinecke about 1915. Note the train in the background.

was built in 1887 or 1888 at about 121-8th Ave. S. and was moved to 801-803 2nd Street South about 1894. It was the first hotel in Hopkins and housed workers for the M.T.M. Company, the Red Wing Sewer Pipe Company and the railroad and streetcar workers. There was not one clothes closet in the entire hotel, because in those days, men lived out of their suitcases. Initially, the owner, Samuel Smith, also worked at the M.T.M. factory. Hotel guests were charged $3.00 to $3.50 per week for board and rent. Meals were furnished and some lunches were put in lunch pails for the workers. Laundry was not furnished except for fresh bed linens and towels. The roomers would go to the lakes in the summer or to the public baths at barber shops along Mainstreet to bathe, where the going rate was 25 cents for a bath and towel. There was a laundry in town to get clothes clean.

ing work at the M.T.M. Co. It got its name from the many families living there with lots of children, who were always moving about inside or out. Most of the families were of Bohemian descent. The beehive apartment building was torn down on March 31, 1932.

A neighborhood grew up on the east side. Campbell's store was there, the M.&St.L. depot, a blacksmith shop, the Harley H. Hopkins home and the Hopkins Post Office.

The Smith Family lived on the first floor where there was a 35-foot room that served as both living and dining room. Seven tables were used to feed the guests. The home was furnished in black walnut when it opened and it had a carriage house out back. But it depended on the M.T.M. boarders for its business. During a bad period when men at the factory were being paid in notes

The West Minneapolis House

Dwellings began to be built on land to the north and the south of the M.T.M. factory to provide homes for workers. The "West Minneapolis First Division" extended from Excelsior Avenue on the north, 13th Ave. S. on the west, 7th Street S. on the south and approximately 5th Avenue S. on the east. North of the factory, this was land previously owned by the Dows and their home had a prominent position in the center of the neighborhood. Besides small worker homes built for families, many larger boarding houses or hotels were built to house single or transient workers. By the mid-1890s this part of town began to develop quickly as the commercial focus shifted away from the east end toward what is now Mainstreet Hopkins.

The 13-room West Minneapolis House

The West Minneapolis House, 802 2nd St. S, Front view, with the Samuel Smith family standing in front.

instead of cash, the black walnut furniture was burned for fuel to keep the hotel warm.

Chester Smith was born July 7, 1902 and grew up in the West Minneapolis House. He was one of the first newspaper delivery boys in Hopkins. He also was a projectionist at the first movie theater in town. In 1941, he took over the West Minneapolis House after his parents had died. He recalled that a few pieces of original hotel furniture were stored in the basement and brought out at Christmas each year along with the crystal-bowled kerosene lamps used for decorations in the later years.

The hotel continued to take in transients until the 1920s and then it evolved into a boarding house. Chester Smith worked at Dahlberg Motors in addition to having boarders. The West Minneapolis House was showing a lot of wear, Smith could not find a buyer to renovate the old structure, so through an urban renewal program, the house was torn down in the winter of 1973.

Barefoot Valley

By the middle of the 1890s, the M.T.M. factory was straining to enlarge its work force. They were able to attract additional Bohemian immigrants, but housing was still a major problem. By 1905, the M.T.M. Company decided to construct some simple houses for these new workers. Lots were purchased on 12th, 13th and 14th Avenues North of the M.&St.L. railroad tracks. About a dozen one-and-a-half story houses were built and rented to the new employees. When all these

houses were built, they had no plumbing, electric wiring, heating or insulation. All of them had open front porches and they all had those famous two-holers near the back of the lot.

From 1905 until about 1920, all of the residents of the area were Bohemian immigrants except for two families, the Milberts and the Blomquists. Because the new Bohemian families were too poor to buy shoes, they often went barefoot, so the rest of the town christened this area "Barefoot Valley." Since there were no street numbers in those days, some method had to be used to denote each area. The result is that the part of Hopkins opposite Barefoot Valley was known as "Finland" reflecting the Scandinavian settlement of Swedes, Danes and Fins.

Up until about 1920, the neighborhood had a rural atmosphere. Nearly every family had a large garden, a cow and a flock of chickens. Clint Blomquist tells of the 100 hives of bees his father kept. The honey was sold in his father's store for $1.00 per gallon. Unlike other boys, Clint always wore shoes—his lawn was clover and that was no place for bare feet!

The Avenues

What is now known as "**The Avenues**" developed north of the factory and the emerging commercial area along Excelsior Avenue. It extended north to Minnetonka Mills Road and what became Highway 7 and on the west to 15th Avenue North and extending east to 5th Avenue North (to Burnes' farm). This area was platted as "West

Homes along Eleventh Avenue published in the *Hopkins News,* July 26, 1906.

Newly planted trees and freshly poured sidewalks grace the street of Eighth Avenue, photo also from the 1906 *Hopkins News*.

South Hopkins

In south Hopkins, the neighborhood that housed the M.T.M. workers became known as **Peaceful Valley**. It is unknown how this area was named but perhaps it was the more pastoral setting amidst farms that gave it its name. In contrast to the more bustling neighborhoods or to the noisy factory and railroad area to the north, this must have seemed a peaceful place. Peaceful Valley extended from 8th to 5th Avenues South and 5th to 7th Streets South. Its northern border was the M.T.M. factory property (now Supervalu) and its eastern border was the Hennepin County Poor Farm property. Some of the worker homes built in this area about 1900 can still be seen today. Peaceful Valley was literally on the "other side of the tracks" from city services for many years. It wasn't until 1952 that it was hooked up to city water service. There was an old dump on 6th Avenue South that was ordered closed in 1914, the same year 11th Avenue South was extended to reach the southern neighborhoods.

Minneapolis 2nd Division." By 1910, Hopkins had 468 dwellings and 533 families. The most common dwellings were neat 1 1/2-story frame family homes. Farmland surrounded this neighborhood, but the belching smokestacks of the trains and factory could be seen to the south.

"Gibb's First Addition to Hopkins" extended the western border of Hopkins to 17th Avenue before 1940 and "West Minneapolis Third Division" further extended this border to approximately Shady Oak Road in June 1949. As Hopkins got larger, Minnetonka Township got smaller. To this day, the borders of Hopkins are jagged and it is sometimes hard to tell what is in Minnetonka and what is in Hopkins.

In the 1950s, Steiner and Koppelman builders developed the western half of the poor farm property into a neighborhood adjoining Peaceful Valley and named it **Park Valley**.

A devastating tornado ripped through the east end and south area of Hopkins on June 2, 1925, destroying many homes in its wake, in addition to doing a huge

Tornado damage to homes at 2nd Street S. and 5th Avenue S., June 2, 1925.

amount of damage to Justus Lumber, the M.T.M. factory and the Harley H. Hopkins home. Because of the tornado, though, many photographs were taken of simple worker homes in early Hopkins that we might not otherwise have.

The last farmers to sell their property for development were the raspberry and produce farmers in south Hopkins. As these farmers sold out, large apartment complexes or industrial campuses grew up.

Interlachen Park

With the incorporation of St. Louis Park Village (October 4, 1886) and Golden Valley Village (December 17, 1886), all that was left of the former Minneapolis Township was about 800 acres in portions of Sections 19 and 20. This was not enough acreage to maintain a township government, and the Minneapolis town hall, then at Lake St. and Lyndale Ave., was deemed too far away, so the area that now encompasses Interlachen Park was attached to Minnetonka Township for administrative purposes. Residents voted at Minnetonka Mills, but many did their day-to-day business in Hopkins Village.

In the 1850s, an Indian trail crossed the southwest corner of Interlachen Park. There was a huge oak tree at 150 Maple Hill that helped mark the way for the Indians. This trail went from Ft. Snelling and St. Anthony Falls to Lake Minnetonka. As late as the 1930s evidence could be seen of the route of this trail.

The neighborhood became known as "Interlachen Park" when on July 1, 1911 the plat of the original (south) half of the area was filed by Fred A. Savage, for its owners, Lester A. and Arthur E. Boyce. These two men had acquired the land from their father, John Rand Boyce, on September 16, 1886, who had bought it in 1878 from Calvin G. Goodrich, a former president of the Twin City Rapid Transit Company. That same year (1911) the Interlachen Golf Club had been built and a few enthusiastic members wished to build their homes nearby. The first lot to be sold in the development went to Charles E. Purdy, one-time president of the Minneapolis Board of Education. The first house was built in 1913 for Lester Boyce at 136 Maple Hill Road, and that home is still in the family. That same year the Charles A. Tuller home at 200 Homedale and the Charles Wilkins home at 236 Interlachen Road were built.

The original F.A. Savage plat records the names of the roads in Interlachen Park as Monk (now Blake), Boyce (now Ashley), Murray (now Holly), Purdy (now Oak-

wood), Interlachen (unchanged), Tuller (now Maple Hill), Homedale (unchanged), Wilkin (now Hawthorne) and Lyons (now Meadowbrook). The name changes were made sometime around 1930 when the Interlachen Park Needlework Guild decided on a beautification program for street names.

The northern part of Interlachen Park was platted in three separate additions: (1) the Charles H. Preston's Interlachen Park filed on July 17, 1947, (2) the Frank H. Hutchinson Addition filed on Nov 19, 1947, and (3) the Ripley B. Brower, Jr., addition on Oct. 18, 1949.

Interlachen Park was annexed to Hopkins in two parts in 1949 and 1952. Always a tight-knit neighborhood, Interlachen Park grade school children attended the Harley Hopkins School and now attend Eisenhower Elementary or private schools. Until March 1940, telephone calls to Hopkins cost 10 cents, and within Interlachen Park homes were either in the Hopkins or the Minneapolis telephone exchange—a situation that created another link in neighborliness. It was sometimes cheaper to make a visit than to make a call!

Neighborhoods Platted before 1942

The Hopkins Historical Society has a property assessment log kept by Thomas J. Kosanda from 1940-1952 as City Tax Assessor that shows the neighborhoods established before 1940 in addition to the original West Minneapolis subdivisions already mentioned.

"Anderson's 1st Addition to St. Louis Park" is the area north of the Blake School property to 2nd Street North, with Monk Avenue being the easterly border. Several homes were in the 800-1100 block of Excelsior Avenue west of Blake Road before 1940, but the bulk of this area was commercial property, which included the Massey Harris Company.

"L.P. Crevier's 1st Addition to West Minneapolis" was a small neighborhood in southwest Hopkins from 13th-17th Avenue South, wedged between the M.&St.L. and Chicago, Milwaukee and St. Paul Railroad tracks south of 5th Street South. "Davidson's Addition to West Minneapolis" was an even smaller neighborhood in south Hopkins having homes on large lots on just two streets by 1940, platted as the 1000 blocks of 9th - 13th Ave. S.

"Gibb's First Addition to West Minneapolis" extended the Avenues to 17th Avenue North. "Stevens' Oakwood Park" had homes in the 200 and 300 blocks of Tyler, Van Buren and Monroe Avenues. "West Minneapolis Center" near Harley Hopkins School was developed in what is known as the "Presidents Streets."

The Campbell Farm was developed into neighborhoods after World War II.

The "West Minneapolis Annex" subdivision extended 7th and 8th Avenues South below 7th Street South by 1940, too.

The **Hobby Acres** neighborhood, (Lohman-Aarhus Division) east of the newly created 5th Avenue and south of Highway 7 had a few homes on Althea Lane and Sweet Briar assessed in 1940 and by 1942 had more homes built on Wayside Road, Holly Hock, 5th Avenue, Hazelane and Farmdale.

The **Parkridge** neighborhood began in 1942 with homes on Washington, 1st St, Ridgewood Drive, Park Lane, Oak Glen Drive and 5th Avenue, although it was platted in 1929. The homes built in the 1940s were considered "war housing." The land was available, but home building materials were scarce. The Parkridge neighborhood is known for its small homes built on relatively large lots.

Still not platted or developed in 1940 were slightly less than 40 properties, consisting of the two Hopkins family's heritage homes, various farms, including much of the huge Campbell farm (formerly the Burnes' homestead), dairies, industrial properties including the Minneapolis Moline acreage, as well as the Poor Farm and Fair Ground properties owned by Hennepin County.

Neighborhoods Annexed After World War II

Hopkins' growth slowed down during the depression of the 1930s and during the big war, but after World War II, it really took off. Census statistics show a population of 4,100 in 1940, 7,595 by 1950 and 11,370 by 1960. Hopkins had almost tripled in 20 years!

Cecil Kloss, who followed in his father Herman Kloss' footsteps after World War II as a homebuilder in Hopkins, recalls they built 227 single-family houses within the Hopkins city limits in a twenty-year time span. Many of these homes were along 5th Avenue and in the new neighborhoods established on the former Burnes/Campbell farm as property was sold by Ann Campbell Borland. "We always got local Hopkins people to work with us," recalled Cecil Kloss in a talk he gave to the Hopkins Historical Society in 1997. There was Buzz Arlt on the cement crew, Arthur Shelby built the fireplaces, carpenters were Clem Stifter, Ralph Souba, Jim Stepanek or Charlie Sanderson; Henry Pokorny provided the plumbing, Gustafson & Fuxa (with Red Corey and Catherine Schutz) the electric, A.W. Hammerlund the sheet metal. Heating was completed by Eddie and Alvin Plehal, painters were Hennig Anderson and Harry Douglas, excavating was done by Mel Johnson and after he retired, by Bollig and sons. The lumber came from the local yards: Justus Lumber, Lampert Yards with Bob Berchek as manager, or from Dan and Dennis O'Leary at Pioneer Lumber.

Kloss also recalled the early years working with his father when Fred Swanson would excavate with a large scraper pulled behind a horse. The tractor style excavating was a real improvement in construction. One of the reasons so many of the pre-World War II homes in Hopkins have steps leading up to the first floor, and thus relatively shallow basements, was because excavating was done with primitive equipment in the early years.

Some of the growth of Hopkins can be attributed to annexing areas previously located in Minnetonka Township. The most common reason for a neighborhood choosing to join Hopkins was because they wanted city services such as sewer and water that Hopkins could provide. The fact that Hopkins' city sewer connected to the Twin Cities Sewer system in June of 1950 probably helped some neighborhoods make a decision.

The **Bellgrove** neighborhood is a case in point. It has about 70 homes, many on spacious wooded lots. It is the northernmost protrusion of Hopkins just north of Oak Ridge Golf Course and straddling Minnetonka Boulevard. It is a quiet secluded place where many yards slope into the untamed overgrown flood plain of Minnehaha Creek, ending at the creek itself. It is surrounded on three sides by Minnetonka but Bellgrove chose to be annexed to Hopkins in 1950 to get city water.

Other areas annexed by Hopkins were: the Oak Ridge Country Club (March 1946); West Minneapolis III, the "Avenues" from 17th to Shady Oak Road (June 1949); Drillane Addition (October 1949); Interlachen Park (1949) and East Interlachen Park (1952); and Bellgrove Addition (1951-52).

Mostly single-family homes were built with a few exceptions. The **Elmo Park Apartments** (now known as **Brentwood Park**) were built in 1950 on former farmland north of Highway 7 and east of 17th Avenue North, which supplied Hopkins' first rental units. In addition, the **H & H Pines Mobile Home Park** was built in Minnetonka Township abutting Hopkins' west side just after World War II to provide both rental and owned low-cost housing. After repeatedly applying to obtain Hopkins city services, the city of Hopkins finally annexed the "Pines" in October 1966. In 1996, the Pines Trailer Court was replaced with the townhouse neighborhood, "The Oaks of Mainstreet."

The Last of the Farm Land Developed

Since after World War II, developers have been ready to pounce on any available land in Hopkins. During the 1960s and 1970s, many raspberry farmers in south Hopkins were ready to sell off their land. Multiple dwellings have been the most efficient use of land since the '60s. 53% of the housing units now in Hopkins were built between 1960 and 1980; most of these are multiple dwellings. The largest multiple-dwelling development in Hopkins is the **Westbrooke Patio Homes** at 11th Avenue South and 7th Street South developed beginning in the 1960s on over 77 acres of farmland formerly owned by the Trombleys, Vaskos and some of the Feltls. Apartments were added, so today over 1,300 units make up the Westbrooke neighborhood. A small commercial center serves the neighborhood, at 11th Avenue South and Westbrooke Way.

Opus II sits on 450 acres of former raspberry farmland in Minnetonka near the south end of Hopkins. Designed by Rauenhorst Corporation, this community was carefully planned to use the land and the natural features to create a clean, functional neighborhood of office, industrial and commercial areas adjoining high-density residential units interspersed with walking paths and ponds. By 1979, over 3,000 people had already been employed at Opus II and it was expected that someday it would be enlarged to employ over 6,000. Most of the old farmhouses were torn down,

The Elmo Park Apartments were the first rental units built after World War II. They are now the Brentwood Park Townhomes.

but many of the original families were honored with streets names.

One relic of a bygone era that sat amidst the Opus development on 3.45 acres of land was the heritage home of the Feltl family. The former home of John Joseph Feltl, pioneer, berry grower and community leader, was built in stages beginning in 1872 and excellently maintained by subsequent owners. In 1993, the home was considered "a rare surviving example of a brick or brick-veneer house of late Victorian/Post Victorian style indicative of those built by relatively prosperous farmers between 1870-1900." However, it was located in an area not zoned for residential use and was put up for sale to be moved. No buyer was found, so the house was leveled. Descendants consoled themselves by saving some of the pale yellow Chaska bricks from the old farmstead. They had previously erected a plaque on a stone monument in honor of John Feltl's daughter Margaret, which reads: "Dedicated to Margaret E. Feltl, farmer and school teacher, whose vision and persistence in preserving the land hereabouts for something other than a solid waste disposal site, provided the opportunity for OPUS II to become a reality for present and future generations to enjoy."

The "Feltl Rock" was placed on October 12, 1988 on Smetana Drive across from the St. Therese Home. The Feltl family home had been located about 300 feet west of this monument.

Built near Opus II in 1987 is **St. Therese Residence** of Hopkins, a 226-unit senior apartment complex with

The John Joseph Feltl Home, built beginning in 1872. Photo taken in 1988.

luxury apartments units and services such as a beauty shop, library, coffee shop, underground parking, nursing and pastoral care, with an attached nursing home facility.

> *Hopkins is about 98 percent developed with little vacant land. It has been in redevelopment mode for a number of years, and has had to deal with financing improvements and increasing its industrial strength while maintaining its hometown feel.*
>
> —Bill Craig, former Hopkins City Manager

Apartments and Condominiums

Since its beginnings, Hopkins has guarded its economic independence by nurturing the industries that employed its people. So, in the early 1960s, when it became time to provide new housing to broaden the tax base and the work pool, Hopkins officials and citizens saw no problem with erecting multiple dwellings. Federal urban renewal money became available in 1965, the city redrafted the zoning map from single to multiple-family dwellings and the apartment building craze was underway.

Clint Blomquist, city building inspector from 1962 to 1972, said the first apartment builder was Elmo Ginkel, who walked into Blomquist's office and laid the plan on his desk for a seven-story building on Blake Road. "I was trained in building single-family homes. Boy was that a shock," said Blomquist. After that, other plans flowed in steadily; the tallest building reached 11 stories. That was the Hopkins Village Apartments at 9 Seventh Avenue S. This created a problem because the Hopkins fire trucks could not handle a fire in such a tall building.

A drive through town in 1980 would reveal the following apartments: The **Dow Towers** erected in 1970-71 at 22 5th Avenue South, **Rosewood West** on 5th Avenue North (155 units), **Hopkins Plaza**, 151 8th Avenue South (102 units), **West Side Village** at 101 Blake Road North (165 units), **Ramsgate Apartments** on 421 North Van Buren Ave. (360 units), **Central Park Manor** on 1510 Mainstreet, built on the site of the old high school (109 units), **Creekwood Estates** on Northeast Lake Street (180 units), and by far the largest—**Westbrooke** in the south of town (1300 units).

By 1980, the U.S. Census figures revealed a shocking

Parkside single-family homes and Citigables townhomes.

statistic—60 percent of Hopkins' dwelling units were apartments. Hopkins had 7,700 renters! This precipitated discussions about the density and aesthetics of so many apartment buildings in town. In an effort to achieve balance, further construction of buildings over four or five stories was banned. But this didn't alleviate the problem of the civic silence of renters. Renters often do not have the stake in the community that homeowners do.

To tip the scales a bit the other way, some housing units built in the late 1980s and 1990s in Hopkins were owner-occupied condominiums or townhouses. The **CitiGables** townhomes opened in 1989 near City Hall is a case in point. Older homes were torn down in the city's downtown and a new "neighborhood" was built. CitiGables has 14 townhouse and 49 Condominium units, with secured building entrances, underground parking and perhaps one of the best locations in the Twin Cities for access to banks, medical centers, a post office, grocery store, library, art center, movie theater and more. **The Oaks of Mainstreet** is another successful homeowner project located on the former site of the Pines Trailer Court. One of the latest medium-density home projects in Hopkins is **Parkside**—58 single-family homes built on 10 acres of land that used to be a parking lot of the former Honeywell Company in northeast Hopkins. Homes in Parkside

were completely sold within one year of the purchase of the land for approximately $150,000-$200,000 each.

Revitalization

Some of the older homes in Hopkins were rehabilitated with Federal Community Redevelopment loan and grant money throughout the 1970s and 80s. The city had been studying the area around its new city hall since 1957, but urban renewal started for real in 1965 with the appointment of the city's first Housing and Redevelopment Authority. In studying the older area of Hopkins, they had found that out of 61 residential buildings, many of which were multiple dwellings or boarding houses, 48 were substandard. In addition, 5 of the 22

The Oaks of Mainstreet is a new kind of neighborhood. These units are owner-occupied, and within a short walk to all the amenities Hopkins has to offer.

These houses are all gone now, replaced by government buildings and apartment houses, but they were in run-down condition prior to their removal. Looking north between 8th and 9th Avenues South.

commercial buildings in the old section of town were substandard. They applied to the Federal Government's Housing and Urban Development department. City leaders were greatly pleased with an announcement in July of 1967 from U.S. Senators Eugene J. McCarthy and Walter F. Mondale that Hopkins had been approved for a $104,850 planning grant for a $1.21 million urban renewal project. It was only the second Twin Cities suburb with such approval; South St. Paul had a similar project approved a month earlier.

Over time, with federal monies, 120 homes in Hopkins were brought up to code. The most visible project was the conversion of South Junior High School into affordable housing for 100 families, now known as **Raspberry Ridge.**

Hopkins received the 1995 Innovative City Award in recognition of its special efforts to improve its multifamily housing and help first-time homebuyers find homes in Hopkins. It offers low-interest loans and forgivable grants to low-moderate income homeowners. It provides subsidized housing for the elderly and handicapped. All rental units are registered and inspected to comply with Hopkins' maintenance code. A neighborhood advisory board meets regularly to discuss issues important to the town. There are real incentives to keep up property maintenance and the community takes pride in its housing efforts.

Historic Homes Project

Hopkins came late to the historic preservation bandwagon. Most of the old homes are gone; they were not elaborate homes to begin with. The Dow House, a Vic-

torian beauty, was the symbolic heart of Hopkins for many years but even that could not save it from the wrecking ball. The Feltl home was well maintained but it was in the wrong place after the new Opus II neighborhood was planned. But there are over 60 homes that were built in the 1890s or early 1900s that are still in use. Many have been lovingly cared for by their various owners. Many times, several generations of a family have lived in the same home.

On October 28, 2001, the Hopkins Historical Society presented the first of its Historic Homes Proclamations recognizing these homes as integral parts of the city's history and the homeowners as those who have provided stability to the neighborhood, character to the community and value to the city. The awards were signed by Hopkins Historical Society President Dean Empanger and Hopkins Mayor Gene Maxwell.

The first proclamation was given to Rick Brausen and Kristin Chalberg, owners of the home at 345 N. 13th Ave, which they purchased from Frances Smykal in 2000 and are renovating with her help. This home was built in 1907. In 1922, Frank Smykal bought the home from Joseph Plehal. In 1954, Frances and Joseph Smykal purchased the home from Joseph's father, Frank. In the early 1900s, Frank owned most of the land surrounding the home and the Smykal family raised a cow, celery and tomato plants. The two-car garage formerly had a hayloft, a cow barn on one side and a chicken coop on the other.

The second proclamation, given to Suzette Steppe, was for her home at 302 N. 19th Ave. Built in 1902 by Joseph Pashina, the home was purchased in 1919 by Joseph Dudycha, a Czechoslovakian immigrant. Dudycha started working at Minneapolis Moline until he incurred an eye injury. He then worked for the railroad and farmed the area around his home. He owned the entire west side of the 300 block of 19th Ave. N., then in Minnetonka. In the early 1950s, Joseph Dudycha's daughter Veronica bought the home along with her husband Thomas Steppe. In October 1999, their daughter Suzette Steppe purchased the home, becoming the third generation to own the home.

Faculty of Hopkins School 1915.

CHAPTER 5

Education and Worship

The early settlers had a cultural heritage with a strong respect for knowledge and education. Soon after building a home, the settlers gave their thoughts to educating their children. Before an actual schoolhouse was built, classes were held in various cabins or available buildings. In 1862, the first school building was built on land donated by George Burnes and it eventually became known as Burnes School.

The Bohemian community was the only distinct ethnic group in the Hopkins area initially, and they banded together fairly early to teach religion and customs to their children. By 1868, the Bohemians were meeting in homes to conduct services in both the Catholic and Protestant traditions. In 1880, St. Margaret's Catholic Church was completed in the Shady Oak area. It was the first church building in the area.

A small group of Protestant Bohemians managed to erect a church building, which was dedicated in 1888, and was known for many years as the Bohemian Presbyterian Church, now Faith Presbyterian located just west of the Hopkins border. Not having the language barrier the Bohemians had, the Yankee settlers had connections to Minneapolis area churches in the early years before they built their first church building in the Hopkins area, a Methodist church, in 1889; this congregation had been organized as early as 1885.

Today there are numerous houses of worship in Hopkins and its school district serves the city of Hopkins, most of Minnetonka, about half of Golden Valley, and portions of Edina, Eden Prairie, St. Louis Park and Plymouth, with a school population of about 8,300 students.

Strong faith traditions and strong schools make a very sound infrastructure for a town. Here, we are proud to explore Hopkins' past as it pertains to education and worship.

Schools

The first known school location and teacher was Mrs. Lamb who conducted classes in her small log cabin, which was the first residence of John P. Miller located south of County Road 3 (now Excelsior Boulevard), in line with the western boundary of Ninth Avenue South.

Around 1857, Mrs. Fairfield opened her home on what is now Washington Avenue and taught a three-month term. The next known "school" was conducted in a shanty on the Harley Hopkins farm and taught by Miss Sarah Gates, who later became Mrs. George Baird. A little later, a person by the name of Allison taught school in a granary in the yard of the Hopkins' home site. Gates and Allison taught for five years.

Archie Miller's father, Frank (son of John P. Miller), used to tell about being carried across the swamp east of his father's cabin on the way to school. For a time the man who carried young Frank was Daniel Dow. The school was located in a granary on the land belonging to Harley Hopkins.

During this time, the children of the Bohemian settlement were being taught by Mrs. William I. (Hannah) Bryant in the vicinity of Bryant Lake. Mrs. Bryant had been a teacher in her native Boston and taught first in her log cabin, then in a log schoolhouse built at the junction of what is now Shady Oak and Rowland Roads about 1856. Although she was not paid, the children's parents helped Mr. Bryant clear his land and rendered other services for payment.

By 1862, some parents were sending their youngsters to the Pratt School in St. Louis Park. A group of settlers,

Burnes School built in 1862, was Hopkins' first school building. Photo 1889.

among them the Burnes, Griswold and Miller families, decided it was time for a school building of their own.

Burnes—The First Hopkins School Building

Hopkins' first school building was built in 1862 on an acre of land donated by George Burnes on the northwest corner of Washington Avenue and Excelsior Boulevard. Burnes School was a one-room frame schoolhouse.

Henry Hicks was employed as the first schoolteacher. He came from Illinois and had been wounded in the face in the Civil War. It is said that he had a profound influence on his students. He taught reading, writing, spelling, geography and arithmetic (up to elementary algebra) to students who ranged in age from six to 20. He also organized spelling bees, a popular competitive activity at the time and conducted a singing school. In later years English grammar, speech, United States history and bookkeeping were added to the curriculum.

Henry Hicks had an interesting life after leaving teaching; he was appointed Hennepin County Sheriff, served as Justice of the Peace in Minneapolis, studied law and eventually became a District Court Judge.

Enrollment increased with the coming of the Minneapolis Threshing Machine Company in 1887, two teachers were hired and a new school was needed. After

> *In selling homes in Hopkins we did so on our school system. Hopkins was always known for the finest of schools. We had the best teachers and the best principals and superintendents. Hopkins, in my time, had the best athletics—we were #1.*
>
> —Donald Milbert, Former Hopkins Mayor

Burnes School in remission, 1910.

1888, the last year the Burnes school building was used as a school, it stood empty for 37 years except for occasional use by churches or for storage (the 1910 photo shows a Gold Medal Flour sign over the door). Talk of preserving it as a historical site ended when it was completely leveled by the tornado of June 2, 1925.

Second and Third Hopkins School Buildings

In 1888, the south half of the new two-story brick school was completed. The school contained four rooms and was located on the west side of Ninth Avenue North one-half block north of Excelsior Avenue (now Mainstreet). During the winter of 1888-1889 all the Burnes School blackboards, erasers, chalk, pointers, globe, maps, dictionary, books and wood box were hauled to the new school. The building had no electricity or running water, but did have gas lights, outside pump and outside privies. These conveniences were later added to the building. Increase in enrollment made it necessary to hire two more teachers, bringing the total to four.

In 1898 the north half of the building and the bell tower were added and in 1902, another eight-room wooden building was built just south of the brick one on 9th Avenue North. These two buildings handled the elementary classes until the Junior High School was built in 1925, at which time this new building housed both elementary and junior high students.

A two-year High School course was added to the school curriculum with the first graduation held in 1898. Soon thereafter, high school was extended to four years; the first four-year graduation ceremony was held in 1902 in the Opera Hall.

Pupils were called to start classes by the ringing of a bell located in the bell tower on top of the brick building. Now and then, a student would be fortunate enough to help ring the bell by pulling the bell rope. Boys and girls were separated during playtime—the girls' playground was south of the schools and the boys' playground was north.

Both of these school buildings were demolished in 1926 after Elementary and Junior High classes were moved to the new school on Excelsior Boulevard north between 13th and 14th Avenues, formerly known as South Junior High, today known as Raspberry Ridge Apartments and the Hopkins Activity Center.

First Hopkins Senior High School Building

In 1908, the first high school building in the area was opened. It was located on the south side of Excelsior Blvd. between 15th and 16th Avenues. Students from all

The high school and grade school buildings on 9th Ave. N. were the second and third schools built. The brick building operated 1888-1926. The wood frame building operated 1902-1925. They were both demolished in 1926.

The Hopkins Senior High School Building between 15th and 16th Avenues facing Excelsior Boulevard. Built 1908, demolished 1974. Photo – 1943.

the surrounding districts (Shady Oak, Glen Lake, Burwell, Oak Knoll, Eden Prairie, Harley Hopkins) came here for their higher learning. The school housed the 7th and 8th grades and the four-year high school.

High school education emphasized book learning to prepare students for the University or Colleges. In 1912, two classes a week of manual training were introduced as well as a sewing class. By 1914, these and a cooking class were taught on a full-time basis. In 1918-19, a commercial department was started with classes in shorthand and typing. In 1923-24, under arrangement with the University of Minnesota, courses in agriculture were taught.

As some of these pupils lived quite a distance from the school, a few came by horse and buggy. In the early 1920s, the students from Eden Prairie came by bus that was driven by a junior or senior student.

Separation of the sexes continued in this building by having two entrances, front and back; the girls' entrance was on the west and the boys' on the east. It also had stairways inside designated in the same manner. The front doors were protected by heavy iron gates that were padlocked each night. Every Halloween these gates were lifted off the hinges by some energetic youth and hidden somewhere in the neighborhood.

On the second story of the building was the Assembly Room—the home-room for all high school students, where they started their day and spent any free time they had. Here on nice days with the large south windows wide open could be heard the outside noises, especially the merry-go-round music and the roar of the crowds at the harness races during the County Fair days in September. The Assembly Room was host to any all-school meetings or entertainment.

What a climax to a long career of teaching! Mike W. Zipoy, commercial instructor at Hopkins High, was issuing report cards last Friday, his last day of school before retiring after 25 years of teaching at the senior high. Some 30 students picked up their report cards and left the room. Mr. Zipoy and three students remained. Suddenly, one shouted that the ceiling was bulging. Mr. Zipoy and Co. backed against a wall, whereupon a sizeable chunk of plaster crashed to the floor of the old room B4 in a shower of dust. No one was injured. Maybe it means "hurry up" with that new senior high—Hopkins certainly needs it!

—*The Hennepin County Review*, June 17, 1954.

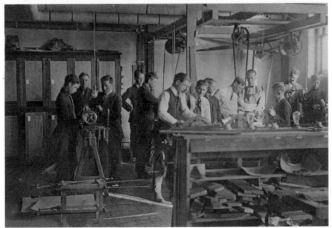

Imagine yourself here… in a 1915 Hopkins High School cooking class or woodworking shop!

After the new Hopkins High School was opened north of Highway 7 in 1956, the old high school was called "The Annex." Various classes and other school functions were held in the building until the late 1960s. After deteriorating badly from lack of maintenance, it was demolished in 1974 to provide the site for the Central Park Manor Apartments.

East End School—Harley Hopkins School

At the start, Hopkins was served by School District #19. After the school was built on 9th Ave. N., the students from the East End became dissatisfied with the arrangement, so in 1898 the East End seceded and formed their own School District #135. They built a four-room frame building known as the East End School near Jackson Ave. and First St. S.

Until 1909, classes were held from the first through the sixth grade at the East End School and students finished the balance of their schooling "uptown" or what we would now refer to as "downtown" Hopkins. In 1909, the first eighth-grade class was graduated from the East End School. In 1926, a new 14-room School was opened and the old school was demolished. The new school was named after Harley H. Hopkins, a staunch advocate for education. His granddaughter Augusta Hopkins Winter was on the school board at the time, but she was absent when the school name was selected; descendants note she was very pleased with the name. Harley Hopkins School was expanded in 1942, in 1948 and again in 1953. By 1957, the school population was so large the Kindergarten classes were temporarily housed in the new Hopkins High School on Highway 7.

Harley Hopkins School, 125 Monroe Avenue South, Edina, operated as a grade school for about 45 years. In 1981 due to declining enrollment, it was converted to the Harley Hopkins Family Center and was used for Early Childhood Family Education (ECFE) and the Kaleidoscope Preschool for 3 to 5 year olds, sponsored by Hopkins School District 270. The old building was torn down in October 1990 and was replaced by a new structure, which was the first facility of its kind in the State to be built specifically for early childhood and family education programs. Now called the Harley Hopkins Family Center, the building also houses Early Childhood Special Education for children with delayed development and Family Literacy, which provides English language skills for immigrants. In addition, a preschool program for children who are deaf or hard of

East End School 1898-1926.

Harley Hopkins School 1926-1981.

hearing and the Hopkins Early Learning Center rent space in the building.

Junior High Building—South Junior High—Hopkins Activity Center

By 1923, the two Hopkins grade schools were dilapidated and outdated, and the school board decided to get a bond issue approved to build a new school. State law required approval of a majority of registered voters. With 1,400 voters registered and a turnout of 150 voters a rarity for a school election, bond approval was out of reach. They tried three times and failed. In 1923, the school board legal counsel got a ruling from the Chief Justice of the Minnesota Supreme Court requiring only a majority of the votes cast on the bond issue if the building was to be built at a new site. The result was that on the fourth attempt, a $150,000 bond issue was passed, and along with $30,000 reserve already on hand, enough capital was available to build and equip the original section of what was to become South Junior High.

This building was first occupied in January 1925 and was located between 13th and 14th Avenues on the north side of Excelsior Boulevard. It had two stories and two wings—one for the elementary school and one for the junior high. These wings were divided by an auditorium (main floor and balcony) seating over 900 and a gymnasium, which doubled as a stage for school and community events when divided by a backdrop of drapes. The gymnasium had a full-size basketball court where for several years the district basketball tournaments were held. Previous to this building, basketball and many school events were held at the

Opera Hall. High school physical education, music and agriculture classes were held here and later the industrial arts department was moved to this building.

A northwest addition was completed in 1936, which included a new thing—the first school cafeteria. Early on there were no school buses and many children walked several miles between home and school each day. Some carried their lunches and some walked home for lunch. In 1936, with help from the government's W.P.A. program, it became optional for children to have school lunches. Local summer garden produce was used to supply food for the winter months. Under the supervision of Hugh Firmage, the "Hopkins Canning Project" got underway. Garden vegetables were canned by local women with the help of the Home Economics Department to give students practical experience in canning.

In the late 1940s, the elementary students were transferred to the Katherine Curren Elementary School

This photo was taken from the steps of South Junior High looking at the High School.

South Junior High School built in 1925 has been remodeled as apartments.

The façade looks the same as the old South Junior High but the stairway leads to the courtyard of the Raspberry Ridge Apartment complex completed in the early 1980s.

Harmony Hill

The site of the Hopkins Activity Center seems to have always been a location for human activity. The old Indian trail from Fort Snelling to Minnetonka Mills came up Nine Mile Creek to its source, then skirted the east side of the high hill before heading for the Mills. Around the year 1900, two houses were built near the summit of the hill on lots facing east on 13th Avenue. One of them was occupied by Herbert M. Newland, who was the Justice of the Peace of our new village.

One day two factions came before Justice Newland and demanded a jury trial. While Officer Al Cooper was rounding up a jury, the Justice settled the argument to the litigants' satisfaction, shook hands and left. Harold L. Hollister, publisher of the first newspaper in Hopkins, The Hopkins News, *was so impressed by the Justice's action that he named the hill "Harmony Hill."*

Before the new school could be built on this site, the two houses were skidded down the hill to 12th Avenue and relocated. The hill was leveled to one-half its former height.

From 1925 through 1955, all high school graduates received their diplomas on Harmony Hill.

—By Clint Blomquist [with editorial changes]

and the entire building was used for Junior High School classes and a few special high school classes. In 1959 after North Junior High was built, it became known as South Junior High.

Another addition was completed in March 1957 on the north and northeast that provided more classrooms, a band room, boys' locker room with shower room and a cafeteria facility. This is basically the area later acquired by the City of Hopkins for its Activity Center.

In 1977, because of declining enrollment, it was decided to close the school by the end of the school year. Efforts were immediately begun to find a new use for the structure.

The building reopened in 1981 as the Raspberry Ridge Apartments and Hopkins Activity Center. Through extensive remodeling, former classrooms became 65 comfortable apartments. The auditorium and gymnasium were gutted when the conversion took place, but the front of the building was retained and still stands. Most of the ground floor of the north portion of the building became a community center, housing the Hopkins Historical Society, the Hopkins Area Congregate Dining Program for seniors, and other activities sponsored by the Hopkins-Minnetonka Recreation Department.

In 1981, the Hopkins Historical Society moved its headquarters into the former band room of South Junior High on the north side of the building.

Katherine Curren Elementary

Both Katherine Curren and Alice Smith Schools are named after long-term elementary teachers and are two

Dr. Frank J. Kucera presents roses to Katherine Curren at the dedication of Katherine Curren Elementary School.

Katherine Curren Elementary School built in 1946.

Plaque in downtown park reminding us where the time capsule is buried.

changed to "Katherine Curren" school to honor a teacher who had taught in the Hopkins School system for 44 years.

Katherine Curren's teaching career began in Hopkins in 1905 when she became the fifth grade teacher in the school system when it only employed 12 teachers from grades one through high school. Later she taught other grades and music. Her first year's salary was $45 per month. In 1908, she witnessed the cornerstone laying for the senior high building and in 1924, the cornerstone for the junior high building.

Because of her long service as a teacher, she taught third-generation students from some families in her later years. Already ill when she retired in 1949, Katherine Curren passed away at the age of 66 on May 22, 1952.

Katherine Curren school students buried a Halley's Comet Time Capsule on June 6, 1986 in the Downtown Hopkins park to be opened June 6, 2062 after Halley's Comet has come again.

Alice Smith Elementary School

Alice Smith Elementary School is on the north side of Minnetonka Mills Road approximately between 8th and 10th Avenues, just south of Highway 7.

Alice Smith School opened in 1952, and had an addition in 1961. The school was originally designated "Minnehaha School," but the District 19 school board

of the three schools of Hopkins School District #270 that are physically located in Hopkins proper. Katherine Curren School is located on the south side of Main Street between 16th and 17th Avenues.

Katherine Curren School was built in 1946 when the increase in both elementary and junior high students made it necessary for a new elementary school. More students made it necessary for an addition in 1957. A realignment of students and bus service closed the school in 1975, but it reopened in 1981 when the Harley Hopkins and Burwell schools were closed.

Originally called "Washington School," on January 13, 1949, its name was

Alice Smith School.

Some favorite teachers about 1934-35. On the highest step: Alice Smith, Barth Snyder, Katherine Curren. Middle step: Rodene Holme, Doris Elliott Empanger, Celeste Rudser, Irene Schwan. Lowest step: Margaret Hughes Henke.

A unique feature of Eisenhower High School was the window-lined library built over the front entrance. Here, students study in 1967.

decided to honor Alice Smith with the name. Alice C. Smith was a teacher who came to Hopkins in 1919 for a two-year stay and remained a first grade teacher here for 29 years, retiring in 1949. She had only missed four days of teaching in all those years!

Miss Smith began teaching when Robert Mayo was superintendent of schools and the main elementary building was on 9th Avenue. Her first-grade classroom was in the four-room frame annex to the main brick building. She had 30 pupils in her 1919 first grade class and taught for a salary of $70 per month for the nine-month term. Four years later, Alice Smith's classroom moved to the new elementary wing of the new Junior High building and kindergarten was established.

When Miss Smith retired in 1949, she did so just a few months too early to be able to hold classes in the new Katherine Curren School. When asked how school had changed throughout her teaching career, Alice Smith replied:

"I could see almost a year-to-year improvement in facilities and teaching materials.... Textbooks are more attractive and better planned, making the study material much more interesting for the children."

Hopkins High School—Eisenhower High School—Eisenhower Elementary and Community Center

Located on the north side of State Highway #7 approximately between the extension of 8th and 12th Avenues going north, a new state-of-the-art high school opened in 1956 due to the age and lack of space in the old High School. Besides the usual rooms for high school academic classes, rooms were provided for woodworking, metalworking, auto repair, chorus, orchestra, a fully equipped lunchroom, library and school district offices. In addition, the building has a swimming pool, a well-equipped "Little Theatre" seating approximately 500 and a full-size gymnasium with a stage, folding bleachers, which together with chairs provided room for large crowds. A unique feature of this building was the addition of a bubble on the roof with a telescope

Eisenhower School built 1956.

Students lining the circular stairway near the Hopkins High School front lobby in 1957.

made by Lawrence Sauter, a teacher, for those interested in astronomy.

This building became overcrowded in the late '60s and Hopkins Lindbergh High School opened in 1970 to alleviate the problem. For twelve years, the former Hopkins High School on Highway 7 was known as Eisenhower High School. Hopkins Eisenhower closed in the spring of 1982 as a cost-saving measure during a period of declining enrollment. All of the students were consolidated at Hopkins Lindbergh, which was renamed Hopkins High School. Eisenhower's purple and gold "Warriors" and Lindbergh's maroon and gold "Flyers" were replaced by the new Hopkins High School's royal blue and silver "Royals."

The Eisenhower building became Eisenhower Community Center, with headquarters for the Community Education Department, other school district administrative services, various tenants and community use of the theater, swimming pool, gyms, cafeteria and several classrooms.

The 1980s brought a new period of increasing enrollment and Eisenhower Elementary School opened in a remodeled wing of the Eisenhower Community Center in 1988. It was upgraded in 1993 along with all the other elementary schools, the two junior high schools and the high school thanks to the community

passing a $49.5 million bond referendum to upgrade its schools.

Tanglen Elementary, North Junior High, Hopkins High School, Lindbergh Center

Today, Hopkins High School is one of a complex of school buildings located about a mile east of Hopkins Crossroads (Co. Rd. 73, also known as 17th Avenue) north of Cedar Lake Road in Minnetonka. The High School opened as Lindbergh High School in 1970 and became simply "Hopkins High School" after Eisenhower High School closed in the spring of 1982.

Sharing the large plat of land with the High School are North Junior High, dedicated in December 1958 (opened in 1959) and Tanglen Elementary School, opened in 1968 and named for long-time Superintendent of Schools L.H. Tanglen. A totally remodeled Hopkins High School, including a multipurpose activity center wing called Lindbergh Center that is jointly funded and operated with the City of Minnetonka, opened in the fall of 1996.

L.H. (Tang) Tanglen retired in August 1966 after serving 22 years as the Hopkins School district superintendent of schools. During his tenure, seven separate school districts were combined into the Hopkins School District and enrollment jumped from 900 to 9,500 students while the teaching staff increased from 39 to 440. The Hopkins School Board honored him by naming Tanglen Elementary School, 10901 Hillside Lane in Minnetonka, after him. L.H. Tanglen passed away at age 86 on August 24, 1987.

West Junior High School, 3830 Baker Road, Minnetonka, was built in 1967 to serve the western portion of the Hopkins School district. For about ten years, Hopkins had three Junior Highs—South, North and West. Today, two Junior High Schools serve the 7th, 8th and 9th grades, "West" and "North," and the High School houses grades 10-12.

Gatewood Elementary, 14900 Gatewood Drive, Minnetonka, serves the Glen Lake area of Minnetonka. This school opened in 1970 and is located south of Glen Lake off of Eden Prairie Road. Gatewood earned the National School of Excellence award in 2001 and is an International Peace Site.

Miscellaneous Schools

Various grade schools are now part of Hopkins School District #270 but started out in other districts. Some are closed and torn down or have been put to other uses,

The Glen Lake School in 1942. Elementary school from 1911-1956.

while some remain as schools in the Hopkins district. In addition, Hopkins has some private and parochial schools within its borders.

Glen Lake Elementary (District #115) at 4801 Woodridge Road, Minnetonka, is actually the third Glen Lake School. It was built in 1956, with an addition in 1961 and substantial remodeling in the mid-1990s.

The first school in the Glen Lake area was a one-room schoolhouse built in 1882. It was called the Country School or Jackson School, named for the Jackson family that owned the property near the school and boarded teachers in their home. This school was located on the corner of Woodridge Road and Excelsior Blvd.

In 1911, a two-room red brick school was built at the corner of Woodhill Road and Excelsior Boulevard. Later, that was enlarged to include four classrooms, a library, an office and a gymnasium/auditorium. When the addition was built about 1945, the school had eight grades. The office was converted into a two-month kindergarten in April and May, complete with a sandbox, graham crackers and warm milk for snacks. The first grade teacher doubled as the home economics teacher and the principal taught seventh and eighth grades; she was also the superintendent of schools.

By 1946, more and more families had moved into Glen Lake and the school was bulging with children. Glen Lake merged with Hopkins in June of 1946 in a consolidated school district whereby Junior and Senior High School students were bussed to Hopkins schools and Glen Lake school had six grades in its four classrooms. By the early 1950s the school could hold only the first grade students and all other elementary children were bussed to Hopkins. The building of the new Glen Lake Elementary on Woodridge Road brought the elementary students back to their own neighborhood. The old school building was sold to Hennepin County in July 1960.

Shady Oak School (District #97). Some of the children in the Bohemian Settlement walked three miles to school at Rowland and Shady Oak Roads in Eden Prairie to attend the school that had been started by William and Hannah Bryant. Their parents decided to build a

Shady Oak School with students and teacher about 1914.

The second Shady Oak School built about 1923.

new school closer to their homes in Minnetonka Township. A one-room schoolhouse was erected on land donated by Winslow Cerveny on the east side of Shady Oak Road in a hollow approximately where Crosstown Highway 62 is today. Built of cream-colored brick manufactured in Chaska, Minnesota, the first classes were held in 1891. Many wanted to call this school the Hannah Bryant School in honor of the first teacher, but the name Shady Oak, District 97, was agreed upon. About 1923, a new red brick Shady Oak School was built to replace the older school.

On June 4, 1946, the parents in the Shady Oak School district voted to dissolve and join the Hopkins school district. The little brick schoolhouse was demolished in 1961.

Burwell (School District #52). Built in 1921, opened in January 1922, the Burwell school located on Minnetonka Boulevard was built to replace the old one-room school in use since 1875. It was also known as the Minnetonka Mills School. The school site, on the north bank of Minnehaha Creek, was donated by the Burwell family in honor of Charles Burwell, who had served on the District #52 school board for many years and for whom the school was named. The first teachers were Marie Swanson (grades 1-3) and Miss Thorson (grades 4-8). It became part of Hopkins School district by 1955. School additions were built in 1947, 1952 and 1958. In 1981, the school was closed and used as a community center. In June of 1990, Hopkins School District #270 sold Burwell to St. David's Child Development & Family Services.

Oak Knoll Elementary (District #133) at 2000 Hopkins Crossroads was built in 1927 to serve the Oak Knoll area of Minnetonka, which was annexed to Hopkins in the early 1950s. The school served as a neighborhood school until 1972. It had additions in 1935 and

Minnetonka Mills School (Burwell) built in 1921.

1952. Initially it was used as Groves School after closing; it is now Omegon Corporation.

Westview School (District #138), located at 628 Mendelssohn Avenue North (north of Highway 55 and west of Highway 169) was built in 1927. After attending grade school at Westview, students would attend high school in Minneapolis. It was in an awkward location for consolidation with other districts. There was talk in the early 1950s about consolidation with Meadowbrook, Wayzata or Hopkins, but the old Hopkins High School was overcrowded and could not take on any new students. In 1955, after the new Hopkins High was built, the Westview District #138 voted to dissolve and merge with Hopkins. In 1963, Golden Valley District #281 tried to acquire Westview, but they were turned down by the Hennepin County school commission. Westview School had additions in 1952, 1954 and 1958 and closed in 1978. It is now incorporated into Westview Business Center, 622-708 Mendelssohn Avenue N.

Meadowbrook Elementary, at 5430 Glenwood Avenue, Golden Valley opened in 1981, at about the time the Golden Valley School District #275 merged with Hopkins #274. Today, it has a K-6 population of 540, with a staff size of 85. The Ronald B. Davis Community Center attached to the school was built in 2002 and dedicated Monday, April 29. It was named after Ron B. Davis, long-term Hopkins School Board member and chairperson who died on July 30, 2001.

The $4 million, 24,000 square foot community center was built jointly by the Hopkins School District #270 and the city of Golden Valley to provide expanded space for the Hopkins School District's early childhood family education, Kids and Company (latch-key), parent/adult education programs and Golden Valley's Park and Recreation Department-sponsored programs.

St. Joseph's and St. John's Schools. St. Joseph's Catholic School opened in 1923 and served as both church and school until a free standing church was built in 1954. The St. Joseph's complex is north of Excelsior Boulevard between 14th and 15th Avenues. St. John the Evangelist Catholic School opened on October 15, 1951 and is located in Interlachen Park. Classes are held through the eighth grade at which time the pupils continue their education in the Hopkins High School or at one of the area Catholic high schools. The three Hopkins area Catholic schools—St. Joseph's, St. John the Evangelist and Immaculate Heart of Mary in Minnetonka—have combined for educational purposes and are now known as the John Ireland Schools.

The Blake School. Blake School is an independent day school for students in pre-kindergarten through 12th grade. It began in 1907 when William M. Blake opened a private boys' school in his Minneapolis home. In 1911, a corporation was formed that wanted a day school to match the quality of eastern preparatory schools. The corporation purchased the Mendelssohn farm between Interlachen County Club and Hopkins and the school building was dedicated On Oct. 30, 1912. Blake school became co-ed on August 15, 1972 after merging with Highcroft and Northrop girls' schools. It has campuses in Hopkins, Wayzata and Minneapolis. Blake school is considered to be among the best preparatory schools in the nation.

In December 2001, Blake School announced plans to create the Gordy Aamoth Jr. Memorial Stadium on its Hopkins campus to honor an alumnus who died in the September 11, 2001 attacks on the World Trade Center in New York. Gordy Aamoth Jr., 32, a 1988 graduate of Blake School and native of Wayzata, worked for Sandler, O'Neill and Partners Investments in New York City and died when the hijacked United Airlines Flight 175 crashed into his building.

Hopkins School District #270

At the start, Hopkins proper was divided into two school districts, #19 was west and #135 was east of Fifth Avenue. Students from all the surrounding areas—Glen Lake, Shady Oak, Burwell, Oak Knoll, Eden Prairie and Harley Hopkins—came to Hopkins High School to receive their grades seven through twelve education.

Big changes began in 1944 when L.H. Tanglen was appointed Superintendent of Schools. Bussing of students began. By 1955 many of the surrounding school districts had consolidated to form Hopkins School District #225, which included: Hopkins District #19, Harley Hopkins District #135, Westview District #138,

As a caring community of learners, embracing diversity and constantly striving for excellence, the Hopkins School District declares as its mission: 'To instill in each learner a passion for learning and a commitment to reach one's potential throughout life by creating participatory learning experiences that are challenging, relevant, and dynamic.'

—The Mission Statement for the Hopkins School District

The Woodworking Project
"You remember woodworking class—where you made a set of bookends or a wooden trivet for your mother. Well, Woodworking 3, Al Peterson's class at Charles Lindbergh High School in Hopkins, Minnesota, got tired of making bookends, so they made an airplane…" Thus began Charles Kuralt in his "On the Road" broadcast during the CBS News.

Kuralt and film crew were on hand June 1, 1974 as the two-seat French-designed Emeraude powered by an 85 hp engine, Experimental Aircraft N74LH, took off on her maiden voyage from Flying Cloud airport. North Central Airlines test pilot Captain Lloyd Franke flew the plane for almost 25 minutes before landing and saying "it flies… like a rocking chair."

"What do you remember from your Senior year in high school?" asks Kuralt. "Not much, probably. Well, this is what Woodworking 3 will remember from theirs."

Burwell District #52, Oak Knoll District #133, Shady Oak District #97, and Glen Lake District #115. In 1964, the state changed the number for this consolidated district to Hopkins School District #274.

In 1980, Golden Valley School District #275 merged with Hopkins School District #274, and the consolidated school district was given the name Hopkins School District #270. Golden Valley's Meadowbrook Elementary School continued to operate, but the secondary students were merged into other Hopkins schools. Golden Valley Middle School and Golden Valley High School closed and were sold to Breck School.

Now School District #270 serves the City of Hopkins, the greater part of Minnetonka, a large section of Golden Valley and parts of Edina, Eden Prairie, St. Louis Park and Plymouth. The Hopkins schools always demanded much of their students and we can be very proud of the district's education ranking.

The Hopkins School District has a well-established tradition of educational excellence and community commitment to high expectations and support. All three secondary schools are National Schools of Excellence and were the first in the Twin Cities to receive this prestigious award. National awards have also been earned by a variety of programs, including art, writing, community service and technology applications.

The Eden Prairie School System transported their 11th and 12th grade students to Hopkins Schools with their own school buses until about 1928. In 1945 Hopkins Schools consolidated with Harley Hopkins, Shady Oak and Glen Lake Schools. Superintendent Tanglen asked Ed DeVeau to transport those school children as of 1946, thence started DeVeau Bus Company's thirty-year association with Hopkins. Photo cir. 1947. Two 1939 buses; two 1946 buses shown.

Every year, students receive numerous national honors in areas such as music, writing, visual arts, creative problem solving, video production, business education, mathematics and other areas. Hopkins students also consistently outperform their counterparts in the state, region and nation on standardized tests. The District is annually a state leader in the number of students honored in National Merit Scholarship competitions.

Approximately 8,300 students attend seven elementary schools (K-6), two junior high schools (7-9) and one senior high school (10-12). The district also provides programs for infants at an early childhood family resource center and for senior citizens at a community activity center. The District is a partner and major tenant in a multi-disciplinary community arts facility—the Hopkins Center for the Arts on Mainstreet Hopkins.

Through its participation in the West Metro Education Program, Hopkins School District 270 offers two magnet school opportunities. The **Interdistrict Downtown School** is an intercultural magnet school and the **Fine Arts Interdisciplinary Resource (FAIR) School** is a fine arts magnet school.

The Ron B. Davis community center, built jointly with the city of Golden Valley at Meadowbrook School, opened in October 2001. This facility enables the

School District to expand its early childhood family education programs to the northern part of its territory.

When the **Hopkins Online Academy** (HOA) opened its virtual doors in September 2002, it became the first online charter school in the state of Minnesota. And it is the first time that a regular public school district has created its own online charter school.

Changing demographics are first noticed in the school system. With an increase in immigrant populations since the early 1990s, Hopkins has implemented English as a Second Language (ESL) programs for both youth and adults. A tradition began at the High School graduation in 2001 whereby the flags of foreign-born graduates were displayed in addition to the American flag. Twenty-five countries were represented in 2001 and 19 countries in 2002, celebrating and embracing the diversity of the student body and the community.

School Photos Through The Years

The true class photo is a tradition that was discontinued sometime in the 1950s. The face-only photographs we get today for school photographs do not have the charm and character of the older full-class photographs. Nor do they tell such an interesting story. Following are some exceptional class photos from years past.

1890—The entire school population poses in front of the grade school on 9th Avenue North; boys on the left, girls on the right.

1898—This is the entire Hopkins High School posing in front of their building on 9th Avenue North.

1907—An East End School Class.

1910-1912—The Second Grade Class at the 9th Avenue North School.

1927-28—Hats were the fashion for the girls of the Second Grade Class at the 9th Avenue North School.

1934-35—Sixth Grade Class at the Hopkins Public School.

1940-41—Burwell School's 3rd and 4th grades.

1958-59—There were only six boys in this 8th Grade Class at St. John the Evangelist Parochial School.

The first church in the area was St. Margaret's Catholic Church, completed in 1880. It served the Bohemian community. Merged into St. Joseph's in 1921, the church was torn down in the mid-1920s. St. Margaret's Cemetery is still in use, on Bren Road east of Shady Oak Rd.

Churches and Synagogues

Prior to 1890, the Bohemians were the only distinct ethnic group concentrated in the Hopkins area. Because they could speak very little English, they banded together to share and preserve their common interests, the most important of which were their customs, religion and language.

By 1868, the Bohemian community felt a need for religious instruction for the children and a plan was adopted whereby church services were held in the homes of the settlers. When the home was Protestant, the services were conducted in that tradition; when Catholic, the services were conducted by a Catholic. The Catholics far outnumbered the Protestants initially; at the close of the Civil War, there were 120 families in the settlement and only seven of these were Protestant.

This practice continued until 1879 when the Catholic members of the Bohemian community decided to build their first church on the site of today's St. Margaret's Cemetery, on Bren Road, east of Shady Oak Road. St. Margaret's was the first Catholic Church in the area.

Beginning in 1877, the Bohemian Protestants arranged for annual visits from a Czech pastor, the Rev. Francis Kun of Ely, Iowa, to administer the Sacraments. He challenged them to build their own church. It took a few more years until they had a large enough population to erect their own church building. On July 15, 1888, the John Hus Church was dedicated. This was the first Protestant Church building in the area.

After the M.T.M. factory attracted immigrant workers from other nationalities, the community acquired conclaves of Scandinavians, Irish and German, all of which followed the same pattern by establishing the Norwegian Lutheran, Swedish Lutheran, German Lutheran and Irish Catholic churches. This pattern of churches serving a specific ethnic group continued until about the 1920s, when the national churches slowly changed to requiring services in the English language. By then, the second and third generations knew the English language, but the older generations were extremely traumatized by the transition.

St. Margaret's Catholic Church.

In 1879-1880 Winslow (Vaclav) and Anna (Popelka)

Dvorak donated land for the first Catholic Church–St. Margaret's. The church faced west on Bren Road east of Shady Oak Road in Minnetonka Township. Winslow, with the help of his brother-in-law Josef Petrak and other parishioners, built the church in which Rev. Father Tichy of New Prague conducted the first mass on Sunday, July 1, 1880. This was the first religious service in a church in the Hopkins area. Father Tichy served the mission church as pastor until 1886. Other priests who served were: Fr. J. Rynda of St. Paul (1886-1890); Fr. F. Simonek (1890-1893); Fr. F. Hrachovsky (1893-1904); and Fr. Joseph M. Hovorka (1904-1921).

Winslow Dvorak served as the sexton as well as maintenance man for the building and cemetery for thirty years or more. The first person buried in St. Margaret's cemetery was Mrs. Joseph Kopecky (Mary Portel) who died Feb. 20, 1881. Sadly, the second burial was Winslow Dvorak's nephew Joseph Petrak, Jr.

Between 1905 and 1910, the church building was extended, plastered, painted and decorated internally; a new altar (hand-crafted in Shakopee, MN) was added as well as new pews and other furnishings. The photographs we have of this church date from this period.

After World War I, the Catholic Church leaders decided to merge the St. Margaret's congregation with the St. Mary's congregation to form St. Joseph's parish in 1921. By the mid-1920s, no longer in use, the St. Margaret's church building was dismantled. Some of the wood from the original church was used in building the Frank H. Dvorak home northeast of the church; he was a grandson of Winslow Dvorak. This home is no longer there, but St. Margaret's Cemetery is still in use.

The Hopkins Historical Society has on display the large painting of St. Margaret, patron saint of the first parish, from the old church. It also has the original altar cloth and other artifacts.

St. Mary's Catholic Church

After the M.T.M. Company built its plant in 1887, the population exploded. A group, predominantly of Irish origin, formed St. Mary's Catholic Church and built their small church, only 20 by 42 feet in size, at 51 Sixth Ave. S. in 1895. It was known as the Irish Catholic Church to distinguish it from the Bohemian Catholic Church (St. Margaret's). St. Mary's was a mission church sponsored by the Immaculate Conception Parish of

St. Mary's Catholic Church, 6th Ave. and 2nd St. S.

Built in 1922, this St. Joseph school building doubled as both elementary school and church. In 1953 it became the school building after the current Church of St. Joseph opened.

and one of Mary, from the Church of St. Mary are on display at the Hopkins Historical Society Museum.

St. Joseph's Catholic Church

St. Margaret's had purchased a site for a new church on the south side of First Street North between 14th and 15th Avenues. During the same time, St. Mary's had bought the site of the present St. Joseph's on Excelsior Avenue between 13th and 14th Avenues to replace their small church on Sixth Avenue South. By the time money and materials were available after World War I, Archbishop Dowling had taken a firm stand against ethnic churches for being inconsistent with American nationalism, so the Catholic hierarchy decided to merge the two Catholic churches into one. This was a blow to the many elder Bohemians who still leaned heavily on their native language. There was a period of rebellion when some members of St. Margaret's transferred to the Bohemian Presbyterian Church, some left the church altogether, but many finally accepted the merger.

In 1922, St. Joseph's parish completed a school, parish house and nuns' home at the Excelsior Avenue location. The parochial school was opened in 1923. Initially, the school building was designed so it could be used as a "temporary" church, with the hope that a church building would be built in 10 or 15 years. But the depression of the early-1930s and World War II made them delay their plans. Fr. Hovorka remained at St. Joseph's during the great depression of the 1930s and was still there to see the current Church of St. Joseph, completed in 1954, built to the east of the school. On July 6, 1955, Fr. Hovorka died suddenly. Father Vacek, then pastor at St. John the Evangelist parish in Interlachen Park, was asked by the Archbishop to transfer to St. Joseph's, which he did on August 31, 1955.

Fr. Vacek served 24 years in Hopkins. Joseph Vacek immigrated to this country with his parents when he was six years old. The Czech language was spoken in his home. He first came to Hopkins as a priest in 1932 where he listened to confessions in Czech, German and English. At that time, the parish extended as far west as

Minneapolis. During its first seven years it was served by the Rev. Father J.M. Egan, assistant pastor of the Immaculate Conception Parish. In 1902, St. Mary's was given its first resident priest, Father Martin Mahoney.

Father Mahoney was well known and well loved. He was well known because of his love for fast horses, which he used in performing his church duties, including a mission responsibility at Cahill. He was well loved because of his lifelong devotion to helping anyone who needed help. A typical case happened one real cold winter day when F.E. Kenaston, the president of M.T.M., met Fr. Mahoney on Excelsior Avenue without a winter coat. He informed Kenaston, when asked, that he had no overcoat. Kenaston removed his expensive coat and put in on Father Mahoney. The next day a beggar rapped on Mahoney's door asking for a handout. He looked frozen in his skimpy clothes. He left wearing Kenaston's coat. Fr. Mahoney gladly suffered the winter's cold. This story is only one of many similar ones that endeared Fr. Mahoney to everyone in the community. In 1913, Fr. Mahoney was returned to his previous post at the historic old church in Mendota from whence he had come to Hopkins.

Rev. Fr. Benjamin F. Audus followed Fr. Mahoney and stayed until Archbishop Dowling assigned Rev. Charles E. Hovorka as pastor of the new parish of St. Joseph, a merger of St. Mary's and St. Margaret's, in 1921. Father Hovorka continued as pastor of St. Joseph's for many years.

Two statues, one of Joseph holding a young Jesus

Excelsior. Since then, 14 parishes have sprung from the original St. Joseph's Church.

After his first stint in Hopkins, Vacek served two parishes in St. Paul (St. Andrews and St. Stanislav's) and was a pastor at St. John the Baptist in Savage before he was asked to come back to Hopkins to found St. John's parish in 1950. After serving there a few years, he returned to St. Joseph's for 20 more years. He would give the invocation at the Czech Heritage Fest every year in the Czech language until very few people could understand the language any more. He was elevated to the rank of Monsignor by Pope Paul VI in 1966, retired in 1975 and lived his remaining years in Hopkins. He passed away Dec. 8, 1987 and is buried in St. Margaret's Cemetery.

Bohemian Church, John Hus, Faith Presbyterian

The **Bohemian Church** was organized in 1887 when the small group of Protestant Bohemians decided to go ahead and build a church. In the autumn of 1887, Frank Bren donated the land for the church and cemetery. Other families contributed as much money as they were able. $736.13 came from the Bohemian churches of Ely

and Cedar Rapids, Iowa and Silver Lake, Minnesota. With additional donated materials and labor, the church and cemetery were dedicated on July 15, 1888. The first Board of Elders includes the names of Vincent Plehal, Joseph H. Empanger, Joseph Bren, Joseph Lapour and Joseph F. Kucera.

At first, there was worship in the small church conducted every Sunday by various pastors from St. Paul or conducted by the church elders. Beginning in 1891, the Rev. Francis Pokorny of the Bohemian Reformed Church of Silver Lake became their guiding pastor. He came once a month from Silver Lake to teach the Bible on Friday evening, instruct the children in the Bohemian language on Saturday and then conduct worship on Sunday. He encouraged them to affiliate with the Presbyterian Church of the U.S.A., which the 96 members did in April 1900, and they became the **Bohemian Presbyterian Church**.

The Rev. William Schiller became their first resident pastor, and served devotedly until he died in February 1904; he is buried in the now Faith Church Cemetery opposite the former main sanctuary entrance. The Rev. Joseph Bren was elected as pastor on April 5, 1904, installed as pastor on June 12th 1905 and served the

The John Hus Presbyterian Church and Cemetery, now Faith Presbyterian, 12007 Excelsior Blvd., built in 1934.

The Bohemian Presbyterian Church was built in 1912 and burned down in 1933.

church for 16 years. Under his leadership, a chapel was built about three miles south in Glen Lake to provide Sunday school for that community. In 1912, a new church building was erected to care for the increasing membership. Every piece of sound timber from the old church building was used in the construction of the new building and again, much work was done by the members themselves. The second church was dedicated on June 30, 1912.

By 1918, the church had 185 members. The Rev. Ludvik Burian became pastor in 1920, the Rev. Joseph Bren having accepted a call to the Hus Memorial Church of Cedar Rapids, Iowa.

The congregation received a heavy blow when on September 30, 1933, in the space of about two hours, the church was completely destroyed by fire. A new $3,650 pipe organ had been installed just a year earlier, and the Ladies Aid Society had started a fund to enlarge the kitchen. The country was in the midst of a depression; if any congregation was put to the test, this was it. Almost before the fire was out, they were resolved to rebuild another house of worship. Amazingly, less than a year later, on August 5, 1934, they dedicated their third church sanctuary, which is currently the social hall of Faith Presbyterian Church, 12007 Excelsior Boulevard, Minnetonka.

Rev. Burian accepted a call to move to Ely, Iowa, and

the Rev. Joseph Havlik became the Bohemian Presbyterian Church's new pastor in 1938. In 1940, he led the congregation to dedicate themselves to serve the whole community irrespective of race or nationality. Two different services of worship began to be conducted–9 a.m. in the Czech language and 11 a.m. in English. The church's name was changed to **John Hus Presbyterian Church**. The congregation was named after John Hus, a Protestant Reformation leader born in Bohemia in 1369, who believed that God's message should be read and studied by everyone, not just the priesthood. After ten years, Rev. Joseph Havlik accepted a call to the First Presbyterian Church in Minneapolis and the Rev. Orrin H. Moore began as pastor on June 15, 1950. Thus ended the era of the Bohemian national churches in the Hopkins area, an era that lasted nearly a hundred years.

An education addition was built onto John Hus Presbyterian beginning in 1952, but the congregation was to encounter significant changes throughout the 1960s. The Czech immigrants were growing older and becoming fewer in number. Yet, the area was rapidly increasing in population. The Glen Lake Presbyterian Church, located at 5339 Beacon Hill Road in Minnetonka, was overcrowded and could not expand. The Presbyterian Church recommended that these two churches combine.

The **Glen Lake Sunday School Union Church** began as a non-denominational Sunday School established by the Rev. John Ferris in 1912. It attracted a number of people from diverse religious backgrounds, but by 1917, many families felt the need to affiliate with some established denomination. The Presbyterian Church responded with interest and support, so by 1921, this church took on the new name, the **Glen Lake Presbyterian Church**.

A joint congregation meeting was held on October 29, 1967 of the John Hus and Glen Lake Presbyterian Churches of Minnetonka Village for the purpose of merging the two congregations. The new church became known as **Faith Presbyterian Church of Minnetonka**, initially having 1,100 communicant members.

Ground was broken in July 1975 to build a new sanctuary and education addition onto Faith Church. In 1992, it added a gymnasium, classroom wing, choir room and changed the old sanctuary into a modern kitchen and social hall. During the remodeling, an entire side wall of the old church was removed, but the heritage stained glass windows, many dedicated by the old settlers' families who so lovingly rebuilt the church after the devastating fire of 1933, were carefully remounted to a place of honor between the new social

hall and the narthex. This new social hall was named "Faith Hall."

United Methodist Church of Hopkins

While the area south and west of Hopkins was settled by Bohemians, Hopkins proper was settled mostly by Scotch-Irish and English settlers. By the 1880s, they also were feeling the need for religious opportunities for their families. The Methodist church assigned an older pastor, Edwin S. Bunce, to the Minneapolis Circuit. In 1885 that included the West Minneapolis and the Parker's Lake Church (now known as Messiah United Methodist Church.) During Pastor Bunce's first year he was assisted by James S. Garvin, a man of 35 but who was in poor health. Crop failures led to lean times and within three years the Minneapolis Circuit was reduced to 9 full members and 5 probationers. It looked as if the Methodist Church was not going to survive in this area.

Then came Mr. and Mrs. Levi Longfellow of Minneapolis who donated two lots on 9th Avenue South in the village of West Minneapolis to this small band of Methodists. Levi Longfellow was one of the dealmakers that brought the M.T.M. Company into the area. He also

Methodist-Episcopal Church and Parsonage at 28-9th Ave. S.

was a charter member of the Hennepin Avenue Methodist Episcopal Church of Minneapolis.

The real push in establishing the Methodist church here came from Christian Tosteson, the mechanical genius who came here from Racine, Wisconsin, with the M.T.M. Co. He had been attending Methodist prayer meetings in St. Louis Park and met others he encouraged to move to West Minneapolis: Fred, Bill and Burt Anderson who soon opened up a dry goods store on main street, and the Johnson brothers who established a meat market in town, which later became Hovander Foods. Tosteson was really motivated to build a Methodist church, so with the help of Paul Swenson, a man who would later become the core of the threshing machine company and a few others, he put up the white frame chapel at 28 Ninth Avenue South called the **West Minneapolis Methodist Episcopal Church** in 1889.

The Rev. J.E. Henderson served as pastor the first year. He served 26 members and 6 probationers. Five children and 12 adults were baptized that first year. $15 covered the year's expenses (light, heat, etc.). $300 was allowed for rent for the minister for one year, jointly paid by Parker's Lake and West Minneapolis congregations. In those days before St. Mary's Catholic Church was built, the Irish Catholics conducted Sunday afternoon services in the Methodist Church. The Methodists had the first and only church bell in a Protestant church of the village.

The Rev. L.P. Smith served the church in 1891, coming by horse and buggy (cutter in winter) from Hamline University to lead an 11:00 service Sunday mornings. He also led services at Parker's Lake and Golden Valley.

Over the years, some additions and improvements were made to the church. On September 27, 1928, the church became **Hopkins Methodist Episcopal Church** due to a change in the village name. In 1950, the church changed its name to **First Methodist Church of Hopkins**. In October 1953, ground was broken for the modern church at 717 State Highway 7, where the congregation still resides. The structure was built in stages. In 1954, services were conducted in the new church. The sanctuary, church offices and choir room were completed by Thanksgiving of 1956. In May 1963, an education wing added 10,000 more square feet. In August 1968, the church's name was changed to **United Methodist Church of Hopkins**, reflecting the union of the Methodist and the Evangelical United Brethren denominations.

In 1969 when Charles Sweet became senior pastor,

two major developments happened. The Administrative Board approved the concept of a nursery school, which continues to this day and plans were approved to build a nursing home with the support of three churches: Hopkins Methodist, Gethsemane Lutheran and Mizpah Congregational. **Chapel View Nursing Home** was completed in October 1971 and has been a valuable asset to the community. Pastor Sweet later became the Chaplain at Chapel View and after several years of comforting the elderly, he stated: "This is the finest ministry of my life."

To commemorate their centennial as a congregation, in July 1985, a plaque was placed in the Hopkins Downtown Park to designate the site of the original Methodist Church built in 1889.

Mizpah Congregational/United Church of Christ

In the early years while the Methodist Church was moving toward reality, so too, was the group that became the **Mizpah Congregational Church**. In 1885 Rev. George Hood and Joseph Hamilton of the Union Church located in St. Louis Park, instituted Cottage Prayer meetings in the rural homes near the Hopkins railway station. The first of the meetings took place in the Dow home. Later meetings were held in the Bates, Basset, Boyce and Empanger homes. A Sunday school was formed in those early days.

In the fall of 1888, C.O. Anderson, a student of Lake Forest University, came to Hopkins and held regular preaching services on Sunday. He led a movement to organize a church and on September 9, 1888 the constitution, by-laws and creed were adopted for the small church of 18 members. Representatives from the Union Church of St. Louis Park, from Plymouth Church, Pilgrim Church and Vine Church, all from Minneapolis, formed the advisory committee. The following September a church building was started on the southwest corner of Eighth and Excelsior Avenues. Charles Sedgwick was the architect. It was dedicated Nov. 17, 1889. Due to its small membership and generally hard times, money shortages caused many problems. Ministers stayed only a short time. A parsonage at 13 Van Buren Street South started in 1892 was lost by foreclosure because of the panic in 1893. A little known newspaper *The West Minneapolis Recorder* was being published in the spring of 1892 by a Rev. G.W. Jackman. He is also listed in the Church Directory in the paper as pastor of Mizpah Congregational Church, an obvious effort to survive the adverse times.

In 1906, Mr. H.D. Truman offered to trade the church lots 7 and 8 on 8th Avenue for its Eighth and Excelsior Avenue location. He agreed to move the church and pay $1000 besides. The proposition was accepted and in 1907, the church building was moved about a half block south to 14 Eighth Ave S. where it was Mizpah's home until 1953. A parsonage was built on a third lot adjacent to the south side of the church. The little congregation had trouble retaining pastors and the membership had dwindled so much that in 1916 there was talk of uniting with the Methodist Church, who was in a similar predicament. (The Methodists rejected the merger.) The Reverend James E. Earle, who had been pastor in 1912 and 1913, came back again in 1917 and put some new vigor into the congregation. By January 1919, there was $39.00 in the treasury! Although he didn't stay long, the congregation had turned a corner.

Membership reached 154 by 1922. That year a basement was constructed under the church and a social hall and kitchen were added. In 1951, there was talk again of joining forces with the Methodists, but this time the Congregational members turned it down. Instead, land was purchased in 1951 for a new church located at 412 Fifth Avenue N., which was dedicated January 10, 1954

by about 300 active members. It had a seating capacity of 250, overflow area for 100 more, with 20 classrooms. In August 1956, the Rev. Charles L. Heuser and his family moved into the new parsonage at 305 Campbell Drive. In January 1961, Mizpah adopted the constitution of the **United Church of Christ** and added 7,754 square feet onto their building.

Mizpah is locally well known as the home of the Jack and Jill Preschool, which has operated out of the church for many years.

Gethsemane Lutheran Church

After the Minneapolis Threshing Machine Co., came to the area in 1887, Scandinavians began to move here. Some worked for the factory and others established businesses in Hopkins.

During the late-1880s, Andrew Olson arranged for Pastors C.J. Petri and J. Ternstedt and Student J.H. Nelson to conduct services in the old Burnes School at Highway18 (now 169) and Excelsior Avenue for the Swedish and Danish group. During 1889, they purchased two lots at Second Street and Ninth Avenue N. for $700, on which they erected their first church building for $2,000. On September 17, 1890, the Swedish

Mizpah Congregational Church and Parsonage, 20-24 8th Ave. S. in 1950.

The Gethsemane Lutheran Church, Northeast corner of 9th Avenue and 2nd St. North built in 1936.

Lutheran Church of West Minneapolis was officially organized. The charter members were the families of A.T. Anderson, C.O. Anderson, John Austin, John Goldborg, Andrew Olson, Frank Strobeck, John Lock and Frank Sackrison.

Various pastors and students served the congregation in the first years. In June 1894 the first resident pastor to serve the new church, Rev. E.O. Stone, took over his duties. Not long after, the Rev. Stone became the first to be married in the church when he married Andrew Olson's daughter Florence. Rev. Stone moved in 1896 to a church in Minneapolis. Sixteen pastors and students filled the church's needs between 1896 and 1914. Rev. E.A. Bongfeldt became pastor in the spring of 1914. During his tenure, the church basement and an addition were added.

At the annual meeting of the church in 1931, the decision was made to henceforth conduct all services in the English language, thereby ending the nationalistic aspect, which had prevailed from the beginning of the church. The 1930s marked the end of most ethnic languages and customs in churches.

In May 1936, a decision was made to build a new church on the same site. On October 11, 1936, the cornerstone was laid on the distinctly Gothic structure. Pastor Lasse Stohl came to Gethsemane in 1943 and

served the church longer than any other pastor. During his tenure, a parish building was added in 1948 and on September 24, 1962, he helped dedicate the new church at 715 Minnetonka Mills Road.

In 1987, Gethsemane was given back a beautiful altar window that had been hidden behind a baptistery wall when another congregation had occupied their former church building on 9th Avenue North. This window had been purchased in honor of pioneer Frederick Dahlberg who had died in 1937 and given his grandchildren some money. Their legacy was to purchase a stained-glass window as a memorial.

This had been hidden for some years until the Bet Shalom congregation was preparing the building for their use, and in their kindness, returned the window to its former owners. The Dahlberg grandchildren arranged for its restoration and installation in the stairway leading down from the choir room in Gethsemane's present church.

Today, Gethsemane Lutheran Church is a 2,000-member congregation of the Evangelical Lutheran Church in America. Recognizing that Hopkins has become more ethnically and economically diverse, Gethsemane has adapted its ministry through the years to meet the changing needs of the community.

Norwegian Lutheran Church

Not very much is known about this short-lived parish. Anton Walstead built the Norwegian Lutheran Church at 41 Twelfth Ave. N. about 1908 or 1909. English services were held at the Norwegian Lutheran Church on Sunday, December 22, 1910. The photograph of the church was taken about 1914. In 1915 the German Lutheran Church (Zion Lutheran) purchased the building.

Zion Lutheran Church

Zion Lutheran Church was established by the Germans, the last ethnic group in the area to assert its nationality by starting a non-English language church. As early as 1903 Professor E.L. Arndt, of Concordia College in St. Paul, began conducting services in Hopkins for a few families. These services were conducted in private homes and under various leaders until January 1915,

The Norwegian Lutheran Church about 1914.

church flourished as the community grew and in October 1950 they sold their old church building to the Hopkins Baptist Church and dedicated their new church at 241 Fifth Avenue North in Hopkins.

The first pastor to serve Zion was Rev. Paul Walther. He introduced English in every Sunday morning service as early as 1915. He was followed by Rev. Charles Hornburg (1918-1922); Rev. Edwin Kurth (1922-1926); Rev. Carl Mundinger (1926-1936); Rev. Walter P. Clausen (1936-1946); Rev. R.W. Brill (1946-1960); Rev. J.E. Hakes, assistant pastor (1960-1962). The Rev. H.E. Sieving served Zion from April 1961 until he retired as pastor in September, 1973, and continued to serve as Pastor Emeritus for some years. The Rev. Roy Karner had assumed assistant pastor duties in 1969 and assumed the pastorate in September1973. The Rev. John T. Huchthausen was the associate pastor from October, 1976 until August of 1978. The Rev. Howard A. Krienke assumed those duties on September 16, 1979.

when the Rev. E.N. Nachtseim organized the congregation. In its early days, the church was known as the **German Lutheran Church**. In 1915 they purchased the former Norwegian Lutheran Church at 41 Twelfth Avenue North.

Zion built the first addition to their little church, a tower and basement, in 1926. A second addition, a sanctuary and a full basement, was built in 1935. The

After the new church was built in 1950, the member-

Zion Lutheran Church, 41 12th Avenue North front and parsonage on October 16, 1949. Groundbreaking for their new church at 241 5th Avenue North was also on the same day.

ship expanded. In 1957, an educational wing was added to the church. The latest substantial addition to Zion was the Van Daalen organ dedicated on June 6, 1976.

St. John the Evangelist Catholic Church

Due to the large increase in population of the area following World War II, in May 1950, land was purchased for a second Catholic Church and school in Hopkins. About an acre and a half was purchased from George and Anna Miles in Interlachen Park. About 350 people gathered for the first mass as a parish on June 25, 1950 held at the Hopkins Theater and celebrated by Fr. Joseph Vacek. St John's served the eastern edge of St. Joseph's parish in Hopkins and portions of St. Louis Park and Edina. They continued to hold mass in the Hopkins Theater on 5th Avenue until their new facility at 1503 Boyce was ready. St. John's school opened on October 15, 1951 with 84 students and only four classrooms. Fr. Vacek celebrated the first mass in the new building on Sunday, October 28, 1951. The pews and kneelers had not been delivered yet so the eager parishioners sat on folding chairs and knelt on the cold, cement floor.

A new $750,000 contemporary style sanctuary was dedicated on May 10, 1969 and since it faced a different direction, the new address for the church became 6 Interlachen Rd. This structure has a unique design that has won numerous architecture awards. The building was described in 1982 in *Architecture Minnesota* as "surely one of the handsomest religious buildings to be found in the upper Midwest today…" St. John's celebrated its 50th Anniversary in 2000.

Immaculate Heart of Mary Catholic Church

Immaculate Heart of Mary Catholic Church was established in a Quonset hut next door to the Glen Lake School on Williston Road and Excelsior Boulevard shortly after World War II in the Glen Lake area of Minnetonka. Services were held there until the new church building was constructed on the corner of Mayview Road and Excelsior Boulevard in the 1950s.

The three Catholic schools in the area—St. Joseph's, St. John's and Immaculate Heart of Mary—consolidated their parochial schools in 1970. Students are bussed to the school that houses the appropriate grade level for them. This combined school system is known as the **John Ireland Schools**.

Bet Shalom Congregation

In 1981, the Bet Shalom Reform Congregation was organized by four families who, after growing to 32 fam-

The Bet Shalom congregation moved into the former Gethsemane Lutheran Church at 201-9th Ave. N. in 1985. This photo was taken after the Gethsemane parish building was built in 1948.

ilies, invited the Rabbi Norman M. Cohen to become their spiritual leader, their first rabbi. They began to hold Sabbath services in the Jewish Community Center in St. Louis Park. Over the next four years, the congregation experience rapid growth and in 1985, the 200-family congregation purchased the former Gethsemane Lutheran Church building at 201 Ninth Avenue North in Hopkins for their synagogue and religious school. Several different congregations had used this building since Gethsemane had moved out in 1962. It was dedicated as the Bet Shalom Synagogue in November 1985. This was the first Jewish house of worship in Hopkins.

While readying the building for use as a synagogue, the congregation discovered a baptistery formerly used by a Baptist congregation. They also uncovered some stained glass windows installed as a memorial by Gethsemane church members in 1937. At the initiative of Rabbi Cohen, the stained glass windows were kindly returned to the Gethsemane congregation, where they were restored and incorporated into their current church building.

After 17 years in Hopkins, the Bet Shalom congregation, at 687 families and growing under the vision of Rabbi Cohen, built a new synagogue in 2002 on Orchard Road in Minnetonka. On April 28, 2002 an emotional "Torah March" occurred, in which the congregation removed the sacred artifacts from their old building and walked with them four miles to the new building. These were the Torah (the sacred scrolls) the Mezzuzot (parchments containing several passages from the Bible enclosed in a case posted on doorposts), the Chupah (the marriage canopy) and the Ner Tamid (the "Eternal Light," which was extinguished, to be lit again at the new location). During the march, the congregants stopped at three area churches with which they have special relationships—Mizpah United Church of Christ, Hopkins United Methodist Church and St. Paul's Lutheran Church. Especially moving were the choirs at each church who sang a Hebrew song with the words "Shalom my friend."

Bet Shalom held their first service in their new building on May 3, 2002. Formal dedication of the building was on May 31, and the school was moved in the fall of 2002, after finishing out its school year at the 9th Avenue North Hopkins location.

Cross of Glory Baptist Church
Cross of Glory Baptist Church, 4600 Shady Oak Road, Minnetonka, began as a merger of the Park Baptist Church of St. Louis Park and the First Baptist Church of Hopkins (housed in the former Zion Lutheran Church at 41 Twelfth Avenue North) in October 1969.

The **Park Baptist Church** had its beginnings in 1943 when a group of people from Bethlehem Baptist Church met to consider the establishment of a Baptist General Conference church in the western suburb of St. Louis Park. Thirty-two people attended its first meeting in a former tavern converted for church use. In September of 1946, several lots were purchased on Vernon Avenue and 41st Street and a basement church was dedicated June 6, 1948. The superstructure was built and dedicated on November 22, 1953 with a membership of 120.

The **Hopkins Baptist Church** congregation started services in 1942 and was incorporated in 1944. They initially met in the American Legion hall, then in 1950 purchased the Zion Lutheran property in Hopkins. They had 75-100 members in 1965 when they added on the front addition to the church at a cost of $18,000. They were a mission-aided church of the Minnesota American Baptist Convention and their pastor was the Rev. Albert Snyder in 1965. They changed their name to the **First Baptist Church of Hopkins** in September of 1964.

In September 1970, the Cross of Glory congregation moved from the Park Baptist site to the First Baptist Church of Hopkins site on Twelfth Avenue North. In July of 1972, the church moved to the Katherine Curren Elementary School in Hopkins. In August of that year, the **Bush Lake Church** indicated it wanted to join this congregation also, and the properties of the Bush Lake Church were deeded to Cross of Glory and new members welcomed.

On Sunday, October 29, 1972, the congregation met for the first time at its current location in a new facility at the intersection of Excelsior Boulevard and Shady Oak Road on the Minnetonka-Hopkins border. The Rev. Leonard Karlberg was the first pastor of the new church called Cross of Glory Baptist and served during the construction of the main building and its addition in the 1970s. He accepted a call to the Foothills Baptist Church in Tucson, Arizona in 1982. He was followed by the Pastors William Malam 1983-1992 and Jon Herring (1993-) with interim pastors and directors hired as well to lead the growing congregation. Cross of Glory celebrated its 25th Anniversary on October 25, 1997.

Fairview Evangelical Lutheran Church

Fairview Evangelical Lutheran Church was built in 1955 at 4215 Fairview Avenue, Minnetonka. The Reverend Fred W. Golke was their first pastor and the initial congregation had 85 members. A new sanctuary and annex were dedicated in June of 1974 after the congregation had grown to over 600. Fairview Lutheran, Missouri Synod, advertises as being in Hopkins in some publications and as being in Minnetonka in others.

Assemblies of God/West Oaks Community Church

Assemblies of God/West Oaks Community Church at 11901 Excelsior Avenue west of Cross of Glory Church and east of Faith Presbyterian Church is yet another Minnetonka church that serves the Hopkins area. The assemblies of God congregation dedicated their present church in July of 1965. Prior to this, they had met at 28 Ninth Avenue South.

Living Waters Christian Church

Living Waters Christian Church was a congregation about nine years old when it moved into a former health club at 1002 2nd Street Northeast in Hopkins about 1994. It is the newest congregation in the Hopkins area.

The houses of worship in the Hopkins area have expanded and advanced with the development of the community. They have been one of the most important influences in the community. They fill a vast community need just as they did over a century ago.

Cemeteries

There are no cemeteries within the city limits of Hopkins, although a potter's field was located at the Hennepin County Poor Farm, which operated in Hopkins from 1865-1953. When the Poor Farm closed, 380 sets of "no name" remains were re-interred at Woodside Cemetery in Tonka Bay through the efforts of the Huber mortuary of Excelsior.

There are several cemeteries very near Hopkins that have traditionally been the final resting place for Hopkins residents.

Grandview Park Cemetery, established about 1868, is east of Highway 169 at 6901 Maloney Avenue. It is officially in Edina, but is primarily considered a Hopkins burial place. Grandview is nonsectarian and was established by Johnston Mealey and his wife Ann. It was first known as Mealey's Cemetery and incorporated in 1902 as Grand View Park Cemetery. The Mealeys operated a horse collar factory from 1904 to 1910. Their daughter married John Lindberry, and the Lindberry family has operated the cemetery ever since.

The Hopkins water tower can be seen through the trees from the Grandview Cemetery. Photo taken in 2002.

Faith Presbyterian Church Cemetery at 12007 Excelsior Boulevard, a short distance west in Minnetonka, is for church members, many of which are Hopkins residents.

The Catholic cemetery is St. Margaret's located on the site of the former Catholic Church, southeast of Shady Oak Lake at Bren Road in Minnetonka.

Very near St. Margaret's Cemetery is Shady Oak Cemetery located on the west side of Shady Oak Road near Lone Lake Park. This was the old Bohemian nonsectarian burial ground.

Today, of course, there are many burial alternatives available, such as at Ft. Snelling National Cemetery, Lakewood Cemetery in Minneapolis or at other secular or religious cemeteries in Minneapolis or neighboring communities. Cremation is an increasingly popular option.

This large crypt in Grandview Cemetery is the final resting place of Paul Swenson, the most powerful man in Hopkins from about 1887-1927.

A funeral procession to the cemetery was a lot different in 1914 than it is today! This procession is going south on Shady Oak Road from Excelsior Avenue (now Mainstreet) to Excelsior Boulevard. Photo taken from the viaduct over Shady Oak Road.

The Hopkins Lions Club started to develop Shady Oak Beach in the early 1940s. This photo is dated 1944. Shady Oak Beach has been a favorite recreation site for the community and was recently totally remodeled by the Hopkins-Minnetonka Recreation Department.

CHAPTER 6

Leisure Time

Leisure amusements, athletics and recreation were not a priority in the first few decades of the community's existence. Pioneers worked ten hours a day, six days a week in the M.T.M. plant. A farmer's work was seemingly never done. Homes and schools had to be built. Children had to be fed and clothed. Family entertainment was a lot simpler and included hayrides, picnics in the summer, and ice skating and sleigh riding in the winter.

But it has always been important for people to get together to socialize, exchange ideas and have some fun together. Because the village of Hopkins was the commercial center for the area, it also became the focal point for social activities. Clubs and organizations abound. Lodges and service organizations have provided community service in addition to social outlets for Hopkins citizens. Community festivals, music and theater groups and athletic teams contribute to a strong com-

munity spirit that endures despite the encroachment of the big city.

In this chapter, we will explore the many activities that Hopkins folks have enjoyed over the years when they were not working.

Lodges and Service Organizations
Masons—Albert Pike Lodge #237

In 2001, the Albert Pike Lodge celebrated its 100th anniversary as a Freemason fraternal organization. Around 1900 some Hopkins area members of the Masonic Lodge in Wayzata decided they wanted to meet closer to home, so together with some Wayzata members, they started the charter process. They received permission to operate from the Grand Lodge of Minnesota on Oct 15th and officially adopted their charter on January 24, 1901. There were 66 members initially. The first Master of the Lodge was S.S. Kellington, a

The Masonic Temple at 907 Mainstreet (Excelsior Avenue).

physician from Wayzata. Other names of interest on the roster of initial members are A.H. Nash, Fred Kenaston and Sam Campbell.

The Albert Pike Lodge first met at Sam Campbell's Store, beginning construction in the summer of 1901 on its temple on Excelsior Avenue between 9th and 10th Avenues (now 907 Mainstreet). The first meeting held in the new temple was in October 1902. The new temple had a regal look and sat a few feet off the street with property on either side. The building was remodeled in 1949 when there was a surge in membership following World War II. In 1955, it was jacked up and a basement was dug under it. The two lots on either side were sold to defray the cost of construction and remodeling. In 1963, the building was painted white and the iron fence and wall were removed. With the mindset of historic preservation, in 1987 the white paint was removed, the building was restored to its brick beginnings, and replicas of the stone wall and wrought iron fence were reinstalled.

William Smetana, told Emil Souba this story many years ago. When the Albert Pike Lodge was looking for a location to build its headquarters in 1901, they were considering two lots: one was near the Hopkins depot on the east end of town and the other was to the west nearer the M.T.M. factory. The lodge initially bought the lot on the east side near the depot. Smetana bought the lot at 907 Excelsior Ave because he believed the town would develop to the west of the tracks and the Lodge

would later regret their purchase. Sure enough, the Lodge reconsidered and bought the 907 Excelsior lot from Mr. Smetana for the home of their temple. And the town of Hopkins did indeed develop west of the tracks. Today, the temple looks a bit out of place, set back from other Mainstreet shops and on a hill but it has been part of the action on Mainstreet Hopkins for over a hundred years.

Ida McKinley Chapter No. 178, Order of the Eastern Star

The women's O.E.S. in Hopkins began through the efforts of Charlotte Straub and her husband B.F. Straub. They held their first meeting on April 28, 1904 in the Masonic Temple in Hopkins. The Past Grand Matron of Minnesota, Louise Lyon Johnson, was present. They required a name and Johnson, seeing a portrait of slain President McKinley hanging in the room, suggested Ida McKinley, the president's invalid wife, who was a member of the O.E.S. There were 74 Charter members. The first officers were: Charlotte Straub, H. Martin Peterson, Lida Seiberlich, Minnie Feudner, Diana Campbell, Minnie Truman and Eleah Hosp. The largest membership year was 1965 with 388 members.

Ida McKinley Chapter is a part of the "family organization" in the related Masonic bodies, but is not part of the Masonic Fraternity. They work closely with the Masons in projects such as aiding the Minnesota Masonic Home and the Masonic Memorial (Cancer) Hospital at the University of Minnesota. Their most ambitious national project is the Eastern Star Training Awards for Religious Leadership to assist men and women studying for the ministry. Through the years, dinners, bazaars, socials and such helped provide funds for its various community service projects. There are records of Social Clubs, Red Cross Units, a Thimble Bee, Areme Sewing Club, Areme Girls Club, Past Matrons Club, etc. They have an excellent working relationship with the Albert Pike Lodge.

Women's Club of Hopkins

The Women's Club of Hopkins, originally the Women's Improvement League, has the following purpose: "to unite for the purpose of mutual benefit and to carry out a civic, welfare and study program." This group was chartered in 1908 as part of the International Federation and met in the homes of members until 1915. Dues were twenty-five cents a meeting.

Numerous activities of the Women's Club have positively benefited the Hopkins community. In 1911-1912, they were responsible for the first park and bandstand at Excelsior and 11th Avenues. Under the category "environmental improvement" they were responsible for getting the men off of the benches in front of the I.O.O.F. (Oddfellows) Building at 9th and Excelsior Avenues and stopped them from spitting on the sidewalks.

Led by Mrs. W.B. Anderson, this group started the first library in Hopkins. They collected books and did many other things to get the shelves stocked. In 1912, the library was located in the upstairs rear of the new city hall on the northeast corner of 8th and Excelsior Avenues. Lillian Wheeler was the first librarian. The women's club held a children's story hour every Saturday at the City Hall. Attendance was often 150-175 children.

The women's club also raised funds to have garbage cans placed at each intersection on Excelsior Avenue in 1913 to help beautify the community. In 1916, they put on a campaign to raise funds for a women's building and a women's rest room at the Hennepin County Fair Grounds in Hopkins.

These women were a dynamic energetic group that in 1947 sponsored a Victory Garden, aid for Native Americans and rolled bandages. In 1951, they developed the loan closet, which is still going. In 1954, they sponsored an A.F.S. Foreign Exchange Student and provided scholarships for two Hopkins High School students. In 1957, they provided for a water fountain at Burnes Park. This same year they withdrew from the International Federation. On their 60th anniversary, Mrs. Myrtle Johnson Bjorklund interested the group in starting a garden club and an antique shop.

In 1979 the Women's Club pushed for and achieved a passive park in downtown Hopkins and celebrated its opening. They celebrated their 75th anniversary in 1983 and had to restrict their membership to 250 in 1987-88 because it was getting too hard to manage its large meetings. They often meet at Faith Presbyterian Church and are still a strong contributing force in the community.

VFW—George R. Wolff Post #425

The Hopkins Veterans of Foreign War post was organized June 30, 1920. It was named after the first soldier

The Women's Improvement League of Hopkins at their 40th anniversary gathering on May 1, 1947.

VFW Members posing with cannon in front of the Junior High School Building in the late 1920s.

from Hopkins killed in World War I. Both Spanish-American War and World War I veterans were part of this first group. The Cross of Malta from the Knights of St. John on the Isle of Malta, is the VFW symbol, which was established nationally in 1899.

Currently the Hopkins post has 1,000 members and they are active in rehabilitation services for veterans, volunteering millions of hours at the Minneapolis Veterans Administration (VA) hospital and at the Minneapolis Soldiers' Home, for which they lobbied the legislature to upgrade in the 1990s. The Cooties are affiliated with the VFW; they are an honorary group that do extraordinary volunteering on a regular basis. The VFW Ladies Auxiliary is also very active in service and hospitality work.

VFW Post #425 met at the old City Hall on 8th and Excelsior Avenues in the years after World War II and in 1951, they purchased the lot where the American Legion is now, at 10 Twelfth Avenue

South. They built a basement meeting room and began meeting there about 1950. They ran a carnival at the Hennepin County fairgrounds that paid their mortgage. They ran the Hopkins Raspberry Festival for 5 or 6 years after World War II. They are best known for their

VFW Members after World War I.

Flossie Park and Isabelle Beckman—VFW Poppy Sale, 1924.

camp at Quantico, Virginia. He refused medical help there saying: "My dad knows more about these things than any man living and I'm going to him." He was sent to Swedish Hospital in Minneapolis. As the newspaper reported: "Despite the high faith of the patient and the skilled and unrivaled care of the father, the ailment was not to be subdued. The young man died." Distraught over the loss of his son, Dr. G.W. Moore went personally to Washington D.C. to apply to serve in the medical reserve corps to take the place of his son, whose untimely death deprived the country of a first-rate fighting man.

The Hopkins Legion building at 17 Excelsior Avenue was fashioned after a Virginia plantation and was built with volunteer labor on land donated by M.B. (Punchy) Hagen. Wally Hamilton designed the building. When the building was torn down to make way for Highway 169, the Post bought the VFW building at 10 12th Avenue South.

The American Legion places great emphasis on youth programs. They sponsor Boys' State, (a program to expose youth to government), teen dances, baseball teams, scholarships, etc. They also lobby and raise funds for the betterment of veterans. They have an exceptional auxiliary working side by side with them to support their various causes.

Memorial Day services honoring our war heroes held every year and for the poppy sales that fund the rehabilitation programs of the VFW. They are active in many civic causes, despite the elderly age of many of their members.

Nationally, the VFW helped establish the GI Bill after World War II, giving veterans the ability to afford college and/or occupational training. For families of soldiers killed in the war, they helped establish widows' pensions and GI bill eligibility for deceased soldiers' children. GI home loans helped returning soldiers afford housing. These programs alone helped upgrade the education and living standards for generations of Americans since the 1950s.

Interlachen Park Needlework Guild

The Interlachen Park Section of the Minneapolis Branch of the Needlework Guild of America adopted its by-laws on December 9, 1929. The purpose of the guild was to aid in providing warm and suitable garments and bedding for the needy of Minneapolis through the organ-

American Legion

The Hopkins John Wilbur Moore Post #320 of the American Legion was chartered in 1928 with about 26 members. Dr. V.T. McHale was the first commander. It is part of the national organization started in 1918 to assist servicemen when they came home from France after World War I. The local post was named for John Wilbur Moore, the son of Dr. G.W. Moore, who died of appendicitis on Jan. 8, 1918 before he went into active duty in World War I.

John Wilbur Moore, a Corporal in the Marine Corps, was taken ill while in

Old American Legion Building, 17 Excelsior Ave., Built 1941.

> *"Father, of all mercies, we are clothed, we are fed, we are sound in mind and body. In gratitude for these great blessings, we offer these material things to those less fortunate. Add Thy blessings, we beseech, to the work of our hands and hearts, so that each garment may carry to the wearer, not only decency and warmth, but courage, comfort and hope for brighter days."*
>
> The Needlework Guild Prayer

ized activities of that Branch. The Interlachen Needlework Guild was founded as the Nissa Club prior to World War I. When the war broke out, Mrs. Henry Perbix, who lived at 240 Interlachen Road, expanded the group with a call for volunteers to sew for the Red Cross.

The Hopkins Historical Society has copies of the minute books of the guild beginning in 1925. In that year the guild made 198 items of clothing: 1 apron, 4 baby comforts, 30 bloomers, 33 dresses, 71 diapers, 27 infants' gowns outing flannel, 2 girls gowns outing flannel, 10 ladies gowns muslin, 2 towels, 16 underwaists, and 2 union suits. There were 28 members in 1925-26 and they were all listed by their husband's name (Mrs. John Doe), except for two who used their own given names. This group was still functioning in 1982 as part of the Methodist church "ingathering."

The Hopkins Rotary

The Hopkins Rotary Civic Club was organized and became a member of the worldwide Rotary International in June, 1938. The Rotary Club met weekly for many years at Bursch's Restaurant and it now meets at the Hopkins Center for the Arts.

The Hopkins Rotary Club has sponsored activities that have helped make the Hopkins community a better place to live. On the first birthday of the club in 1939 about $30.00 was spent to sponsor four boys at summer camp. (These were depression dollars and if you had these, you could accomplish things!) About 1949 it put luminous tape on all the bicycles in town and donated a movie projector to the Hopkins Public Library.

The club has continued to offer projects to help the youth of the community. The Rotary Club gives college scholarships to Hopkins High School students. It also cooperates with the American Field Services (AFS) and Rotary International Student Exchange in sponsoring foreign students at Hopkins High School by supporting a fruit sale during the winter holidays. It recognizes outstanding citizenship with its annual "Rotarian of the Year" and "Community Person of the Year" awards.

In 1987, the Rotary Clubs of the world began an international fund-raising effort to eradicate polio worldwide. In 2002, the Bill and Melinda Gates Foundation selected the Rotary Foundation to receive its second annual Gates Award for Global Health citing its leadership for this and other international health causes. The Rotary Club of Hopkins continues to support both local and international causes, with its Books for Africa program being a prime example of a creative way to link the local and worldwide communities.

Lions

Lions International was started in 1917 by Melvin Jones and has become the largest civic club in the world both by number of clubs and number of members. Currently, the Lions International prime projects are helping the blind, the deaf and diabetics.

The Hopkins Lions Club was started a few months after the Rotary, in 1938/1939. The following were charter members: Bill Mallery, Russ Carroll, H.W. Lorentz, Art Neider, Richard Beckman, Robert Gustafson, Herb Williams, E.N. MacLaughlin, Charles Herzan, Earl Ger-

Shady Oak beach after it was remodeled in the 1990s. *City of Hopkins photo.*

rard, Max Moore, Vern Williams, R.S. Gordan, Lloyd Lindahl, Louis Malbie, Dr. Picha, Earl Homer, Carl Anderson and Ralph Miller. It is the oldest Lion's Club in the suburbs and was sired by the Minneapolis Central Lions Club.

One Lions Club project that has become a major recreational attraction for Hopkins and the surrounding communities was Shady Oak Beach. They bought abandoned property from the Chicago Milwaukee and St. Paul Railroad for one dollar and additional land from Virgil Miller and the Brokl brothers. In 1943, they started developing Shady Oak Beach. Even though the beach was eventually taken over by the Cities of Hopkins and Minnetonka, the Lions regularly contributed to its improvements. They added diving towers, slides, floats, fireplaces, parking spaces, lifeguards, refreshments, restrooms and a shelter through the years. Shady Oak Beach was totally remodeled in the late 1990s by the Cities of Hopkins and Minnetonka and is still as popular as ever.

Other Lions Club activities have been building shelters and warming houses at Central Park, delivering baskets to the needy at Christmas, awarding scholarships to Hopkins High School students, sponsoring Little League, Mighty Mites, Babe Ruth, Boy Scouts, Girl Scouts and other youth activities. During the evening meetings, the Lions often entertained the Hopkins Policemen, Firemen and Butzie Maetzold's athletes.

A number of persons have been active for many years in the Hopkins Lions such as: Dr. J.J. Hersman (1939), Palmer Sveen (1939), Svante Severson (1941), Norm Gustafson (1943), Don Caroline (1949), John Lutter (1949) and Lyman Hamilton (1951). The Hopkins Lions have had three District Governors: J. Russ Carroll (1946), John Lutter (1959) and Tony Tesarek (1962).

The Lionesses, the women's Lions auxiliary, was started in 1976 by Eileen Lutter.

Knights of Columbus

The Council of Hopkins #2232 named after Christopher Columbus was founded on February 20, 1921. They were first housed in the Olson Building on the third floor. They moved to St. Joseph School when it was first built in the early 1920s. The Knights bought property on 7th Avenue South and met there for many years. This building was sold to help finance the red brick colonial building at 34-10th Avenue South built in the fall of 1964, which was remodeled in 1978 and sold

in 1993 to the West Suburban Adult Day Care, known as Open Circle.

The Hopkins Knights of Columbus were off to a good start with eighty-six candidates in the first class adding forty-five transfers for a total of 131 Knights. The first Grand Knight was John Dolan.

They sponsored Boy Scout Troop #274 in the 1920s and early 1930s. Harry Haskins was the first Scout Master. Since that time, the Knight's Council #2232 has sponsored many other activities such as youth athletics, dog derbies, skating contests, carnivals, firefighter appreciation dinners, blood drives and others. Charities have always been stressed. To keep the St. Joseph school open during the depression, the Knights of Columbus raised over $7,000. The State Convention was hosted in Hopkins in 1932. The Knights contributed to the funding of Benilde High School in the 1950s.

In 1988 the name of the council was changed to "Monsignor Joseph P. Vacek Council 2232." This organization celebrated its Diamond Anniversary in 1996 and continues to use St. Joseph Church as home base, with some office space in their former building on 10th. In 1996, its membership was 464 members (29 Honorary and 120 Honorary Life) and it continues to support the churches, schools and community of the greater Hopkins area.

Hopkins Jaycees

The local chapter of the U.S. Junior Chamber of Commerce, the Hopkins Jaycees, was founded in Hopkins in 1951, and celebrated its 50-year anniversary in 2001. The Jaycees is a constructive organization of young persons between the ages of 21-39 who devote a portion of their time to community service in the public interest. Through the act of serving, members receive hands-on experience, which translates to the enhancement of personal growth and the development of valuable leadership skills.

The Hopkins Jaycees have been very active in the community. They assumed responsibility for the Raspberry Festival in 1962 and expanded its features. The Raspberry Committee runs the festival today, but the Jaycees continue to provide funding and run some events. The Jaycees initiated the Hopkins Distinguished Service Award, which is awarded annually to a Hopkins citizen between the ages of eighteen and thirty-six who has contributed to the community. They also award a Boss of the Year award.

The Jaycee Women's Club was founded in 1954. In

C.Z.B.J. Picnic. Snapshot photo processed on September 20, 1929.

of this second organization, the **Western Bohemian Fraternal Association (W.B.F.A.)** in English.

The Z.C.B.J. was considered "progressive." It made progress toward achieving a better state, kept up with the times, and made changes as modernization required. Its very start was caused by the change required by a more modern concept of life insurance—that of each member paying dues according to his or her age and occupation.

By 1899, women were admitted to full, insured membership. This seems common now, but back then this was a daring and outrageous thing to do. The Z.C.B.J. was a pioneer in this aspect and also in admitting youth. By 1922, English had become the official language of the lodges but the Czech language was encouraged. Thus, younger folk who could not speak Czech felt free to join and become active in the group. One stated goal was to continue to strive toward "the

the early 1980s, the U.S. Supreme Court ruled that the Jaycee organization nationally must allow women into their clubs, so about 1982 the Hopkins Jaycees opened their membership to women, which by 1987 had evened out to a 50-50 ratio of male and female members.

Western Bohemian Fraternal Association (Západní Cesko-Bratrská Jednota), or Z.C.B.J.

The Bohemians had several organizations that were very important to their community. The description of the Z.C.B.J. from its 50th anniversary convention program, Omaha, Nebraska, 1947 explains this importance:

> Founded nationally in 1897, the Czechs banded together for mutual welfare and betterment, to provide insurance protection for the family, to better enable its members to cope with the new language, customs, and way of life which they, as immigrants, found in their new home, to furnish opportunity to relieve sharp loneliness, to enlarge acquaintances, and to furnish meeting places and occasions for talking their native tongue, singing their old songs, their music, staging their plays,—all these things were present.

The Z.C.B.J. was started to counteract inequalities in an older Czech society, the Szechoslovak Benevolent Society, founded in 1854. For insurance purposes, the C.S.P.S. (as it was known) charged a flat rate to all members that varied month-to-month depending on how many mortalities they had. C.S.P.S. had been started in the east and had spread west. The people in the east were much older and their mortality was higher than the younger people who had more recently settled in the west. Yet, the people in the west had to pay the same mortuary dues. Instead of reforming this society, a new society was formed, thus "western" was put in the title

Many fraternal organization pins and badges have been donated to the Hopkins Historical Society. Some are very colorful and ornate on one side and could be reversed to black for funerals. The C.Z.B.J. badge on the left shows the red, white and blue side. The C.Z.K.J. badge on the right displays the black side.

highest American citizenship and the most noble in the brotherhood of man."

Sometime in the 1880s, a small building was erected in the Glen Lake area on land donated by Frank Kinsel as a Czech community center and library. The men who built it and equipped it with Bohemian language books were Frank Kinsel, Joseph Soukoup, John Popelka, Joseph Holasek, Phillip Dominick, John M. Chastek, Henry Souba, Henry Dominick and John Makousky. This same group also formed a chapter of the C.S.P.S. Lodge, receiving a charter and operating under that name until 1897. In 1898, the members withdrew from the original lodge and affiliated with the Z.C.B.J. under the name of **F.B. Zdrubek Lodge No. 11**. This unit functioned until 1930 when members of the Hopkins order of the same lodge, **No. 169 Hradcany**, voted to merge with the Glen Lake group. Hopkins Hradcany Z.C.B.J. lodge had been established in 1907 and met in the Hopkins Opera Hall. After the merger, the lodge's name became **Hopkins Lodge No. 11, Z.C.B.J.**

On New Year's eve morning, 1933, the Z.C.B.J. lodge in Glen Lake burned to the ground. A silk flag valued at $135 was saved by John Jeppesen and Bob Ferris who were among the group of neighbors gathered to watch the blaze. Although the Hopkins Fire Department was notified of the blaze, they were unable to respond because the lodge had not made an agreement with the fire department to provide fire protection to them and they were outside of the Hopkins fire district.

Thankfully, the library books were not burned in the fire. 1200 Bohemian language books had been magnanimously given to the Hopkins Public Library when it opened in 1912. In 1933, there were about 200 of these Bohemian books remaining at the Hopkins library. These books were turned over to the Hopkins Historical Society, but since very few in Hopkins could read the Bohemian language any more, these books were donated (in the 1990s) to the new University of Minnesota Immigration Library.

Oriole Lodge Number 302 of the Z.C.B.J. was organized on September 28, 1928. They merged with Hopkins Number 11 in November 1948. In 1984, this lodge was still meeting in the I.O.O.F. Hall.

Western Bohemian Catholic Union (W.B.C.U.)

Lodge St. Joseph #86, a Catholic fraternal organization of Czech people, was chartered in 1911 under the Western Bohemian Catholic Union (W.B.C.U.), or Zapadni Caska Kalolicka Jednota (Z.C.K.J.) emblem. At first, the insurance rates were very low, but as time passed the insurance rates became exorbitant for younger people so many left the organization. Those who remained were so old they couldn't afford to drop out. A sister lodge, St. Prokop, affiliated with St. Margaret's Catholic Church in Minnetonka, was faced with similar decline in numbers, so for a while the two groups met together in the St. Prokop lodge building near St. Margaret's church. The Catholic decree that St. Mary's and St. Margaret's Catholic Churches were to be merged in 1921 was a hard blow to these elderly lodge members, some of whom left the Catholic church. Those that remained Catholic merged with the Catholic Workmen (Katolicky Delnik) lodge in 1929. The Hopkins council retained its Patron "Saint Joseph" designation, but was assigned the branch number 141.

Miscellaneous Lodges and Organizations

Hopkins had numerous other lodges and organizations; many are now defunct. Several were affiliated with the Bohemians or other ethnic groups. Some were organized for a specific purpose and ended when their goals were achieved. We tried to list those organizations we have run across, with

Clubs were always active in making floats for the Raspberry parade. This is a 1939 photo.

The first Hopkins Boy Scout troop.

apologies that we can't go into any more detail or that we most surely have missed some.

Listed in the *Hopkins News* of July 26, 1906—Masonic, Eastern Star, Odd Fellows, Rebekahs, A.O.U.W., Degree of Honor, Woodmen, Royal Neighbors, Royal League, Hibernians, Danish Brotherhood, Danish Sisterhood, Yeomen, Eagles, Good Templars and Bohemian Workmen.

The **Hopkins Independent Order of Odd Fellows (I.O.O.F.)** was formed in 1893 for men. The Hopkins Jewel Rebekah lodge #152 for women was formed in 1896. Many of the early members also were M.T.M. Company leaders and the membership usually boomed in depression times. Meetings were held in the Koblas Building and about 1901 or 1903 they built the I.O.O.F. building at 823 Excelsior Ave. The lodge had an insurance plan and credit union and sponsored many dances, picnics, dinners and card parties. It had a famous annual lutefisk dinner for many years. In 1975, they were still active sponsoring little league baseball and other events.

Sokol is a fraternal organization started in Prague in 1862 and in the USA in 1896 founded on the principle that an individual must be physically fit in order to be mentally and emotionally healthy. It provided gymnastics and calisthenics training for boys and girls from ages 6 and up, had a life insurance component and sponsored camps and social activities. Among the various Bohemian clubs was the **Czech Relief Fund** established in 1917-1919 (name changed in 1935 to **Sokol Damsky Osveta Club**), a women's organization helping the Z.C.B.J. Lodge and other civic causes.

Bethel No. 42, International Order of **Job's Daughters** of the City of Hopkins, started after March 9, 1948 and was open to girls between the ages of 12 and 20.

The **Women's Christian Temperance Union** (WCTU) started in Hopkins in 1943. Hopkins only had 25 members but statewide there were over 8,000 members in 1949. Their goal was to educate about the dangers of alcoholic beverages. They worked hard to help pass the 9:00 p.m. curfew ordinance.

General James Knapp Chapter, D.A.R. (Daughters of the American Revolution) was organized in Hopkins on April 17, 1925. Hopkins was selected as the post office, although a majority of the members initially lived in Minneapolis. At its first meeting in Hopkins, Mr. Levi Longfellow, pioneer and patriot, was the chief speaker, telling of the history of the town he had helped lay out and to which he had given its name.

General James Knapp (1764-1818), for whom the chapter was named, enlisted as a drummer boy on Feb. 8, 1777 at the age of thirteen and served for six years in the Continental Army. He was the ancestor of Mrs. Marshall H. Coolidge, State Regent at the time, who gave the new Hopkins D.A.R. chapter its name.

The **Boy Scouts** were started by Dan Beard in England in 1909. It did not take long before Boy Scout Troop #52 had started in Hopkins. It met upstairs in the City Hall and was sponsored by one of the churches in Hopkins. Some of the boys in the first troop were Lee McNally, Clint Lofgren, Ted Williams and Stewie Beckman. In 1919, the Scout Master ran off and took along the troop's money.

Troop #52, which became the Chamber of Commerce Troop, was reorganized in March 1920 by the Mizpah Congregational Church, and then helped to form two other troops, #152 at St. Joseph's Church and #252 at Gethsemane Lutheran Church. Troop #274 was formed by the Knights of Columbus in 1929 and #278 was formed in Interlachen Park in 1933.

One fundraiser the scouts had was selling American flags to merchants in Hopkins. The boys encouraged each shop owner along Excelsior Avenue to buy a 3 x 5 foot flag on an eight-foot pole for $7.95. The scouts then dug holes in the concrete along the curb for the flags.

Excelsior Avenue was a pretty sight on a holiday with all the flags flying!

In 1922, a group of boys in Troop #52 went camping at Woody Point on Lake Minnewashta. They prevailed upon Austin 'Ham' Hamilton, who normally got off his mail route by 1:00 or 2:00 p.m., to go to camp with them and leave for work from the camp each morning. Ham was an outdoorsman and an excellent cook as well. It cost each boy only $7.50 for two weeks of camping, which was earned by caddying, picking berries and such. The troop was able to get an Eagle Scout from a Minneapolis troop who acted as an assistant leader.

One day, the scouts captured three nice big snapping turtles after Reveille. The next day 32 boys gobbled up 10 gallons of turtle stew. Many boys enjoyed fishing, so every morning those who had permission went out in the four boats that were rented during the two weeks of camp. A lot of fish were needed to feed 32 kids but there was always plenty for a couple of fish fries.

The **Girl Scouts** started in the United States in 1912. Girl scouts were in the Hopkins schools by at least 1937. It was announced in the February 11, 1937 *Hennepin County Review* that twelve girls became girl scouts in front of the Parents and Teachers Association. Miss Lucille DeLeeuw, the high school librarian, led the troop. At this assembly, Dorothy Upham, Hennepin County Girl Scout Director, urged greater public interest in activities of the girls' organization.

The Lewa Council of the **Camp Fire Girls** originally was organized in September 1929, with Mrs. A.R. Lofgren, guardian for the girls. They held weekly meetings at the Community House on the Hennepin County fairgrounds until the weather became too cold. Another Camp Fire group was started at St. Joseph's Church in 1934, but didn't last very long. Later, several Bluebird groups were started. The Rotary gave each group $10 per year; by 1949, the Rotary was contributing $60 a year to each group. The Camp Fire Girls made useful items for residents of the "old people's home" or the Glen Lake Sanitarium and helped serve at P.T.A. dinners. In 1949, there were 150 members in Hopkins.

The **Hopkins Senior Club** was founded in 1951 to provide events and entertainment for senior citizens in the Hopkins and Minnetonka area. Its heyday was in the 1970s when membership grew to 163. Many senior social clubs have been replaced by community-based senior center activities, but the Hopkins Senior Club continues to meet twice a month in 2002.

Clubs in the 1960s. We turned to the Hopkins phone books to see what clubs were popular in more recent decades. The 1960 Hopkins phone book listed these clubs: American Field Service, Parent Teacher Association of Hopkins, Barracks of World War I No 2594, Catholic Workmen Lodge, Chamber of Commerce, Concert Association, Daughters of Isabella, Elks Club and Elkettes, Garden Club of Hopkins, Hops Tubby Tops, West Suburban Kiwanis Club, League of Women Voters, Letter Carriers Auxiliary, Military Order of the Cootie, Mrs. Jaycees, Optimist Club, Opti-Mrs. Club, Royal Neighbors Lodge, Toastmaster Club 49ers, Welcome Wagon, Y's Men's Club and Y' Menettes, Hopkins Newcomer's Club, various church groups such as the Gethsemane Church Women and the John Hus Mariner's Club and Women's Association, Junior Women's Club of Hopkins and Minnetonka, Local 337 UAW-AFL-CIO, Methodist Men's and Women's Club, DFL Ward Club of Hopkins and Edina-Morningside, Meadowbrook Men's Golf Club, Nursing Auxiliary District 6 of Rural Hennepin County, Hopkins DeMolay, Hopkins Hand Ball and Exercise Club, Hopkins Republican Party, Santa Anonymous and Gloria Deo No 16 White Shrine Hopkins Area Chamber of Commerce.

Clubs in 1985, had taken on socially conscious, lifestyle and support group themes not seen in earlier times—Big Brothers/Big Sisters of Greater Minneapolis, American Lung Association, Heart Association, Cancer Society and Diabetes Societies, Senior Nutrition Program, Parents Without Partners, Toughlove Parents Support Group, Courage Center, Hopkins Loan Closet, Interchurch Community Association, Friends of the Library, Christian Business and Professional Women, American Association of University Women (AAUW), Welcome Wagon, Art Center of Minnesota, Kiwanis, American Association of Retired Persons (AARP), LaLeche League and the Minnetonka Choral Society. Not all clubs had a social service theme—"The U.S.S. Phoenix" was a Star Trek Fan Club.

Civic and Community Service Organizations today, listed in the 2002 *Hopkins Community Guide*, have a decidedly social service theme—Adult Options in Education, Autism Resource Network, Bethesda, Goodwill and Salvation Army Thrift Shops, The Children's Chance, Choices for Children, Community Action for Suburban Hennepin, the Depot Coffee House, Empty Bowls Community Education, Friends of the Hopkins Community Library, Harley Hopkins Family Center, Helping Paws of Minnesota, Hopkins Activity Center & Resource Center, Hopkins Historical Society, Minnehaha Oaks Association, Minnetonka Life Care Center, Open Circle Senior Day Center, Sojourner Project, Teens Alone, Vail Place, Washburn Child Guidance Center and West Hennepin Community Builders. The following civic booster associations and veterans groups are advertised—Hopkins Business and Civic Association, Raspberry Festival, St. Patrick's Parade, Jazzberries of Hopkins (a Senior Performing Group), Vietnam Veterans of America and Lynnhurst Masonic Lodge in addition to these long standing Hopkins groups—the American Legion, Elks, Lions, Rotary, Albert Pike Masonic Lodge, VFW and Ida McKinley Eastern Star.

Athletics

A very strong heritage of both school and community-based sports teams exists in Hopkins. In the early years, the school system had strict rules on leisure activities. They frowned on students bringing bats and balls to school. Interscholastic boys' teams were not allowed until 1915.

The first girls' sport in the High School was a swim team in 1956. It wasn't until the 1972-73 school year that girls were allowed to compete interscholastically in a few sports, forced by the passage of Title IX to the Civil Rights Act passed in 1972, which banned sex discrimination in the schools.

Grass roots sports teams and leagues have flourished since about 1900 and even though some of them have changed over time, sports still play a vital role in the life of the community.

Back in 1914, five high school guys—Earnest Goldborg, Harvey Wulke, Benny Berkuvitz, Benny McCormick and a fellow named Larson from Minnetonka Mills—approached the school board to try to organize football and basketball teams in the High School. The school board's response was that if they needed exercise, they should go get an axe and chop some wood. So, the guys each chipped in a dollar, organized their own High School athletic association and started a basketball team with five members. They lost every game they played. By the 1915-16 season, with Professor Mayo's encouragement, the squad grew to seven members and began to play other schools. High school athletics were off to a big start in Hopkins.

Community basketball teams, too, were very popular. The 1911 Hopkins AA quintet was the first organized basketball team in Hopkins. They played in the Opera Hall. When the group first gathered, they discovered that no one knew the rules or any techniques. A relative of Bill and Jake Perbix, Dr. R.M. Rosenwold, a University of Minnesota basketball star, agreed to instruct them. Opponents were hard to find. They went by train to Green Isle, Chaska and Plato, and by streetcar to play Augsburg College or Excelsior.

Baseball was America's favorite sport and always managed to get local sponsors to back a team.

Hopkins' first championship baseball team (1898-1902) was the Minneapolis Threshing Machine team that won 25 straight games before losing to Winona. The team played in three states and all the members worked at the M.T.M. Company.

Bill Carney was the only ex-major league player to play for a local team. He pitched for and managed the 1903-1907 M.T.M. team. After that, he operated a two-lane bowling

The 1912-13 Hopkins Athletic Association Basketball Club team: Einer Jorgensen, George Peterson, A.R. "Butch" Lofgren, Bertram Gaertner, Arthur Nash, William "Bill" Perbix, Joe Kriz, Harvey Anderson.

M.T.M. Co. team cir. 1897. (Front) Bob Sieberlich, mascot Julius Nelson, John Levandusky. (Middle) Billy O'Dell, Sr., Billy Moran, Jack Burns. (Back) Joe Levandusky, Morgan Sweeney, Tommy Tighe, Samuel "Moose" McConaughey, "Snowball" Jeppesen, Frank Levandusky.

team won the state championship in 1951. The M.B. Hagen Little League ball field on 11th Avenue South was the site of innumerable ball games over the years but conceded to development in the 1990s. The Minneapolis Moline Parts Department team won the Slow Pitch championship in 1954 and the Hopkins Legion baseball teams won numerous championships.

Hopkins had a bowling team as early as 1903 and helped organize the commercial bowling league, which was very popular through the 1950s and beyond. Hopkins took the bowling championship in 1934-35 and other years as well.

Hopkins' first horseshoe team began in 1917. Affiliated with the Hennepin County Fair, Hopkins had a racetrack and harness racing was mostly a spectator sport enjoyed by the community. The baseball diamond was in the center of the racetrack. A gun club offered shooting

alley in the basement of the Opera Hall. Later, he was a game warden.

The Hopkins Advertisers baseball team had a different sponsor for each player. We can identify the local sports enthusiasts in the 1912 team photo—Nelson Confectionery, H & B Grocers, Sackrison Grocery, Swedburg Photos, Quist Shoes, K & B Hardware, Anderson Blomquist Dry Goods, H & B Grocery and a feed store.

The Smetana Pillmakers, sponsored by Smetana drug store, was a local team that featured younger players, all buddies that had played for many different teams. They had a wide assortment of uniforms, but the mascot and coach wore Smetana Pillmaker logos. In his oral history, Ernie Goldborg stated that his mother would not make him a "Pillmaker suit" but he played on the team for a little while anyway.

Community baseball has continued to elicit strong local support. The Hopkins Little League

In 1951, this Hopkins Little League team won the State Championship but lost in the final game of the regional playoff in a Chicago suburb.

Hopkins Advertisers baseball team (1912) all have different names on their shirts showing the various sponsors for the team.

The 1915 Hopkins High girls' basketball team.

In the high school, athletics were mostly the domain of the guys until the mid-1950s. The 1956 girls' swim team competed under A.A.U. swim club rules at the Y.M.C.A. The new Hopkins high school was one of a few that was equipped with a swimming pool and the girls took advantage of the opportunity to swim, although there wasn't a school conference for them. By 1958, the Hopkins Year Book shows an organization called the Girl's Athletic Association, advised by Miss Lorraine Stevenson, whose purpose was to stimulate interest among girls in a variety of sports, both in and outside school. Members of this "club" attended invitational play days where members played tournaments with girls from Minneapolis and other Lake Conference schools.

"Play days" were not enough for the young female athletes of the 1970s. History was made on May 1, 1972 when U.S. District Judge Miles W. Lord ruled that two girls may participate in sports as members of boys'

competition and Clyde Snavely won many National Rifle Association medals from 1914-1923.

Women were not totally left out of athletics in the early years. In 1905, the Minneapolis West High School girls' basketball team played Litchfield High School in a demonstration basketball game in the Opera Hall. A photo of this unusual team hangs on the wall of the Hopkins Historical Society. A Hopkins High School girls' basketball team was formed at the same time the boys' team was formed in 1915, but we are unsure how long this team continued.

Because there were so many Bohemians in the Hopkins area, the Sokol Gymnastics Clubs were popular for both girls and boys. We have several 1910-era photographs of Hopkins area Sokol groups, with Frank H. Kriz as the instructor.

The 1910 Girls' and Men's Sokol Classes under Frank H. Kriz.

teams and the teams they belong to could not be disqualified for doing so. This overruled the Minnesota State High School League that had declared girls were ineligible to play on boys' teams and if they played, both their own and the opposing teams in a game would be disqualified.

Antoinette (Tony) St. Pierre of Hopkins Eisenhower High School and Peggy Brenden of St. Cloud Technical High School had brought the lawsuit. St. Pierre had wanted to participate in both the boys' cross-country running and ski teams. When she had turned up at a meet as part of the Hopkins team, the whole team had been disqualified. The Hopkins school board had voted against allowing her to participate perhaps because they feared it would jeopardize girls' interscholastic athletic teams, which they were thinking about instituting, but had not yet done so. But Judge Lord declared St. Pierre was qualified to participate. In addition, the government had ruled that if schools wanted Federal money, they could not discriminate because of gender. Consequently, by the 1972/1973 school year, the girls' High School athletic scene had changed drastically. Hopkins had a girls' slalom downhill ski team, a cross-country ski team and swim team. Tony St. Pierre participated on the boys' Cross Country Ski Team, which had a lake conference record of 12-0 that year. In 1973, girls' tennis was added and in 1974 volleyball and track. Girls' sports opportunities have continued to expand.

In the school year just completed (2001/2002) Hopkins High School teams added five State championships to their athletic record. In November, 2001, Hopkins was the first school to win the state Class AA boys' and girls' Cross Country championships in the same year. In February, 2002, Hopkins swept both the boys' and girls' Nordic Skiing team championships, becoming the first school to achieve two such double championships in one year. When the boys won the state Class "4A" basketball championship in March, it was Hopkins' fifth team championship of the school year, which is believed to tie a state record.

High School Athletic Awards

This list includes state championships that were won by teams in the five high schools that are part of the history of the Hopkins School District: the original Hopkins High School Warriors, Hopkins Eisenhower High School Warriors, Hopkins Lindbergh High School Flyers, Golden Valley High School Vikings (merged with Hopkins in 1980) and the current Hopkins High School Royals:

Boys' Basketball—1952, 1953, 2002
Girls' Cross-country Running—1983, 2001
Boys' Cross-country Running—1998, 1999, 2001
Boys' Golf—1944
Girls' Golf—1980-1981; individual state
    champion—1979, 1980, 1981
Girls' Swimming—1978, 1979
Boys' Swimming—1966, 1967, 1970, 1971,
    1972, 1974, 1975, 1976, 1977
Boys' Soccer—1983
Boys' Wrestling—1963, 1967, 1968; individual
    state champions—1966, 1970
Girls' Tennis—1994
Boys' Tennis—1976 (individual title)
Girls' Nordic Skiing—1993, 2001, 2002
Boys' Nordic Skiing—1995, 1997, 2002
Girls' Gymnastics —1990
Girls' Softball—1997
Dance Team—1997, 1999, 2001
Debate—1959, 1962, 1965, 1966, 1967, 1968,
    1970, 1999

Butsie Maetzold and Maetzold Field.

Maetzold Field, bounded by 1st and 2nd Streets North and 12th and 14th Avenues North was bought by the City of Hopkins in December of 1984 from the Hopkins School District, which had used the field from about the late 1940s until Eisenhower High School closed in 1982

A youthful Butsie Maetzold.

The 1941 Hopkins Football team, Lake Conference Champions. Coach Maetzold is on the left rear.

for Hopkins School's athletic programs. There were plans to develop the land but due to public outcry and the need for more athletic facilities in Hopkins, Maetzold Field came to be used by various community athletic groups.

The field was named for Russell Stanley ("Butsie") Maetzold, a 28-year coach at Hopkins High School (1929-1957) and athletic director at Hopkins Eisenhower until 1969. As a player, he led Red Wing to state basketball titles in 1920 and 1922. He later became a three-sport star at Hamline University. He joined the staff at Hopkins High in 1929 as a math teacher and the coach of all sports.

Maetzold was a really talented football coach. When

he quit coaching football in 1946, his teams had compiled an 88-6-5 record, won 10 Lake titles, were unbeaten nine times and twice were not scored on in conference play (in 1933 and 1937.)

But it was as a basketball coach that he made his biggest mark. Maetzold's teams won or shared 19 Lake Conference titles, compiled a 508-62 record, with five region titles, two state championships (1952 and 1953) and a winning streak of 65 games between 1952 and 1954.

Before he retired, Maetzold hand-picked the next basketball coach for Hopkins, Kenny Novak (Sr.) who is still on the coaching team at Hopkins in 2002. "Maetzold had offers to take college coaching jobs, but he liked Hopkins so well that he never wanted to leave,"

The 1952 State Champion basketball team. Hopkins also won in 1953 and 2002.

Youth soccer is extremely popular now and lacrosse is gaining in popularity. What will be the "in" sports of the future?

Persons attending were Mayor Harlan Perbix, Mrs. Congdon and Dr. MacQueen. At that meeting, it was voted that a Director of Recreation be hired "to act as executive secretary of the Commission and to direct and plan the entire recreation program the year around."

L.A. (Larry) Harris was hired November 7, 1949, to be the director of recreation, first as a part-time position and as of January 1, 1959, to be full-time. Hopkins became the first suburban Twin Cities municipality to provide a full-time year-round recreation department and one of the few in the State of Minnesota to do so.

Harris continued this employment until he resigned and left Hopkins in October of 1961. He was replaced by Richard L. (Dick) Wilson, who was instrumental in bringing the cities of Minnetonka and Hopkins together in 1967 to form a joint recreation program that stands today. Wilson passed away July 17, 2001. The Director of Recreation Services for Hopkins-Minnetonka is now Dave Johnson. Offices are at the Minnetonka City Hall, 14600 Minnetonka Boulevard.

Since 1967, the Hopkins-Minnetonka Recreation Services has continued to grow and offer unique opportunities for area residents of all ages. The Fall 2001 Recreation department catalog is 38 pages long and lists 20 parks in Minnetonka and 8 in Hopkins under its jurisdiction. The Hopkins parks are: Burnes (201 Park Lane), Central (101-17th Ave Ave S.), Downtown (9th Ave. S. of Mainstreet), Interlachen (262 Homedale Rd), Maetzold Field (1215-1st St. N.), Oakes (900 Lake

Novak recalled in his eulogy after the passing of Maetzold in 1982.

Kenny Novak, Sr., was at courtside when the Hopkins boy's basketball team finally won another State basketball championship on March 23, 2002 after 49 years, defeating Bloomington Jefferson 54-40 in the Class "4A" final at St. Paul's Xcel Energy Center. His role was not as head coach anymore—that belonged to his son, Kenny Novak, Jr.

Hopkins Parks and Recreation

Recreation and Parks as a function of the city government began on March 30, 1948 when Hopkins Mayor Joseph C. Vesely organized the first meeting of the "Playground Board." Representatives of twenty-five Hopkins organizations formed a civic unit for the development of a proper playground for the city. Mr. Earl Dahlberg was elected to serve as chairman for the group. Names mentioned at that March 30, 1948 meeting were: Mrs. Don Donovan, Mr. Otto Chermak and Mrs. K.M. Trygstad.

School Districts #135 and #19 voted approval on April 29, 1949 to enter a joint legal partnership with the City of Hopkins for the establishment and operation of a recreation program. With this approval, a "Hopkins Recreation Commission" was created. Its first meeting was held October 3, 1949. Earl Dahlberg was elected chairman and Mrs. Anna Anderson, secretary.

The Pavilion near Hopkins' Central Park.

The 1910 Hennepin County Fair.

Street NE), Valley (801 7th Ave S.), and Overpass Skate Park (100 Washington Ave. S.) Twenty parks in Minnetonka are used by Hopkins' residents, including Shady Oak, Purgatory Park and Big Willow Park and Ski Trail, in addition to playgrounds and playfields at all Hopkins and Minnetonka schools (10 in Hopkins District #270 and 4 in Minnetonka District #276).

Most significant are the many facilities added for recreational use during the 1980s and 1990s: Hopkins Pavilion (ice arena and multi-use, built in 1990), The Depot Coffee House, Harley Hopkins Warming House, Hopkins Activity Center (in the old South Junior High, opened January 1, 1981), the Hopkins Center for the

Arts and in Minnetonka—the Glen Lake Skate Plaza (new in summer, 2001), Minnetonka Ice Arena, the Lindbergh Center, Minnetonka Community Center, Minnetonka Art Center (new, 2001) and the Williston Fitness Center.

It would be interesting to compare what classes are offered now to what will be popular in ten, fifteen, or even a hundred years from now. The Fall 2001 Hopkins-Minnetonka Recreation Services catalog offers the following: aquatics (swimming lessons), adaptive recreation, adult and youth sports leagues, craft classes, health and fitness, safety awareness and self defense, teen and senior programs, open gyms, special interest social clubs, indoor basketball, soccer, T-ball, volleyball, LaCrosse, badminton, broomball, skating, kick boxing, tennis, snowshoe making, hockey and karate. Summer offerings are even more energetic, with playground activities, outdoor youth and adult leagues in baseball, soccer, tennis and golf, senior trips, family gardens and traditional outdoor swimming lessons at Shady Oak Lake.

Community Celebrations
Hennepin County Fair
The Hennepin County Agricultural Society was formed February 26, 1853 and the first fair was held October 20th of the same year. Although the location is vague, it

Top photo: The Hennepin County Fair racetrack was where Central Park is today. In this photo, we are looking north; the high school (between 15th and 16th) is far left. Bottom photo: Looking east down Excelsior Avenue at 11th in 1912.

was probably in the area opposite the Nicollet Hotel on Washington Avenue in Minneapolis. In 1855, the exhibit that attracted the most interest was a display of three apples grown by Gideon Pond. In 1865, the principal speaker at the fair was Horace Greely. Sometime later, this fair was discontinued.

In 1907, the Hopkins Commercial Club decided to hold a harvest festival and solicited funds on the main street for that purpose. Much to their surprise, they found themselves with more than ample funds. Dr. Moore suggested they hold an agricultural fair and an organization was set up—J.O. Harrison (President), Emil Anderson (Treasurer), William Smetana (Secretary) and Andrew Justus, Dr. Moore, Hilmar Olson, Fred Souba and August Hentschel (Directors). The exhibits were held in the local halls, livestock was housed in large tents and all concessions were held on the street. A charge of 5 cents was made to view the exhibits and to the surprise of the managers, the project was self-supporting and even made a little money.

A few of the first superintendents of exhibits have been traced. William Hartig and Joe Empanger were in charge of fruits and vegetables, Mrs. William Smetana and Mrs. MacGillary supervised the women's exhibits.

F.J. Kokesh hardware exhibit, Hennepin County Fair, circa 1910.

H.L. Hollister handled poultry and William or John Nesbitt oversaw the livestock.

For many years prior to 1907, Hopkins had what was known as a "Market Block" located between 11th and 12th Avenues (where the Hopkins Theater is now). Farmers came monthly to the market to display their grain, cattle, horses and hogs in the block-long open-front sheds along Excelsior Avenue. Here, they traded and sold their farm products. At this first agricultural fair, tents south of the market block as well as the Opera Hall and Olson's Hall were used for exhibits. Excelsior Avenue from 8th to 10th was roped off and served as a giant midway. At the west approach into town was a huge triumphal archway and at 8th and Excelsior Avenues a monument towered in the boulevard. There was activity throughout the town.

The first fair was a huge success except for a couple of mishaps. A windstorm leveled the horse tent the first night of the fair and the crisis and near panic that followed was a conversation piece for months. In addition, the fair had a $400 deficit when the bills came in. Dr. G.W. Moore and Hilmar Olson, two board members, took a trip into the city. They made the rounds of the breweries, passing the hat as they went, to pay for the defunct street fair treasury. They picked up a little more than the $400 they needed and the fair was saved.

By 1908, the fair site between 11th and 12th Avenues was expanded south to First Street and a bandstand and platform were erected. Late in 1910, the fair association decided to buy the 22 acres now occupied by Central Park. Buildings were erected at a cost of $9,000. Most of

Some exhibits were particularly hard to fill. The day before the fair, there weren't enough chickens nor were there any bantams and ducks to display. Wilbur Moore and Arthur Maloney, young men at the time, garbed themselves for some night action and proceeded to find fowl to fill the exhibit cages, unbeknownst to the exhibitors, that is. Imagine the surprise of Joe Miller to find some of his ducks exhibited the next morning! The boys filled several cages in this manner, and the strange part of it is, not only Joe Miller's ducks, but even some of the lesser birds "borrowed" from their owners at night, won ribbons!

—Clint Blomquist [with editorial changes]

the improvements were made by merchants, farmers and factory workers, donating their time on evenings and Sundays to improve the grounds.

In 1917, Hennepin County bought the fairgrounds from the Association for about $20,000. Permanent, brick buildings were built and by 1919, there were 13 fair buildings, including a grandstand and central bandstand. Attendance at the fair averaged 7,000 per day.

Four men can be credited with the success of the first agricultural fairs—Dr. G.W. Moore, Andrew Justus, Hilmar Olson and William Hartig. One member of the original group stated that the lumber for the buildings was furnished by the Justus Lumber Company, which waited many years for their money; they were finally paid at a decided discount.

From this small beginning grew one of the most progressive county fairs in Minnesota. The Hennepin County Fair took place at the fairgrounds in Hopkins every year until 1962, which was the last year the fair was held at that site. In 1966, the county sold the land to Hopkins. Most of the wooden structures were demolished in the spring of 1967 but a few of the buildings remain. The area between 13th and 15th Avenues that had been the racetrack was used as the city landfill until it was raised to a suitable elevation and then it was converted into the present-day Hopkins Central Park. The brick structures on the western portion of the fairgrounds were converted for use by the Hopkins Public Works Department and today can be recognized as county-fair type buildings just south of Katherine Curren School.

Even though the Hopkins area had lost much of its agricultural character, the Hennepin County Fair continued to be held at the Hennepin County Highway Department headquarters in Hopkins on Washington Avenue and County Road 18 (now 169). In the 1980s, it moved to Corcoran, where it is still held each summer.

Raspberry Festival

With enthusiasm, the Hopkins Raspberry Festival began during the depression as a way to boost business in Hopkins. Art Plankers, a pioneer Hopkins food merchant is credited with suggesting "raspberries" for the theme. About 75 Hopkins businessmen and farmers were organized and July 21 was chosen as the day to hold the festival, to coincide with the peak of the raspberry-picking season.

Jim Markham, editor of the *Hennepin County Review*, got the word out. Minneapolis mayor Thomas Latimer

There were 11 days in which to get it ready. We did the best we could, with no precedent, about $350 of expense money as I recall, but lots of enthusiasm... The festival drew 20,000 people and it caught on as a natural, from its first amateurish attempt."

—James L. Markham, Chairperson of the first Raspberry Festival in 1935

issued a proclamation urging all citizens of Minneapolis to "motor to Hopkins Sunday to enjoy the hospitality of the Northwest's greatest suburb, to enjoy the entertainment and to have some free raspberries and cream with the compliments of Hennepin County's famous raspberry growers and the progressive businessmen of Hopkins."

By all accounts, the day was a success for everyone, especially the raspberry growers, who were assigned places along the curbs to sell their wares. Perhaps sales went so well because the raspberry mixed with the local libations, or so Markham said: "We used to call it the big

An ad for the first Hopkins Raspberry Festival published in the **Minneapolis Journal July 20, 1935.**

berry bust in those early days." (The five-cent beer might have had something to do with this.)

As 20-25,000 people descended on Hopkins about 1 p.m., German bands took their posts at a number of street corners. The Minneapolis Working Boys' Band followed and at 2:15 p.m., the parade was kicked off by the Hopkins Municipal Band, led by Charles C. Lapic. "The Hopkins band boys, dressed in their flashing new uniforms, which arrived just in time for the occasion, covered themselves with glory, and played and marched like a band inspired," said the Review.

The Hopkins Raspberry Festival has become a Twin Cities institution, held the middle of July to coincide, but not overlap with, the Minneapolis Aquatennial Celebration. It was a natural fit for the town and continued this year with the 68th annual festival held July 11-21, 2002. The raspberry farms are long gone, but the town has cause to celebrate anyway and so it does.

At the 15th Raspberry Festival in 1949, the parade alone drew over 70,000 fans. The Friday and Saturday programs drew about 15,000. A baton twirling contest and amateur talent concert were part of the 1950 festival, with a carnival show and midway at the Hennepin County Fairgrounds. BeBe Shopp, former Miss America from Hopkins, crowned Bernice Rogers as queen in 1949 and Marjorie Higgins as queen in 1950.

By 1960, there was a Junior Raspberry Parade consisting of about 800 children from the Hopkins Recreation summer playground program marching in their own shorter parade on Saturday. There was a mutt contest, pie-eating contest and a doll buggy parade. The *Hennepin County Review* advertised that 400-500 raspberry pickers were still needed and that housewives with young children were encouraged to apply as a family group. 50-75,000 people were expected for the big parade, which ended up being hot and long, with some people needing help from the fire department's respirators.

Politicians were always a large part of the parade. The 1960 parade had Senator Hubert Humphrey, Congressman Roy Wier and Governor Orville Freeman marching under the DFL banner. "Twelve-year veteran Humphrey still licking his wounds from the presidential candidate mauling he received from John F. Kennedy, filed for reelection the day after the Hopkins visit declaring: 'the challenge to serve one's country and state has never been more critical,'" explained the DFL-leaning *Review*. The Humphrey-Wier-Freeman contingent were guests at an after-parade party sponsored by Hopkins druggist Floyd Alcott and his wife, Kitty. Humphrey's discourse at the party was the high cost of campaigning! Wier's political opponent, Clark MacGre-

The 1935 Raspberry Festival Royalty. Edna Brokl was Raspberry Queen and raspberry pioneers John Empanger and John Feltl were the grand marshalls.

The parades started at the Hopkins Theater on 5th and Excelsior Avenues. This photo was taken in 1970.

gor and a "Plymouth Republican" were present at the parade working the crowd, but got only disdainful mention from the *Review*. In later years, to keep the festival from becoming too political, the Raspberry Festival directors allowed incumbent politicians to ride in the parade for free, but candidates were assessed a rather high fee to participate.

Hubert Humphrey was back as Grand Marshall in 1970, this time as a former Vice President of the United States. The festival royalty visited Humphrey's private helicopter as it was taking off from the *Sun* newspaper plant on Interstate Highway 494. A photograph of smiling Hubert Humphrey (Democrat) and Clark MacGregor (Republican) was prominently displayed in the paper. Jim Klobuchar, popular columnist for the *Minneapolis Star*, was the emcee of the raspberry coronation. The 1969 Raspberry Queen, Maureen Wagner, was now Queen of the Lakes. The Kiddie Parade represented 17 playgrounds in Hopkins and Minnetonka and the lucky finder of the Golden Raspberry in the treasure hunt won $250. The frogs were training for a frog-jumping contest. Gladys Hanus in the Tonkawood neighborhood of Minnetonka was still growing raspberries. She remembered when raspberries cost a quarter for three pints. Prices escalated to three for a dollar and in 1970,

the early berries were as high as a dollar per pint but had dropped to 69 cents by festival time.

Senior citizens kicked off the 1976 Raspberry Festival with events planned exclusively for them—card par-

The 1984 Raspberry Royalty, ambassadors for Hopkins for a year.

ties, bingo, checkers, ice cream social, a play and old-time music were some of the special events. Frank Brokl, who had come to Hopkins from Czechoslovakia as a 17-year old about 1909 and still grew raspberries in his garden plot, was the Raspberry Festival parade grand marshall. When Frank married Clementine Bren, a woman he met at John Hus Church, his parents gave the newlyweds $30 to help set up housekeeping, which was considered an extremely generous gift in those days. (Frank Brokl passed away in 1977, but his spouse, Clementine Brokl, passed away in 2002 as this book was being written—at the age of 108!)

In 1976, Senator Humphrey and his wife, Muriel, were back in the parade, as well as 3rd District Congressman Bill Frenzel. The Raspberry Festival committee spent weeks trying to track down an authentic covered wagon to give the area youth an historical experience. It was pulled by two very authentic oxen. At "Krazy Daze," the merchants all dressed up in honor of the country's bicentennial. Horseshoe pitching was a new festival event. There was a farmers' market and a corn and pie eating contests for the youngsters. There were baseball, softball and tennis tournaments and

Junior Olympics. A bicentennial costume street dance added to the festivities.

Today, the Hopkins Raspberry Festival has a web site. It explains that in 1934 the first "Annual Picnic of Hopkins Civic and Commerce Association" was held. The following year, the event was named "Raspberry Day." In an effort to help farmers sell some extra produce during the depression, Hopkins invited everyone to the community for a free bowl of raspberries—and the people came in droves. And they still come—to enjoy the revelry of good old wholesome fun in this unique town of Hopkins. The web site is full of information, past and present, about the raspberry festival.

BeBe Shopp never wore the Raspberry Festival crown, but one summer she marched in the Raspberry parade as part of the Hopkins High School band (1947) and the next she rode on a float as the reigning Miss America! She crowned fellow classmate and friend Bernice Rogers queen of the 1949 Raspberry festival.

Beatrice Bella Waring, Minnesota's one and only Miss America, better known as BeBe Shopp, is Hopkins' most famous daughter. In 1948, Daniels Photography Studio of Hopkins entered BeBe in the 1948 "Stairway to Star-

BeBe Shopp returns to her "home town" of Hopkins and is greeted by dignitaries Hubert H. Humphrey (left) and Hopkins Mayor Joseph Vesely (right).

dom" contest held at Excelsior Amusement Park. She became Miss Minnesota and went on to win the Miss America pageant in Atlantic City that same year. BeBe Shopp was a member of the 1948 Class at Hopkins High School and played vibraharp in John Tesar's high school band. She was the daughter of Mr. and Mrs. Edward R. Shopp of Williston Park Road, who had moved to the area from Downer's Grove, Illinois.

Following her reign as Miss America, BeBe attended the Manhattan School of Music between 1949 and 1952 and formed her own professional music group. She married Bayard David Waring of Boston in 1954. The Warings have four daughters. Upon returning for her 25th Hopkins High School reunion, she said, "You know, I didn't move to Hopkins until I was a sophomore in high school, but I've always claimed it as my hometown."

Hopkins' Centennial—1987

The date chosen by city promoters for the official beginning of Hopkins is 1887. This was when the M.T.M. Company opened in the area and what had been merely a few farms started to coalesce into a town. Thus, Hopkins celebrated its Centennial in 1987.

If any town knows how to celebrate, Hopkins does. The celebration lasted from May until September, with each month's events unique and delightful. It involved the entire community of Hopkins, young and old. Some of the highlights were:

- The Centennial kick-off celebration was held at Mainstreet Days in May.
- The Big Party month in June featured on Saturday the 20th a box lunch social, antique displays, a children's play, a barbershop quartet contest, a big

band concert, a Sousa marching band (in the grand Hopkins tradition of marching bands!), a raffle, clowns and a birthday cake. Raspberry Sunday (the 21st) featured the world's largest raspberry sundae, a sing-a-long and concert, former-resident homecoming celebrations, honoring of Hopkins' oldest resident and oldest businesses followed by fireworks at nightfall.

- The traditional Raspberry Festival in July had a Centennial theme and fine arts fair.
- A Grand Old Fashioned Day on August 15th was a charming innovation in recognizing Hopkins history and featured an historical trivia contest, a beard judging contest, a handlebar moustache contest, a fiddlers' contest, a Harley Hopkins look-alike contest and an all-community talent show. A community breakfast-in-the-street brought everyone outside to start the day, old-fashioned buses were brought out of storage to shuttle visitors around town, church choirs and folk musicians performed in the afternoon, artisans demonstrated old-fashioned crafts and games. Picnics were scheduled through the day and a barn dance was held under the stars. A highlight of the day was the presentation of the magnificent Centennial Quilt, now hanging at City Hall. Also, Charlie Maguire, well-known Twin City folk musician, performed his song commissioned for the Centennial entitled "Hopkins is My Name."
- Heritage Days celebrated the community's history plus a Centennial Grand Finale in September featured concerts, folk art shows and children's games followed by a pig roast and live music after sundown.
  - Music in the Park concerts entertained throughout the year.
  - A new book, *The Hopkins Centennial Album*, was published to honor the 100 years of Hopkins community history.

When William Sincock, head of the public relations committee for the Hopkins Centennial, wrote to international VIPs asking them to come to Hopkins to help celebrate, he didn't dream of the many responses he would receive, including regrets from Queen Elizabeth II. The letter was from a lady-in-waiting to the Queen Mother who stated:

Hopkins centennial quilt with 9 sewers, August 1987.

M.T.M. threshing engine #6424 (30 h.p.) 1910.

"Although interested to hear about the celebrations that are being planned, Queen Elizabeth fears that it is not possible for her to do as you have asked. The Queen Mother is sorry to have to send you this reply, which may cause disappointment."

Barbara Flanagan, columnist for the *Minneapolis Star and Tribune*, described a few more interesting responses in her column of July 6, 1987:

Actress Katharine Hepburn wrote, "Good for you, Hopkins, Minnesota. It must be very pleasant to be the Raspberry Capital of the World."

Political humorist Art Buchwald congratulated Hopkins and then added, "It is odd in the world we live in that the raspberry has taken on a negative vocal connotation. To give one 'the raspberry' is to cuss them out something awful. This must be stopped. All monies raised at the Centennial must go to an educational campaign to persuade children not to use a raspberry as a form of displeasure."

The Hopkins Historical Society has a scrapbook of these letters, which is a "who's who" of celebrities at the time. It includes letters from: Jimmy Carter and George Bush, President and Vice President of the United States, Ger-

ald R. Ford, Former President of the U.S.; Cyrille Schott, President of France; Tom Bradley, Mayor of Los Angeles, CA; Dave Durenberger, and Rudy Boschwitz, U.S. Senators from Minnesota; Bob Dole, United States Senator; Bruce F. Vento, U.S. House of Representatives, MN 4th District; Walter F. Mondale, former Vice President of the United States; George Latimer, Mayor of St. Paul, Rudy Perpich, Governor of Minnesota; Anthony V. Bouza, Chief of Police, Minneapolis; Donald M. Fraser, Mayor of Minneapolis; Phyllis McQuaid, State Senator, MN Dist. 44; Sally Olsen, House of Representatives, MN 44th Dist; John B. Keefe, Hennepin Co. Bd. of Commissioners; Larry A. Donlin, Mayor of Minnetonka; Lyle W. Hanks, Mayor of St. Louis Park; Mr. M. Holyoak for Walter Cronkite, CBS News; actors and actresses: Robert Stack, Charlton Heston, Alan Alda, Gregory Peck, Hugh O'Brian, Peter Graves, Bob Hope, Eddie Albert; last but not least, Hopkins' own Miss America Bea Waring, (BeBe Shopp) Rockport, MA, "Proud to have come from Hopkins, High School Band member 1947-48, Float in '49."

Theaters

The first theater in Hopkins opened in 1910. It was located at 819 Excelsior Avenue W. and was owned by Jack Shonka. It sat no more than fifty people and did not

The Royal Theater, 805-807 Excelsior Avenue about 1920-21.

silent movies and piano music was provided by Mrs. Jack Burns to enhance the experience.

The second theater, built on the same block, was the Harrison Theater, located at 817 Excelsior Ave. W. This theater had sloped seating and a stage for live shows. Vaudeville, girly shows and silent movies were presented. The theater seated a couple hundred people. The Harrison Theater later became the Royal Theater. Organizations could rent the theater for presenting plays and musical events. Jack Harrison's daughter Lillie was the ticket seller. Henry Gralow operated the projection machine. The records show that Henry and Lillie were later married.

On the same block at 805 Excelsior Avenue W., another theater was built in 1914 by Jack Shonka. It seated close to five hundred people. This theater became known as the Hopkins Theater and later as the Royal Theater because they purchased the "Royal Theater" sign from the Harrison/Royal Theater when it went out

have a stage, but rather a platform down in the front where acts could be performed. One such early act was a long snake in a wicker basket. This theater showed

The Hopkins Theater had a big presence on 5th and Excelsior Avenues from 1941-1985.

Hopkins Cinema Six opened in 1997.

of business. Lillian Wheeler furnished the piano music in this new location. The *Hennepin County Enterprise* ran a news item on April 3, 1919 stating that Shonka sold the theater to Jacobs, Nichols & Marchoff of Minneapolis-Duluth. Jack Shonka had retained his job at the M.T.M. factory during his theater career and continued with that company until his retirement. The Hopkins Historical Society records show that by November 15, 1924, Abraham and Louis Engler owned the theater.

Chet Smith shared some treasured memories about the early Hopkins theaters. He said the theaters were always full; admission was five cents at first (thus the name "Nickelodeon") but prices went up as shows improved. At some point, candy and popcorn were served. "Talkies" made their way to Hopkins but before sound was synchronized onto the film itself, a record was played simultaneously with the moving picture.

At the second and third theaters, stage shows were presented as well as community performances such as the Hopkins village band, plays or school skit performances by the children. At the Harrison Theater, the small Hopkins orchestra accompanied the feature of the evening. Generally, shows were one-and-a-half to two hours long. The show changed daily and matinees were shown on weekends. Sometimes a "serial" was shown. Serials were shows that did not conclude but were continued the following week on the same evening. A serial guaranteed an audience the following week.

The Engler brothers built a new Hopkins Theater at Fifth and Excelsior Avenues. It opened on August 20, 1941 with a grand program. Mayor Madden was there with Councilmen J. Russell Carroll, E.S. (Al) Brown, Anton Olson and Jasper Jasperson. Skater Dorothy Lewis was there, Merle Potter and Dick Cullum of the Minneapolis newspaper, too. The Hopkins municipal band played in the lobby prior to the first big show. This theater seated 1,200 and had a new concept, a "crying room" facility. It had a balcony and beautiful red velvet curtains that dramatically opened when the feature was about to begin. The columnar art deco "Hopkins" marquis that sat atop the building was exceptionally beautiful at night when it served as a beacon to steer would-be moviegoers in its direction.

The Royal Theater at 805 Excelsior Avenue continued to operate after the modern Hopkins Theater was built. It was not advertised in the Hopkins phone books from 1942-1946 (World War II years). It was again listed in the 1947-49 phone books as being owned by MJ and Wm Engler. It was known as the Star Theatre from 1950-1953. The Star Theatre burned down in 1954.

During the 1970s and 80s, many of the old-fashioned movie theaters having large seating capacity and large screens closed. Technology had changed, home videos took a share of their business and it was becoming more profitable to run multiple screen theaters with many movie choices. In addition, the intersection of Excelsior Avenue and Highway 169 had changed so traffic no longer passed by the theater. Engler's Hopkins Theater was torn down in 1985 and was replaced by a car dealership.

Hopkins was without a movie theater until 1997

when its current six-screen theater opened between 11th and 12th Avenues on Mainstreet across from the Hopkins Center for the Arts. Hopkins Mann Cinema Six shows second-run movies, has reasonable prices and is a real hit with cinema fans; they can enjoy free parking and have dinner, drinks or a snack at one of the local establishments nearby.

Music

"Music," says Don Bates, director of the local Westwind Concert Band and long-time band director at Hopkins High School, "is the ONLY universal language." And we can be assured that music has been "spoken" around the Hopkins area since the beginning—first by native peoples with their lilting melodies and chants, then by the ethnic Bohemian settlers with their accordions and violins playing their native songs and by the Yankee settlers with music tastes transported from the East.

We can only pick up on a few snippets of the musical life of Hopkins in this short space, and we will do this through the marvelous photographs and information found in the Hopkins Historical Society collections.

In the fall of 1898, H.L. Hollister, publisher of the *Hopkins News*, organized Hopkins' first band. The photo we have shows 23 members of the brass band dressed in snappy uniforms. The band played on all

The Hopkins Band in 1899. Director H.L. Hollister, is in the front row, fourth from the left.

The Hopkins Mandolin Club of 1904.

"Hlavacek's Band of twenty pieces, and Claggett's orchestra and Eidam's Orchestra give the village representation in a musical way, while the Hopkins Opera Company, composed entirely of local talent under the direction of Charles D. Hazelrigg, formerly the Andrews Opera Company, has put the village strongly on the map during the past year with highly creditable operatic performances."

—from *Hennepin County Enterprise*, Hopkins, Minn., Oct 14, 1915

public occasions such as picnics, 4th of July celebrations, funerals and at various county fairs. The band's first public gig was the dedication of the Odd Fellows home at Northfield, Minnesota. One of the most popular functions of the municipal band was playing at evening concerts in the park. Hopkins had a municipal band under various directors until it was discontinued in 1949.

A few years after forming the band, Hollister helped start the Hopkins Mandolin Club. This club furnished music for churches, lodges, private home parties and Minnetonka boat rides.

In 1907, the Hopkins Symphony Orchestra was organized with L.W. Ballard as director. The list we have only identifies male orchestra members in the original group. A photograph of the orchestra at the Royal Theater about 1920 shows quite a few women members. The conductor at that time was Archie H. Miller, later a State Senator. The 1915 article about Hopkins also mentions Claggett's Orchestra, Eidam's Orchestra and the Hopkins Opera Company. Music played a tremendous part in the early life of the village.

Joseph J. Chermack, known as Hopkins' "Mr. Music," was a self-taught musician who played six instruments—the trumpet, saxophone, clarinet, accordion, cello and violin. Between 1910 and 1925, he organized and directed four bands. Over the years, he played with many others at dances and church and school programs. He was a prime mover behind forming a boys' band about 1920. Chermack gave free lessons to the kids at his farmhouse, arranged their music, planned their programs and was their leader. William Matchke, who played in this early boys' band, suspects that many times Chermack furnished an instrument for a kid who could not afford one. Chermack's love for music and instruments led him to make violins beginning in 1905. They ranged in size from regulation to a small six-inch model. He also wrote music, including

Musicians don't usually get rich. This is the last check for $12.11 Will Matchke received from the boys' band in 1926.

the "Opera Hall Polka," a song that long-time Hopkins musician Matchke remembers playing upstairs in the Hopkins Opera Hall at a Sokol dance. Chermack did all this, and worked for Minneapolis Moline for 50 years, retiring in 1955. This quiet, unassuming man passed away in Hopkins in 1972.

Hopkins' municipal band has been led by many stellar musicians through the years. H.L. Hollister passed the baton to Ike Claggett and then it fell to Bud Hlavacek. Professor Fleck, regarded by some as the band's most brilliant director, served for a while, then Archie Miller, the future senator, took over, then Frank

The Hopkins Orchestra at the Royal Theatre, 1920-1923. Front row (L-R): Leonard Chmel, Joseph C. Vesely, Irene Faimon, Sylvia Svec, Gladys Jenson Pederson, Elaine Makousky, Archie H. Miller (Conductor), Verna Kroon—composer of "When It's Raspberry Time in Hopkins"—Gertrude Schoen, Mary Lapic, Frank Koss, Lloyd Knuth. Back row (L-R): Arvid Quist, Arthur Wade, Ernie (Sliver) Miller, Henry Wade, William Miller, Henry Pokorny Sr., Reuben Harrison, John Daniels, Irwin (Bux) Smetana, Wilbur (Chops) Zerban, Peter Miller, Carl Nelson.

Hlavacek's Band, Hopkins, Minnesota, at the Hennepin County Fair Grounds (M.T.M. smokestack is in the background).

crucial program. The band had to stop performing its popular weekly band concerts during the depression (1934) because the city had no money to pay the members. Bill Mallery was the band director when the band disbanded in 1949. Many considered the disbanding a huge tragedy.

In 1923, another musical organization came on the scene in Hopkins. Armand R. Christiansen became Director of Music at Hopkins High School and at the grade school an orchestra had its beginning. Initially there was no marching band and the orchestra was the sole contribution to the musical life of the town.

In the 1929-30 school year, Christiansen began the High School marching band. Dick Asplin was the first Drum Major and Bernice Meyer the first Majorette. The band's first uniforms were purple and gold, made by a WPA group in St. Louis Park. The band was a regular feature at football and basketball games and in all the town's celebrations and at the Minneapolis Aquatennial parades through the years.

In 1947, John F. Tesar became the High School Music Director. He would hold summer practices for four or five weeks after school had ended so the band would be

Sefcik, who became president of the Northwestern National Bank, then Charley Lapic. The much applauded and remembered Miles Sherry continued to uphold the band's prestige in future years as second and third generations were listed among its members. Playing a great deal of Sousa, some semi-classical selections and Stephen Foster songs, the band practiced for many years in the City Hall. Occasionally, when the need was great, an outside musician was hired to fill in during a

This is an early 1920s photo of one of the first Hopkins High School orchestras, which won first place in the State competition. Quite a few of the boys from the Hopkins Boys' Band are part of this orchestra. Photo from Ray Matchke who played kettle drums in this orchestra and snare drum in the boys' band.

Marching Band–1911. This is a funeral cortege marching west at the corner of 10th and Excelsior Avenues. Bud Hlavacek is the band director at this time.

in top shape for the Raspberry Festival. Tesar took the High School band into the community whenever a band was needed. He was known as "uncle John" to many, was well respected by the students and community alike and brought the Hopkins school band program into state and national prominence. Tesar mentored many musicians during his 31 years as band director and community booster. One of them was a fellow Hopkins music teacher who succeeded him as "Mr. Music" in Hopkins—Don Bates.

Bates began teaching at South Junior High in 1967. His former office is now the office of the Hopkins Historical Society and the band room is now the society's museum. He taught at Lindbergh High School, West Junior High, then became band director at Hopkins High. Being another strong community booster, Don Bates brought back the community band in 1983. When the Hopkins Westwind Concert Band had its first performance on May 11, 1983, it was one of only eight community bands in the Twin Cities area. Seventy local musicians showed up at the first rehearsals, and it settled out to a 62-piece band. They play about 8 concerts in the summer and about 5 or 6 during the school year. They don't travel very far, but their reputation does. Bates, now retired from teaching, states that wherever he travels, "everyone knows about the Hopkins Raspberry Festival and knows that Hopkins is the town that's always celebrating."

Marching Band–1987. For the *Hopkins Centennial Album*, Jim Marvy, with the help of Don Bates, staged a photo shoot of a small portion of the High School marching band at the same 10th and Excelsior Avenue location as the 1911 photograph.

"Television history was made in Hopkins Tuesday evening when the first bona fide broadcast by a KSTP transmitter was received and seen as clearly as a movie."

Hennepin County Review March 25, 1948

Other Amusements

Television

A good sized crowd had gathered at the Hopkins Appliance shop, owned by Bob and Henry Nelson, to view a 90-minute telecast of the Minneapolis Lakers-Oshkosh basketball game. According to the newspaper account, "only a flicker of local interference was noticeable." Three television sets had already been sold by Hopkins dealers. The local dealers declared: "already satisfactory to many, television will not much longer be regarded as a novelty."

The first television set had been installed in Hopkins in January 1948, in the M.B. Hagen Appliance Store, according to the Suburban Press of January 30, 1948. Station KSTP was already operating experimental television, although Hagen and his son Don had to call KSTP to find out the times of programs.

Telephones

In 1897, there were only two telephones in the area—

April 1907

NORTHWESTERN TELEPHONE EXCHANGE COMPANY

LOCAL AND LONG DISTANCE TELEPHONE

Hopkins.

A re-creation of the 1907 Hopkins telephone book.

one at the M.T.M. office and one at the Hennepin County Poor Farm. When William Smetana set up his drugstore in 1897, he had a pay station installed in his store, so people could phone into the city.

Greeting card perfect is this photo of the Hopkins telephone exchange building in a snowstorm.

...Subscribers on a party line should listen to see if line is in use before calling central. Give one short ring for central. Take the receiver from the hook, place it to the ear and await the operator's request for "NUMBER." Respond promptly by giving the number and the call (when there is a call) in the order printed, thus, two-six-one-ring two, for 261-2. The lips should be about ONE-HALF INCH from the transmitter when talking.... When through talking, hang the receiver up properly (big end down), and give one short ring to signal the operator to disconnect. Operators are expected to be polite and patient under all circumstances; kindly accord to them like consideration..."

Instructions on how to use the phone from
the 10-page 1907 Northwestern Telephone
Exchange Company phone book

Headlines in *The Hopkins News* of September 17, 1903 heralded the coming of age of the telephone: "Are Putting in Local Phones: About Fifty Have Subscribed for Phones and More Will." The exchange was located in the rear of Smetana's drug store and Mae Peterson (later Mae Backman) was the first "central." The charge for business phones was $2.25 and $1.50 for private residences.

By 1907, Hopkins had its own phone book published by Hlavacek and Smetana printers of Hopkins. Prior to this time, a West Minneapolis section was included in the Minneapolis Directory. Public pay stations were at Nelson's Store at 9th and Excelsior Avenues, the M.&St.L. Passenger Station, A.E. Sackrison's Grocery Store and the Commercial Hotel at 8th and Excelsior Avenues.

Barnstormers

Back in the 1920s, flying was still a novelty. The man who gained a reputation as the first aviator in the Hopkins area was Elmer Hinck, a barnstormer who often flew at county fairs. Hinck's landing field was part of Catherine Burnes' farm where Hopkins Honda is today (north of 5th and Excelsior Avenues). He kept his plane under a big grove of trees. Stanley Schnabel, a maintenance man at M.T.M., would often go out flying with Hinck on weekends. Schnabel would stand on his head and perform other stunts on the plane. Hinck died in a plane crash at Monticello in 1942 along with Fred (Fritz) Kraemer, whose parents operated a store in Glen Lake.

Kids' Games and Dress

One might find it entertaining to recall some of the

"Bathing" in Shady Oak Lake looked a lot different in the old days!

games kids played about the turn of the century before automobiles, airplanes, radios, televisions and highways came about. Popular games were Rock on the Rock, Hop Scotch, Hopping Bobs, Pump-Pump Pull Away, Ring Around the Rosie, "May I" and Run Sheep Run.

Hopping bobs was always fun in Hopkins. In the winter, the farmers would hook up their horses to a bobsled and go into town for feed or supplies. The boys would jump on the runners and ride west to the 'V' and when they saw another bobsled coming the other way towards town, jump off and ride back.

In the early 1900s, the sand beach on the east side of Shady Oak Lake just north of the C&MRR was a popular swimming and picnic beach. After the C&MRR built the new crossing of the lake that is just south of the

Clint Chastek with his 15 pound northern pike speared in Shady Oak Lake in the winter of 1926.

This little girl is Edna Mather Alschwager. Playing with dolls has always been popular.

present Shady Oak beach, the popular swimming spot became the north side of the new railroad bank, just west of the connection between the two parts of the lake.

In the winter, sliding, skating and skiing were popular although after clearing off Pear Pond, the present site of Eisenhower School, it was pretty rough. Once your clamp-on skates came off, your hands were probably too cold to get them back on. Most boys wore black cotton stockings with corduroy knickers, shirt, cap and mackinaw.

Of course, fishing in the winter and summer was both fun and a necessity for many boys from the area.

The Hopkins Fire Department in 1964. This is the last group photograph taken in front of the old fire station at 8th and Excelsior Avenue North.

CHAPTER 7

Civic Life

City Government

By the 1940s, Hopkins had become a large and complex town. It was felt that some sort of change should be made in the village charter, the Municipal Laws of the 1890s being too outdated and restrictive. On Feb. 21, 1945, a Charter Commission was created and met for two years to create a charter that would provide for the operation of the community of Hopkins in the years to come. Joseph C. Vesely was elected Chairman of the Commission, Sanfred Gustafson, Vice-Chairman, and Carl Towley, Secretary. Members were: Joseph T. Anderla, Clint Blomquist, Amel Feudner, M.B. Hagen, Dwight W. Holcombe, A.G. Larson, Dr. F.M. Madden (President of the Village Council), James L. Markham, Margaret McHale, Frank Sefcik, William S. Smetana and Harry Westling.

Voters approved the charter designed by the commission on December 4, 1947 and the Village of Hop-

kins became the City of Hopkins, fourth class. With the adoption of the charter, the city became a council-manager form of government with the first actual "Mayor" being Joseph Vesely.

The citizens of Hopkins elect a Mayor and four council members whose duties are to adopt the annual budget, levy taxes and establish the policies and regulations under which the city is to be governed. The Council hires the city manager, who is responsible for carrying out the Council policies and directives. It oversees the work of other municipal boards and committees. Regular public City Council meetings are held.

The first woman elected to the Hopkins City Council was Jennie Arimond on May 15, 1979. Ellen Lavin has been the only female mayor, serving from 1985-1987.

City Hall

A joint City Hall and Fire Department was built in 1912 on the northeast corner of Excelsior and 8th Avenues. It

Hopkins Presidents and Mayors

Presidents:

1893/1894	C.L. Hopkins
1895/1897	Fred Souba
1898/	D.E. Dow
1899/1900	Fred Souba
1901/1907	Paul Swenson
1908	G.W. Moore
1909/	Paul Swenson
1910/	Emil Anderson
1911/1913	Paul Swenson
1914/	A.J. Hentschel
1915/1921	G.W. Moore
1922/	J.W. Pemberton
1923/1926	Paul Swenson
1927/1928	Anton A. Olson
1929/1931	M.B. Hagen
1932/1935	G.W. Moore
1936/1937	Anton A. Olson
1938/1939	E.V. Manchester
1940/1947	Dr. F.M. Madden

Mayors:

1948/1949	Joseph Vesely
1950/1953	W. Harlan Perbix
1954/1955	Joseph Vesely
1956/1957	Dr. F.M. Madden
1958/	W. Harlan Perbix
1961/1963	Donald Milbert
1965/1969	John Hanley
1970/1975	Henry Pokorny
1975-1981	Jerre A. Miller
1981-1985	Robert F. Miller
1985-1987	Ellen Lavin
1987-1989	Donald Milbert
1989-1993	Nelson W. Berg
1993-1999	Chuck Redepenning
1999-	Eugene Maxwell

The Hopkins City Hall in 1938.

more fire trucks. It served as the hub of civic activity for 52 years in Hopkins until the city services moved into their more spacious quarters at 11th Avenue and 1st Street South in November of 1964, where they are still located. The old city hall was torn down in May of 1965, a week or two after the Dow House was demolished.

The current Hopkins City Hall underwent major remodeling to keep up with modern technology in 1989, just 25 years after moving into their new quarters. Today, city hall could no longer be considered "spacious" and there currently are expansion discussions underway.

Public Safety—The Police Force

With the incorporation of the Village of West Minneapolis in 1893 came the appointment of its first full-time police officer—Al Cooper. Cooper served for 30 years and was a real legend. Stories are told that as far away as Montana there were transients who would avoid Hopkins because of the officer named Cooper. During Mr. Cooper's reign, most kids thought all policemen were called "Cooper" and some even as old as ten years old when going to Minneapolis referred to all police officers as "Coopers." Cooper retired in 1926 and passed away in 1930.

In the old days, the village trustees were also constables and when there was a need for some help, or if a fire occurred, the bell would be rung on the Methodist

included police and jail in the rear portion and city offices, library and meeting room upstairs. The fire station was on the main level and in the early days they used horse-drawn rigs; Schutz' Livery a few doors to the east supplied the horses. One would call Lil's Café to alert the police or fire departments and someone would turn on a light in front of city hall to call in the volunteers.

City Hall was remodeled in 1941 to accommodate

There never was noted any vandalism in this area. In fact, that was noted through the whole city of Hopkins. Our police officers were on the main street and they personally knew all the Hopkins children.

—Dr. Frank Kucera's Memoirs

Hopkins City Hall, 1010 First Street South, after remodeling, spring of 1990.

In the early 1970s, there were some grievances between the local law enforcement personnel and the city administration. Ovide (Butch) LaBerge was appointed as Superintendent of Police. Through LaBerge's strong administration, the Police Department resolved its difficulties. When LaBerge resigned to become Hennepin County Chief Deputy in 1983, at the City Manager's request, the Charter Commission and City Council acted to create the position of professional Chief of Police. Earl Johnson became Hopkins' first stand-alone Police Chief on July 20, 1983. He served in that position until August 1999. Hopkins' current Police Chief is Craig Reid.

Currently, the Hopkins Police Department has 24 licensed full-time Peace Officers, two full-time Public Safety Officers, five Dispatchers, a Crime Prevention Specialist, four full-time and one part-time Records Clerks. Two part-time Parking Enforcement Officers also work with the department. In

church to call in all helpers. The women were involved also. Cooper's mother was the cook for any prisoners in the jail. The Village President was considered the Chief of Police. Most of the time, he was just a figurehead. However, Deloris M. Olson remembered when her father, Anton A. Olson, carried a revolver as mayor during a depression-era trucker's strike.

Due to social mores in the early years, very little was heard about child abuse, wife abuse, murder, rape and the like. Thievery was probably the biggest crime and even that was minimal. As a matter of fact, most people did not lock their doors to their homes and many did not even have keys.

Eventually, a night watchman was hired to help Cooper. First, Tom Sullivan was hired, followed by Frank Sitar. Ed Makousky, a policeman from 1928 until 1960, was a colorful character. He drove around with a dog in his Model A. In the 1930s, the police force fell under the control of the Civil Service Commission and a three-man police force was hired. Engner Johnson was appointed Superintendent in 1938; he never wanted to be a policeman, yet stayed on the force for 24 years. Also working with him was Lawrence Schutz and Frank Sitar. Ted Johnson was a temporary police Superintendent after Sitar.

When the city charter was adopted in 1947, the City Manager became the police chief. Patrol duties in Hopkins were relatively low-key until the 1960s. In October 1965, a patrol officer began walking Hopkins' downtown at night in addition to having two night patrol cars on duty.

First police officer, Al Cooper, about 1920.

The Hotel de Cooper lost one of it's star boarders Monday noon when Thomas Wales, gentleman of leisure, took French leave after he had served two and one-half days of a ten day sentence imposed by Justice Nash on Friday. Wales had been picked up previously on July 7th and had been given a six-day sentence for begging, which was suspended, but he just couldn't be good and was taken up Friday for drunkenness. Wales was pulling nails from old planks near the City Hall in company with another prisoner and left without even saying good-bye, leaving Chief Cooper his coat as a souvenir.

—*Hennepin County Enterprise* July 30, 1914

addition, the Police Reserves donate over 4,000 hours of volunteer service to the city each year.

Command of the department is structured with a Chief of Police, a Captain in charge of operations, a Sergeant in charge of Investigations, a Sergeant in charge of Administrative Services and 4 Sergeants in

Ed Makousky with dogs and Model A, 1928.

charge of patrol teams. Hopkins has come a long way from having one law enforcement officer who also doubled as the village lamplighter!

Today, our state-of-the-art HPD operates a Public Safety Communications Center operating 24 hours a day, 7 days a week to dispatch police, fire and medical emergency assistance. The 911 emergency system allows an automatic display of the caller's location for prompt response.

There is a strong emphasis on crime prevention in the community with police-sponsored prevention programs such as Neighborhood Watch, Operation Identification, Crime Free Multi-Housing, National Night Out, Police Bicycle Patrol, K-9 Patrol and Counter Act (5th grade chemical use prevention program).

The Fire Department

The Fire Department was founded about 1893, formally incorporated on October 16, 1902, but all records through 1903 were lost in the fire of the Smetana Drug Store. William S. Smetana was secretary about that time. Henry F. Moore, who was Superintendent of the Minneapolis Threshing Machine Company, was the Fire Chief from its beginning until January 3, 1935, when he was given a leave of absence on account of sickness. He died on April 16, 1936 and his long service to Hopkins is praiseworthy, although he was unopposed as chief during that time perhaps because nearly all the firemen worked under him at M.T.M. John McNally was Assistant Chief for many of those years.

The first hook and ladder was purchased between 1893 and 1903 and was pulled by hand using 5 to 15-20 men. There was an adjustable rope that could be released for a large number of men. The rig had several ladders, including those for the roofs as well as 20-25 rubber buckets hanging in a row on each side of the frame. It also carried pike poles and hooks for pulling down items from a fire.

Later, the Village of West Minneapolis purchased two hand-pulled hose carts. These carts had two wheels and carried a chemical tank. The tank carried water and at the fire, a chemical was dumped into the tank to create pressure. Small hoses were attached to use at the fire.

The early firemen always seemed to get to the fires in these early years, although the streets and sidewalks were not paved and snow removal was crude at best. The earliest snowplowing consisted of a triangular "plow" made of heavy planks, loaded with pig iron and pulled by six or eight big draft horses belonging to the

The first motor-driven fire truck was purchased April 7, 1917. This photo was taken in 1925 at the Hennepin County Fair. Driver is Clarence W. Grover, L-R are: Assistant Chief John L. McNally, Carl Lofgren, Seibold Jensen, Albert Valesh.

M.T.M. Co. or to Mike Schutz that just pushed the snow to the side.

After getting a water tower, mains and hydrants (which were a definite milestone in the progress of the Village and the fire department), two hose carts were purchased, each being mounted on two big wheels loaded with regular fire hose. These were still pulled by hand.

The original building to house the fire equipment was on the north side of Excelsior Avenue between 8th and 9th Avenues. Beginning in 1912, the fire station was part of the city hall on the corner of 8th and Excelsior Avenues. When the fire trucks started to sink through the floor, firefighters led the campaign to build a new city hall and fire station in 1964/1965 at 1010 First Street South, where they are still located today.

The fire losses have been kept to a minimum by the activity and faithfulness of the brave volunteer fire department through the years. Firefighters were initially called to a fire by the person who got to the bell first. They first used the bell on the Methodist Church, then the bell built on city hall. In 1927, a siren was put on the roof of the fire station to alert the volunteer fire fighters who had trouble hearing a bell, followed by another siren on the roof of Brellenthin Dodge. Many of the early firefighters owned stores on the main street and would sometimes have to close up the shop to run to a fire, thus losing income in addition to putting their lives in danger.

When phones came into use, the telephone "central" rang each firefighter in his home when a fire occurred.

In the early days, the fire department was active in the social doings of the village, such as parades, Fourth of July celebrations, horse and bicycle racing on the one-mile track north of the M.&St.L. tracks from 10th to 13th Avenues. The traditional dances on Thanksgiving Eve were the biggest event of the year, with dancing from 9 p.m. to 4 a.m. with a complete turkey supper after midnight—all for $1.

Firemen and wives furnished practically all the food, often soliciting the turkeys from farmers. During those days the Minneapolis Threshing Machine and Smetana Pillmakers were among the best ball teams in the country and often traveled into three states playing local teams and winning a large share of the games.

On the Fourth of July the firemen always assisted "Guns at Sunrise" from homemade cannons and anvils. Streets were decorated with tamarack trees nailed to the edges of the wooden sidewalks to ape the forests of the north. There were fireworks galore—day and night—no sale restrictions, with resultant burned, bruised and missing fingers.

The floats were all home made and depicted wonderfully the activities of the various businesses and public organizations. The elite rode in "horse-in-four" phaetons carrying the mayor, and other celebrities, some in "cut-aways" and "stove pipe" hats, etc. Those sure were the days.

Fred Souba Sr., D.E. Dow and Paul Swenson were right up in front, you may be sure, and of course, A.W. Cooper, our efficient and jovial one-man police force was always on hand. His exploits in cleaning out the "jungles" at Shady Oak and Mud Lakes were known all over the U.S.A. "Jungles" in those days were rendezvous and camping grounds for hobos.

—Jim Markham, editor of the Hennepin County Review from 1928 to 1954, as published in the Hopkins Review, in the 1970s

After dial phones were installed, the restaurant owner of Lil's, who lived in the back of his restaurant near the fire station, took the calls, set off the sirens and gave directions to the firefighters. In 1958, an automatic phone notification system was installed. When the dispatcher pushed a button setting off the sirens, all the firefighters'

Photo of the oldest fire fighting vehicle—with "horse power" and buckets.

There was a favorite story of former Chief Hugh Strawn's about Gil Johnson— "There was a child drowning in a swimming pool, and while other firefighters fiddled with the lock on the fence, Gil just vaulted over it and pulled the child from the pool. He wasn't a young man at the time, either." The department's first rescue truck was bought with proceeds from bingo games. The truck had solid rubber tires and a steering wheel on the right side. The truck rode like it had square wheels. Johnson recalled his wife broke her leg in 1938 and she still remembered how "six big guys, dressed in old work clothes, came rushing into the house, picked her up so gently and carried her out to the rescues truck…. Of course, then she had kind of a miserable ride to the hospital [with] those darn rubber tires."

phones would ring steadily as long as the sirens were operating. When the police department went to full-time dispatchers, they also functioned as the fire dispatchers. Firefighters are now issued beepers for notification purposes.

Records show that in 1906, there were 20 volunteer firefighters, in 1858 there were 37, in 1974 there were 41. There still are 41 active volunteer firefighters who must live within 8 minutes driving time of the fire station.

Firefighters are a dedicated lot. In 1993 when the Hopkins Fire Department celebrated its centennial, three long-term firefighters, Wally Lindahl (on the force from 1934-1969) Gil Johnson (member from 1946-1981) and Eddie Lundgren (1952-still on the force in 1993) reminisced about the department. Together they had 110 years of experience. Hopkins was responsible for handling fires in an area that ranged from Highway 101 in Minnetonka, to Edina and Eden Prairie. Minnetonka owned a fire engine that was stored in Hopkins but didn't have its own force until 1959.

All three veteran firefighters remember the "big ones." For Wally Lindahl there was the Minneapolis Moline fire in May 1940. "It was the spring of the year, 6 a.m. on a Sunday. I was driving toward Hovander's when I saw this thick black smoke. I got out of the truck and blew the siren."

In 1989, the Hopkins Fire Department (HFD) was honored as Minnesota's Department of the Year. Today, the HFD continues to provide one of the most progressive and highly recognized fire prevention and educational programs in the state. Firefighters are highly trained, taking courses in the local technical college to receive various levels of certification. They participate in weekly training sessions and in advanced emergency-medical technician training. In addition to fire fighting, the HFD provides medical care in life threatening emergencies and has a hazardous materials response team for

Fire Department with five trucks including a rescue vehicle taken in front of the old fire department on July 31, 1949.

chemical emergencies. They have an extensive public education program and a mutual aid association with many of the surrounding communities to help each other when needed.

We are truly indebted to these fine citizens for their continuing dedication to our community.

The Postal Service

The very first settlers had to pick up their mail from St. Anthony. On March 28, 1855, a post office was established at Minnetonka along Minnehaha Creek in the "Mills" area in the store of Daniel P. Spafford. From then until January 29, 1873, most of the mail for the Hopkins area was handled by this post office at the "Mills" except for two years when postmaster Tom Moore moved the Minnetonka Post Office to Minnetonka Boulevard and Tonkawood Road from about June 1, 1865 until it was moved back by postmaster Page in September, 1867.

Soon after the Minneapolis and St. Louis Railroad

The Hopkins Post Office was located next to the Fred and W.B. Anderson Dry Goods Store at 702 Excelsior Avenue around 1897-1901.

came through in 1872, a post office was opened in the home of Harley H. Hopkins who was appointed postmaster January 29, 1873. When Anna McKenzie, a 16-year old who lived with the Hopkins family, became proficient in telegraphy, she was made the first permanent station agent at Hopkins for the new railroad in her 17th year. The post office, which consisted of a waste paper basket on the floor for holding the mail, was moved over to the railroad station, which at that time was a box car resting on the ground, where Anna McKenzie, the station agent and assistant postmaster, took care of the mail.

The post office was soon moved across the road to the Hopkins' house at 221 Excelsior Avenue East so Harley's daughter, Florinda, could help with the mail. A desk became the main post office. Many old timers recalled visiting the Hopkins' family dining room post office in those early days.

Harley Hopkins passed away in February 1882. Florinda Hopkins was appointed by President James Garfield to succeed him on April 15, 1882. An old post office record shows that the Hopkins post office sold $6.37 worth of stamps in July 1887. Florinda Hopkins operated the Post Office until November 1891 when Samuel C. Campbell was appointed Postmaster.

Sometime in the 1880s Sam Campbell started a store at approximately 216 Excelsior Avenue East, which was across the road from the Harley H. Hopkins home and near the M.& S.L. station. Back in those days and until

The Eidam Store Building at 710 Excelsior Avenue W. served as the Hopkins Post Office prior to 1899.

The Hopkins Post Office at 918 Excelsior Avenue, located east of the Anderson Brother's Store. W.B. Anderson, Postmaster from 1899-1914, standing in door.

1938, a postmaster job was a reward for dedication to a political party. Every time the political fortunes in Washington changed hands, so did the postmaster appointments all over the country. In 1891, the reward fell to Sam Campbell, who transferred the Hopkins post office to his store on the "east end" about a mile east of the M.T.M. Company offices.

As M.T.M. grew, so did their need for a more conveniently located post office. On July 2, 1892, the M.T.M. Company got another post office approved, at 824 Excelsior Avenue W. in what is now downtown Hopkins, in the grocery store of J.D. Helps. The post office was named "Bushnell" after John B. Bushnell, an officer and future president of the M.T.M. The storeowner, John D. Helps, was appointed postmaster of the Bushnell post office.

In 1894, another political change in Washington caused the Hopkins postmaster job to fall to Ed H. Eidam who operated a grocery store at 710 Excelsior Avenue West. He moved the "Hopkins" post office from the east end to a one-story building at 702 Excelsior Avenue, next to the Anderson Dry Goods Store (which was located at 700 Excelsior Avenue.) On August 15, 1895, the Bushnell Post office was merged with the Hopkins Post Office under Ed Eidam's direction.

Grover Cleveland had appointed Ed Eidem as Post-

master in 1894 and he was reappointed in 1898. However, he died during his second term, so his wife, Anna, better known as "Grandma" Eidam, was appointed to complete his term. At some point prior to 1899, the Hopkins Post Office operated out of Eidam's store at 710 Excelsior Avenue also.

William B. Anderson was appointed postmaster by President Theodore Roosevelt on Feb. 28, 1899. He moved the post office to a one-story addition on the east side of the Anderson Bros. Dry Goods Store, at 918 Excelsior Avenue. During Anderson's second four-year term, because the dry goods store needed room for expansion, a new building across the street at 921 Excelsior Avenue was constructed and fully occupied by the post office.

In 1914, President Woodrow Wilson appointed Patrick J. McCormick, an employee of the M.T.M. and a fellow Democrat, to be postmaster. By this time, the town had expanded substantially. The post office lobby contained banks of private boxes and drawers. A full-time staff was required. There were three rural routes carried out of Hopkins. Route #1 was southeast along the Poor Farm Road (County Road 18) into Eden Prairie and Bloomington. Route #2 was to the southwest into Minnetonka and Eden Prairie. Route #3 was northwest into Minnetonka and Plymouth. A Hopkins news-

Rural mail delivery in Hopkins cir. 1907-1912.

First Rural Mail Carrier

Austin Hamilton became the first rural mail carrier for the Post Office in 1905 and was later joined by George Chastek and a Mr. Pettijohn. Most of the winter when there was snow, Hamilton would drive a horse and cutter. He would go to the post office in the morning and sort the mail. He would then come home and heat a couple of building blocks in the oven, wrap them in newspaper and drop them in a big sheepskin bag. The horses were then hitched up to the cutter, the bag put in and he would leave about 10:00 AM. He would go about one fourth of the total route, the route being approximately 35 miles; he'd stop at a farmer's house and trade horses. He would do this 2 to 3 additional times, which meant he always had a fresh horse, plus the fact that some farmers got their horses exercised.

paper dated August 3, 1915, showed three Model Ts, loaded with mail, parked in front of the post office. The full staff with the three rural carriers was shown with the cars. Hopkins had now become the center for mail distribution for a large area.

William Perbix, another employee of the MTM, was the man whom Republican President Warren Harding appointed on June 22, 1922. A major change took place during his term. On September 16, 1927, delivery of mail to all homes and businesses began. The Hopkins Post Office at 921 Excelsior Avenue was now a much used, permanent landmark in the town.

When Postmaster-General James Farley, acting for Franklin D. Roosevelt, appointed Florence D. Markham as postmaster on April 21, 1934, she became the third woman to fill the job. Florinda Hopkins and Anna Eidam had served before her. Florence Markham struggled with inadequate space until the new post office at 18 Ninth Avenue S. was dedicated on May 29, 1935. This was a modern and convenient post office and it was thought it would last for many years. As it turned out, it only lasted until 1968 and many of those years the postal workers struggled under crowded conditions.

Mrs. Markham resigned on January 1, 1944 and Thomas Kosanda succeeded her. He served for four years. Near the end of his term, long-time postal worker Roy M. Kelley retired on April 1, 1948, after serving 26 years. Alfred Ess served as

postmaster from July 1, 1948 until March 1,1955, when Irving Elmquist, a long-time postal employee, took over. During Elmquist's term, the basement of the Ninth Avenue post office was re-excavated and adapted for postal use, thus extending the life of the building.

Stan Helgerson took over in 1959 and then was succeeded by Cecil Sundquist in 1961. The post office continued to grow and by 1965, the Postmaster-General

Hopkins Post Office at 18 Ninth Ave. S. operated from 1935-1968.

The Hopkins Post Office on Ninth Avenue South had a really unique feature—four murals commemorating the raspberry industry for which Hopkins was famous graced its lobby. The murals were painted by Litchfield, Minnesota, artist David M. Granahan through a depression-era grant from the United States Treasury Department Relief Art Project funded beginning in August 1935.

Models of the murals, depicting the activities in the fields around Hopkins during raspberry picking season, were exhibited at the Whitney Museum of American Art in New York in October 1936 and then transferred to the Corcoran Galleries in Washington D.C., where one of the actual panels was also displayed. The murals portrayed a typical scene as witnessed by the artist from a hilltop in the southwest part of the village of Hopkins called "Little Switzerland" in a 1937 article in the *Hennepin County Review*. One of Granahan's Hopkins murals was also produced in the book, *Art in Federal Buildings* published by officials from the Painting and Sculpture Division of the U.S. Treasury Department. The final murals were installed in the Hopkins Post Office in February 1937 and they were enjoyed by the public until 1968 when the Post Office was moved.

Three City Council members rescued one of the murals—*Cultivation of Raspberries*—from the old Post Office prior to its demolition in 1972. In 1979,

the Hopkins Historical Society donated the severely damaged mural to the University of Minnesota in hopes that it would be restored one day. In the summer of 2001, the Weisman Art Museum at the University of Minnesota commissioned James Horns, a Minneapolis art conservator, to restore the old painting. As this book is being written, the mural is once again proudly displayed as part of the *New Visions of American Heartland* exhibit at the Weisman at the University of Minnesota.

David M. Granahan painting one of the murals for the Hopkins Post Office on Ninth Avenue South in 1935-36. Some of the farmhouses were painted from real buildings in the Hopkins vicinity. Minnesota Historical Society photo.

urged the City to find a suitable site for a new post office. After much discussion and argument, the Hopkins City Council decided to raze the old Dow House and make the former Dow Park site available for the Post Office. The present building, at 910 First St. South, was dedicated November 23, 1968. The post office on Ninth Avenue was demolished November 5, 1972.

In 1971, Robert T. Kosanda, whose father, Thomas, had been Acting Postmaster for four years from 1943-48, became Postmaster. Reform and reorganization of the U.S. Postal Service began under President Richard Nixon and Postmaster General Winton M. Blount when they announced on February 5, 1969 the end of political appointments and an introduction of a merit selection process for selecting Postmasters. When Robert D. Scott became Postmaster in May 1980, he was the first Hopkins Postmaster to be appointed by the merit selection process that began in the late 1970s.

Since then, Hopkins has had the following leadership in the Post Office: Edward D. Beck Officer-In Charge and Postmaster 1987-1992, Larry Cruse, James G. Ramthun, and Richard M. Gallice Officers in Charge from August 1992 until February 6, 1993 when Timothy N. O'Hara was selected as Postmaster.

The Hopkins Post Office has grown to be the fourth largest Post Office in the State of Minnesota. It serves under its jurisdiction all of Hopkins, Eden Prairie and almost all of Minnetonka.

Public Library

The Hopkins Public Library was organized on November 11, 1912 through efforts of the Women's Improvement League and the High School Alumni. The first librarian was Mrs. Lillian Wheeler.

On June 6, 1912, an ordinance was adopted establishing and setting apart public property for the use and

Three librarians at the desk of the Hopkins Public Library in the Dow House; Bloomie Mountain, center.

benefit of a public library. Three rooms on the second floor in the north part of the municipal building were set apart for library use. The Library Association had raised $500, books were also donated and by 1915, the Village was kicking in $700 per year to fund the library.

In 1915 the library had 800 books, which included 100 books for children, 50 books for boys, 100 books on history and science; a 25-volume *Werner's Encyclopedia*; a 25-volume *Funk & Wagnall's Standard Encyclopedia* and 500 books on fiction or miscellaneous. There were 75 volumes of Scandinavian interest and 300 for the Bohemians. The library received the following periodicals: *Literary Digest, Scribner's Magazine, Scientific American, The National Geographical Magazine, Review of Reviews, The National American Review, The Country Gentleman, The Popular Mechanics, Illustrated London News, St. Nicholas, Ladies Home Journal, Woman's Home Companion, Youth's Companion, Pictorial Review, Ladies World* (donated), *Metropolitan, American* and *Collier's Weekly*. Approximately 1,050 library cards had been issued since its inception, with only 400 of these in use. They averaged 458 items checked out a month.

In 1932, the library had 3,600 books and Bloomie Mountain began a long

career as Hopkins' librarian. She supervised the move to the Dow House in 1948. The Dow House was a much beloved library, thanks to the homey touches from Bloomie. She was the wife of long-time Hopkins barber, William Mountain, but she supported herself and her four children after he died, sometimes working around the clock to keep up with household chores in addition to library duties. Mrs. Mountain's office was once the kitchen in the converted Dow home and an old sink and dumb waiter were part of her office décor.

Bloomie Mountain retired at the age of 73 in 1962 after serving as Hopkins' librarian for 31 years. Hugh Firmage, Library Board member, summarized Bloomie's service to Hopkins nicely: "She has been very efficient under trying conditions all these years. She started the library with almost nothing and has made it all it is today. We all appreciate her work." Bloomie was responsible for purchasing over 28,000 books during her tenure as librarian and a new library was being planned when she retired. She passed away in

The Hopkins Public Library was in the Dow House from 1948-1963.

> *"An alert, informed, thinking citizenry is a great community asset. A new public library building with an adequate staff, a superior book collection and a vital service program is an immediate necessity for Hopkins."*
>
> —Recommendation for the Future Development and Planning for Hopkins Public Library, 1962

1963. Bloomie's photograph was prominently displayed in the subsequent Hopkins libraries, but was donated to the Hopkins Historical Society in 2002 when the library shut down for remodeling.

On July 17, 1963, the Hopkins Public Library was moved from the Dow House to 25 9th St. North, formerly the Bridgeman Soda Grill. It was felt the Dow House had deteriorated too much under the heavy weight of the books, so it was unsafe for library use. It was temporarily housed there until a new library structure was built at 22 Eleventh Avenue North, the former site of three residences. Groundbreaking occurred in July of 1967. About February 1968 the new building opened and it has served the Hopkins area ever since.

In 1971, Mary Heiges took over as the Hopkins librarian. At that time the Hopkins and Minneapolis public libraries were the only independent library systems within Hennepin County. All the others had joined forces under the Hennepin County Library system. On January 1, 1972, the Hopkins Library Board entered into an agreement of six months' duration to operate as part of the Hennepin County Library system on an experimental basis. The county library system had begun in 1922 but beginning in 1965 funding was drastically changed when the State Legislature enacted statutes allowing it to raise money for buildings, books, personnel and other library services through taxation and bonding. The city of Hopkins' funding, approximately $90,000 in 1971, could not compete with the vast dollars potentially available under the county system, not to mention access to a wider selection of library materials. So, in January of 1973, the little independent Hopkins Public Library joined the vast Hennepin County library system.

In 1994, the parking lot adjoining the library was redesigned and expanded to alleviate some of the parking problems due to the popularity of the library. On March 2, 2002, the 33-year old library was shut down,

The interior of the Hopkins Public Library in the Dow House.

to reopen again at the end of the year as a totally remodeled and updated facility. The redesign, according to Carolyn Muchow, Principal Librarian, complements the Arts Center and other redevelopment projects on Mainstreet. What was essentially a box building has been remodeled to be an aesthetically beautiful building with accompanying new fixtures, artwork and stained glass windows. Behind the scenes, the makeover allowed for state-of-the-art wiring for 26 flat-screen computers and ergonomic improvements to reduce staff injury.

The Friends of the Hopkins Library group has played an integral part throughout the history of the library. These volunteers provide assistance for library programs with an emphasis on children and teens, encourage community awareness and provide funds from book sales, membership dues, contributions and memorials. They contributed to the new glass window art, as did the Library Foundation. Although part of a mega-library system, the Hopkins Library has been able to maintain its own distinct personality, thanks to a rich tradition of citizen involvement and watch-care over it.

Hopkins Historical Society

The Hopkins area had been settled for well over 100 years when a group of people mobilized to form the Hopkins Historical Society around 1972. Founders were Clint Blomquist, Adolph Sidla, James Shirley, Myrtle Bjorkland, Mary J. Heiges and Deloris Olson.

Mary Heiges explained it this way:

When I became Head Librarian of the Hopkins Library, it was still an independent city library. As such, I was a department head under the city manager (Terry Novak). Clint Blomquist was still working for the city [as building inspector] so we often met at city meetings. I don't remember who had the idea of starting a historical society for Hopkins. It might have been Jerre Miller, Clint, Jim Shirley, or Terry Novak. However, everyone who heard the idea thought it was a good one whose time was overdue, since the city was over 100 years old. Clint was in at the beginning and became a real focal point when he retired.… My involvement was to persuade the society and city to go into an oral history project… The library did the actual taping, provided housing for the project, cataloged the tapes by biographical information and subject matter and made transcriptions…"

The Hopkins Historical Society first was housed in the basement of the city hall and used the City Council

> *Thanks to the consistent four-year effort of Hopkins historical buff Clint Blomquist, the city now boasts one of the most complete cataloguing systems in the suburban area.*
>
> —*Hopkins Sun*, October 8, 1976

Chambers for its meetings. Eventually the city acquired the home of Mr. Landgren and after he passed away, his former house at 2020 Fourth St. N. was converted for use by the historical society. This was near Hilltop Park across the street from where the Elder Homestead is today. Clint Blomquist and others, soon began to accumulate a fair amount of Hopkins memorabilia. Blomquist was known to waylay people on their way to the dump to acquire historical treasures and his tenaciousness is much appreciated by Hopkins history buffs.

The single greatest historical contribution to the society, according to Blomquist, was a gift of the *Hennepin County Review* newspapers dating from 1925-1961. The *Review* was owned by James L. Markham and his business partner Eugene O'Brien. O'Brien donated the newspapers to the Historical Society in the 1970s. Markham wrote many historical pieces about Hopkins over the years. In addition to the actual newspapers, Markham's edited copies and the galley proofs were also donated to the Society.

In 1980, the City Council gave the Hopkins Historical Society space in the new Activity Center located at 33 14th Avenue N. During January and February 1981, the Society moved into the remodeled band room of the former South Junior High, which has been its home ever since.

In April 1983, the house on Fourth Street N. that was the former home to the Hopkins Historical Society was sold to the most deserving bidder, the Walter Ellefson family. In the middle of the night, the house was safely navigated down the Welcomall (Mainstreet) and placed at its new location at 144 Eighth Ave. N.

The Board of Directors of the society has been acquiring objects, photos and documents from Hopkins citizens over the years. They host monthly meetings to share items of historical interest with the public and have faithfully recorded these meetings on audio and video tape. They have published a newsletter since the Fall of 1998. Current board members are Dean

Empanger (President), Jim Zdrazil (Secretary), Henry Pokorny (Treasurer), Marlene Dvorak, Therese Glatt and Mary Raabe (At Large).

Newspapers

In 1954, Harold Smetana, the druggist, was cleaning out the store basement when he found a stack of old *Hennepin County Enterprise* newspapers dating from 1913-1917. Smetana trotted over to the *Hennepin County Review* newspaper office, at 1011 Excelsior Avenue to show his great find to the editor, Jim Markham. The two enjoyed reading the news items from 1913. The Village of West Minneapolis, with apologies, was approving the "high" 1914 Village budget of $8,400, the biggest expense being $3,500 for roads. Houses were selling for an astounding $1,050! Markham published the highlights in the *Hennepin County Review* of 1954.

Early Hopkins was well documented thanks to the *Hennepin County Review* office being located on the main street of Hopkins for over fifty years. Its publisher in its heyday was James L. Markham, who was a colorful personality, humanitarian, first-class journalist and exceptional Hopkins booster. Markham came to Hopkins in 1924 and stayed for 34 years. Markham had faith in "his" town: "A Main Street tough enough to survive the depression… then nothing will ever kill it," he said and wrote frequently in his paper.

The earliest record of a newspaper published in Hopkins was *The Hopkins News*, published on Saturdays by Harold L. Hollister beginning September 30, 1899. Its frenetic ownership indicates a history typical of newspapers in new communities. Publishers were Hollister and J.G. Smetana in 1902, Smetana and A.F. Hlavacek in 1902; by 1907, the masthead again credited H.L. Hollister of the West Minneapolis Printing Company with the publication. It was a Republican affiliated newspaper at first but was classed as "Independent" under the ownership of A.F. Hlavacek and John McNally (to 1911), Hlavacek alone (to 1918), the Hlavacek estate (to 1919)

The tax levee for Hopkins next year has been fixed at $8,400, an increase of $1,000, to provide for the gas works, the road fund, the poor, the building fund and the library.

—*Hennepin County Enterprise*, 1913

"Whenever a town survives a crisis, maintains its friendliness and spirit, and moves on just as vigorously as it began, then there is a man with just as much spirit and force behind it. To Hopkins this man is James L. Markham."

—The *Select Twin Citian* Magazine, September 1962.

---

and finally John Svihel (to 1920). In that year, the paper reverted to Republicanism under Charles S. Steffes. In 1921, it succumbed to consolidation with several other county sheets, under C.H. Hubbell, to emerge for the first time in October as the *Hennepin County Review*.

Competing with the *Hopkins News* was the *Hennepin County Enterprise*, a Democratic paper published by Frank Plachy, Jr. in 1913. George J. Silk ran it as an Independent from 1914-1920. This newspaper survived into the 1920s and survived to be a rival of the *Hennepin County Review*, which spared no details in relating an indictment of Mr. Silk in its April 26, 1923 issue.

There were other Hennepin County newspapers operating in the 19-teens that eventually were consolidated into one *Hennepin County Review*. In the first issue on Oct. 27, 1921, was this legend: "A combination of the *Osseo Review*, the *Hennepin County Herald*, the *Hopkins News* and the *St. Louis Park Rural Messenger*, published at Osseo in the interests of Rural Hennepin County." In the first issues of the *Hennepin County Review*, Hopkins news ran to about two columns under the heading "Hopkins Personal Paragraphs" with subheads "Clubs" and "School Notes."

The *Hennepin County Review* had numerous ownership and location changes and then on April 30, 1925, it moved to downtown Hopkins. Two regular features of the paper were "Farm Bureau News" and "The Minnesota Farm," columns that brought news of individual farmer's activities as well as valuable education information to farmers. Items of interest to women and local news were featured as well, the Hopkins correspondent being Mrs. Lillian Wheeler, who was also the librarian. In August, there was always a County Fair edition.

The *Hennepin County Review* was a forum for Jim Markham's Democratic views. He felt he had a duty to the public, so he spoke his mind. "I'm in no popularity contest," he used to say. That spirit made Markham's *Hennepin County Review* one of the most quoted, admired and oftentimes hated weeklies in Minnesota.

"The job of the editor is to try to stimulate honest thinking, a search for the truth, not to convince people he is right," Markham said. "Salty" is how Markham was described in a 1959 *Minneapolis Star* article. "He comforted the afflicted and afflicted the comfortable," was the epitaph given by his long-time business partner Eugene A. (Gene) O'Brien. "A marvelous person of compassion and sensitivity," was Hubert H. Humphrey's assessment. "We'd have to think a long, long time before we can recall a man who more excited our honest admiration and respect," stated the editor of the *St. Louis Park Dispatch*, which Markham had founded in 1941.

Always in poor health, Markham turned over the *Hennepin County Review* to three Republicans from Pennsylvania, giving up his Democratic forum in March of 1954. Gene O'Brien, the *Review's* advertising manager who had joined Markham nine years earlier, stayed on with the new owners and Markham retained a weekly column for a few years after he retired. The editorial policy of the new owners was to continue to "play up" successes and "down play" failures, with a hope to emphasize the decency in life and let someone else spread the gory gossip.

That is pretty much the philosophy of the suburban press, which was a 1947 offshoot of the *Hennepin County Review* that covered suburban news and eventually became the *Sun-Sailor* weekly newspaper currently serving the Hopkins area. The *Hennepin County Review* was located at 1011 Excelsior Avenue West in Hopkins through 1961, moved to 2100 Excelsior Avenue (12 Suburban Square) in 1962 and left Hopkins for good in 1968. The suburban press also operated out of Hopkins until 1968 when it moved to 6601 West 78th Street in Bloomington and began to be called *Sun Newspapers*.

Jim Markham was elected as honorary president of the Minnesota Editorial Association the year after he retired, but was too frail to actually serve. He was in the real estate business for a while, building the "Minnesota Building" at 1810-1814 Mainstreet and he ran a motor vehicle registrar office in St. Louis Park as his health continued to deteriorate. He passed away on September 21, 1963 at the age of 66.

Currently, Hopkins news is printed in the *SunSailor* (Hopkins or Minnetonka Edition), the *Lakeshore Weekly News* published by Skyway Publications in Wayzata and occasionally in the *Minneapolis StarTribune*.

Banks

The **First National Bank of West Minneapolis**, which opened on October 23, 1905, was the first bank in

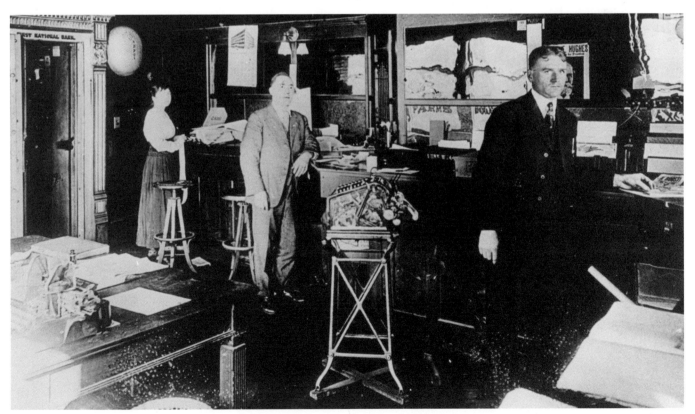

Inside the First National Bank of West Minneapolis, 923 Excelsior Avenue, about 1916.

The First National Bank of Hopkins cir. 1930.

each), but this bank had only four stockholders initially: F.E. Kenaston, Paul Swenson, Bert Winter and W.F. Drews.

The State Bank stayed in its original location for 63 years but expanded several times before moving, first taking over the whole main floor of the Strobeck Building, later building onto the back, providing for a drive-in and also using the upstairs and basement. In 1973, it moved to the present location at 1011 First Street South.

After World War I and during the recession of the early 1920s, many banks failed and the public mistakenly thought the national banks were safer than state banks. Consequently, the State Bank applied for and received a national bank charter and became the **Security National Bank of West Minneapolis** in 1924, changing the last part of its name to "Hopkins" in 1929.

During these years, Union Investment Company, of which Bert Winter was Secretary-Treasurer, became a majority stockholder. In 1929, when Northwestern Bank Corporation came into existence, Union Investment Company sold their holdings in several banks, which included the Security National Bank of Hopkins. Many years later, on Jan. 1, 1947, the name was changed to **Northwestern National Bank of Hopkins**, later still it became Norwest Bank Metro West and is now **Wells-Fargo**.

Hopkins. It was capitalized for $25,000 (250 shares at $100 each). The original shareholders were J.G. Lund, Frederic Souba, Frank Dix, Andrew Justus, J. Van Valkenburg, E.A. Close, W.B. Anderson, B.S. Potter, Alois Plut, Emil Anderson, Albert F. Anderson, J.F. Koblas, Hilmer Olson and E.L. Schultz. They paid 4% on savings until the 1930s. Banking hours were from 9:00 a.m. until 4:00 p.m. Their first bank building was erected on the northeast corner of 10th and Excelsior Avenues. The name was changed to the First National Bank of Hopkins in 1930. It became part of the holding company First Bank Stock Corporation in 1948 and was known for many years as **First Bank, Hopkins**. The First National stayed in its original location for 45 years, adding 20 feet to the back of the building in the early 1940s. In 1950, it moved to its present location, 16-9th Avenue North, almost doubled in size in 1960 and had another major remodeling in 1977-78. A drive-in service unit was built at 44-10th Avenue North. It is now known as **U.S. Bank**.

Amidst the activity of industrial and population growth in 1910, a second bank, the **State Bank of Hopkins**, was chartered. It opened its doors in the east half of the main floor of the Strobeck Building, on the southwest corner of 10th and Excelsior Avenues. It, too, was capitalized for $25,000 (250 shares at $100

The State Bank of Hopkins, located in the Strobeck Building in the southwest corner of 10th and Excelsior, was chartered in 1910.

Midwest Federal's ad from the 1962 Hopkins phone book.

Northwestern National Bank ad from the 1967 Hopkins phone book.

There was a time when all banks in Hopkins were closed for business. On March 6, 1933, President Roosevelt closed all the banks in the United States. Hopkins banks did not experience a run on their banks as had other villages during this time, but it was the one time in the history of Hopkins banks when deposits went down—about 40%. Banks had to sell securities, some at a loss. At the same time, all the assets had decreased in value—even good loans were not collectable. Bonds had decreased tremendously in value, including U.S. Government and Municipal bonds. During this enforced closing, the bankers received instructions that they could: 1) open new accounts with cash only and would have to keep them segregated; 2) cash U.S. Treasury checks; 3) cash checks drawn on their own banks up to a limit of $10.00 and with an affidavit that the funds were required for necessities; 4) make change for cash; 5) allow access to a person's Safe Deposit Box. A news article stated that $12,000 in gold coins came in at the Hopkins banks.

Out of this came the Banking Act of 1933 and many of the bank regulations that endured for many years regarding deposit insurance, how banks could be capitalized, bank examinations, etc., were established.

The two Hopkins banks were fortunate to reopen on the 15th of March. The savings interest rate decreased several times until it bottomed out at 1 1/2% interest.

Although no other banks opened in Hopkins, in 1952 the **Hopkins Savings and Loan** received a state charter. The original board consisted of: Art Koppelman, Russ Zakariasen, Russell Carroll, Peter Jorgensen,

Don Donovan, Irwin Smetana, Dr. Art Carroll, Sever Paulson, John Hersman, Guy Knuth, Elmo Ginkel, Earl Dahlberg and Everett Nygren. They sold to **Minnesota Federal Savings and Loan** in 1961. They were located at 31 Ninth Avenue South, but now no longer exist.

The banks in Hopkins have been very fortunate to have dealt with very industrious, thrifty people from Hopkins and the surrounding areas of St. Louis Park, Edina, Bush Lake, Cahill, Eden Prairie, Minnetonka, Deephaven, Groveland, Plymouth and Golden Valley. Bank deposits have steadily increased. Although the banks were bought out by larger banks, there still is the home-town touch of familiar faces among the employees and strong community participation in Hopkins civic affairs.

No discussion of banking in Hopkins can be complete without mentioning some of the sensational bank robberies of the past. On October 4, 1918 at 10:45 a.m., the First National Bank was held up by four bandits with guns; three inside, one outside. After being handed the money, the robbers locked the three employees (Frank Kriz, Gustie Olson and J.G. Goodspeed) and four customers, among them Stanley Svec and Mrs. Alfred Johnson, in the vault. The captives set off the alarm from inside the vault after the bandits had left. Frank Topka hurried over from the other bank to work the combination and open the vault door. Two of the hold-up men were caught doing a crime later that year, identified and sent to prison for the deed.

Fifteen years later, on November 7, 1933, at noon, a similar robbery took place at the Security National Bank. There were five bandits, one in the get-away car, one outside the door and three inside with guns. Two bank officers, G.J. Albrecht and Frank Sefcik, and two customers, Drs. James Blake and G.W. Moore, were in the bank. All except Albrecht, who was needed to get the money out of the vault, were herded into the back room under guard. During the hold-up, James Koblas came into the bank and was ushered to the back room as well. The robbers got away with about $5,000. A stolen car used in the heist was later recovered in Glenwood Park.

Hennepin County Poor Farm

On the day the Hennepin County Poor Farm opened its doors in Hopkins, these first entries were recorded in the record book:

- Ivory Witherall, male, born in Maine, crippled, admitted Jan. 4, 1865.

- Josephine Cobb, female, born in Maine, paralyzed, admitted Jan. 4, 1865.

The Hennepin County Poor Farm, also known as the Hennepin County Home, operated in the south part of Hopkins between 5th Ave S. and Washington Ave. S. (along County Road 18, now #169) for 109 years until it closed in April 1953. Although the farm labor was supplied by the poor farm residents, many Hopkins citizens were employed at the farm in various capacities throughout the years.

Preceded only by Goodhue County, Hennepin was the second county in the state to provide a home for the poor. The Hennepin County Board of Commissioners, organized in 1852, unanimously decided in 1864 that Hopkins would be the perfect site for a facility to house the indigent or handicapped, who had previously been cared for at private homes with county assistance. The board wanted a site to be near Minneapolis, but not in it. Hopkins was 9 miles away—a good distance. During the first two years the home operated, some of the reasons for admittance were: sore leg, laziness, consumption, old and feeble, intemperance, mental derangement and extravagance.

The county originally owned about 400 acres in southeast Hopkins on the former Mary Gordon property in Section 25. Initially, the Poor Farm was bounded by the Sarah Basset farm at the northeast corner; the John Feltl farm at the southwest corner; the Mary Smith and Joseph Makousky farms on the east side and John P. Miller farm on the southwest corner. By 1898, a map shows only 40 acres held by the county at that site.

The first poor farm building burned about May 8, 1878. The Hopkins Historical Society has an original

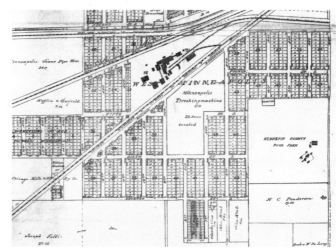

Map of South Hopkins showing Hennepin County Poor Farm from 1913 Hennepin Co. Atlas.

bill that records aid given to the residents by the Hopkins community—60 meals were furnished at a cost of 20 cents each and 5 dresses at 50 cents each were given to the "destitute paupers" at the time of the fire.

A second permanent building was constructed on the site in 1884. The facility had a potential capacity of 150, but only housed 120. A study on the state's welfare system said the situation was an "exception to the rule" because most such homes were overcrowded and understaffed.

Hennepin County was also one of the few in the state to pay a salary to the wife of the farm's superintendent, who received compensation for fulfilling the role of matron. These duties were expected of superintendents' wives elsewhere in the state.

In 1925, when Albert Moore was superintendent, the Grand Jury condemned the wooden building that had been built in 1884 and a new H-shaped building was built, this time housing 200 residents. The open house was held December 8, 1926 for the 2 1/2-story brick and concrete facility that was built for less than the appropriated $250,000. The old building was demolished by the American Lumber and Wrecking Company in 1929.

The old facility did not have any bed-ridden patients; they were cared for by Minneapolis General Hospital. But the new facility accommodated bed patients, and staff included a registered nurse and two orderlies. There also was a cook, laundress and several girl helpers. Meals were simple but good: dinner was meat, potatoes and vegetables; breakfast was cereal (oatmeal) with fruit. Most food was raised or grown on the farm that all residents worked. A Grand Jury report in 1925 said there were 85 inmates ranging in age from 50 to 90 years. An employee at the farm in the 1920s stated that some of the residents were rough characters but some were better types that were down on their luck. The help worked six days a week with an additional every-other Sunday off. They often worked more than 8 hours a day.

A.C. Ekelund became superintendent on March 17, 1930. By that time, there was a laundry equipped with steam washers, dryers and presses. There was a cook and two helpers cooking for 234 residents. This was too many residents and the overflow were housed in the old laundry facility. At Thanksgiving and Christmas, 95 chickens were butchered and cooked in 75-gallon steam kettles; parts were saved and later served creamed on baking powder biscuits.

In 1930, 30 cows, 100 hogs, a flock of chickens and

The main building of the Hennepin County Poor Farm built in 1926 was used by Honeywell from 1953-1972. Photo processed in 1932.

horses were still used for farming. The supervisor of the farm operation was paid $30 per month plus room and board. Sometime later in the 1930s, the farming operation ended.

Because State law prevented people over 65 to live in public institutions if they received old age assistance, by 1952 the occupancy of the home was down to about 100. No one with mental disorders or contagious diseases was admitted and residents had to be unemployable. Most of the residents ranged in age from 25 to 88 and had physical disabilities. Prior to admittance, all residents were examined by Dr. Blake of Hopkins, the County Medical Officer.

In 1952, the home had 24 full-time employees, including two practical nurses. The superintendent was A.C. Ekelund, who had been in charge since 1930. Farming had dwindled to a large garden and about 500 chickens and a few hogs in an effort to keep the food bills down. Many residents were too infirm to work in the garden. The County sold 12 acres of land to Boran Building and Steiner and Koppelman in 1952 for $21,000. The two firms would develop 48 lots for home sites for a new neighborhood called "Park Valley." At this time, lots were selling for about $435 per lot.

A map of the Poor Farm site of July, 1953 shows the following buildings on the site: 2-story main building, milk house, meat storage building, wood house, implement shed, cattle shed, hog stable, corn crib, creamery, ice house, smoke house, root cellar (dirt covered), chicken house and two privies.

On April 16, 1953 the main building with 10 acres was sold to Honeywell for $150,000 to be used by the industrial giant as the company's first corporate research center. The facility was used as a materials oriented research center where study was done on many

The Smetland Funeral procession went along Excelsior Avenue to the girls' final resting spot at what is now Faith Presbyterian Church Cemetery.

advanced products, including ultra-violet sensors. It served them well for over twenty years until Honeywell outgrew the facility and this portion of its business moved to Bloomington in 1972.

The last remnant of the poor farm, the brick building known in its later life as the Honeywell Research Facility, 600 2nd St. North, was demolished sometime after May 1974.

Jim Markham of the *Hennepin County Review* wrote much of the above history of the Hennepin County Poor Farm about 1950. Clint Blomquist of the Hopkins Historical Society tried to find the old Log Book Markham referred to, but was unsuccessful in finding out what happened to this book after the building was destroyed.

"A worker town is always friendly. Hard times make for a common humility—provided the hard times aren't too hard."

—Judge Vince Day as told to Feike Feikema (Frederick Manfred) in 1937

Hopefully, the Log Book has been preserved and someone will someday donate it to a historical society.

Surviving Disasters

While putting this book together, we were reminded of some of the disasters that have occurred in the Hopkins area over time. Some of national importance we have already mentioned—the depressions of 1857 and 1893, and when all U.S. banks closed in 1933. Hopkins has had its share of local tragedies, too. Through the strength of character of its citizens, it has always managed to pull through hard times.

The Smetland Tragedy

Two little girls, Annie (age 11) and Lothie (age 6) Smetland died in a cave-in at the Hennepin County Poor Farm on May 16, 1914. They were local residents and were playing on a dirt pile possibly created when the railroad trestle was being built. Just about the entire town participated in the funeral procession, the town band leading the way as two horse-drawn funeral carts slowly made their way down the main street to the girls' burial spot in the John Hus Church Cemetery.

Someone took a series of photographs of the funeral march and it is from these images we get some of our most interesting glimpses of Hopkins at that time.

1925 Tornado

On June 2, 1925, Hopkins was hit with a tornado that seemed to follow the railroad tracks from the west, causing considerable damage to M.T.M. The main office and parts buildings were the hardest hit. The storm damaged houses, hit the Justus Lumber Company and then damaged the Wade home (formerly the home of Harley H. Hopkins). It irreparably damaged the old Burnes schoolhouse and the Chicago, Milwaukee and St. Paul Railroad Depot.

The Centennial Rain

While Hopkins citizens were celebrating their centennial, in August 1987, a torrential rain sent the "big band" Music in the Park crowd heading for shelter in the Hopkins Office Building where they entertained themselves for three hours before the rain let up and they could try to get home. Roads were washed out, gas lines leaked and basements flooded.

A car had been swept away down nine-mile creek in south Hopkins and a life was lost. Neighbors joined together in a common effort to pump out, dry out and clean up what was declared one of the biggest rains of the century.

The Depression

M.T.M. was one of the few tractor manufacturers fortunate enough to survive the post-World War I deflation period. However, the depression of the 1930s was the most difficult days for M.T.M. and also Hopkins. The factory was closed from September 1931 to April 1935, but problems were already abundant by late 1930. On November 24, 1930, the Hopkins Civic and Commercial Club met to discuss the unemployment problem and the suffering likely to result from it. Subsequently, a village council subcommittee on poor relief was formed.

The Depression, which local lawyer Joseph Vesely characterized as "a searing experience," struck Hopkins full force in the early fall of 1931. James L. Markham, the newspaper editor, remembered "men following him on the streets at night, men with tears in their eyes, begging, not for a job or a week's work, but a day's or an hour's wages—men ready to do anything, anything that would help fill the empty stomachs at home for at least a day."

Under the leadership of Vesely and Markham, a committee of concerned Hopkins citizens conducted a house-to-house fund drive, eventually raising $7,650. It distributed food, clothing and fuel to those in need. Vesely recalled that from October-April, the committee "fed and kept body and soul together" for some 235 families in Hopkins. The committee met every Monday in City Hall and carefully screened proposed aid recipients. Most people were too embarrassed to come and ask for help; someone would appear before the committee and say, "I have a neighbor you should see...."

Neighbor helping neighbor was what it took to keep going during the depression. The Reverend Carl S. Mundinger suggested the village council hire unemployed men to cut wood and he found owners willing to let wood be taken from their land. The council selected 14 men, each the father of at least 6 children, to work

Shoes collected by Nelson Shoe Store for the needy, early 1930s. 917 Excelsior Avenue.

for 30 cents an hour. By March 1933, 151 cords of wood had been cut under the municipal plan.

Roosevelt's New Deal programs helped alleviate the economic misery in Hopkins. The largest government plan that benefited Hopkins was instituted in November 1933. The Hennepin County Board of Commissioners approved the opening of Fifth Avenue from Excelsior to what is now Highway 7. This was funded by the Federal Government's Civil Works Administration (CWA). Men were hired to build the road by hand, which involved leveling a large hill. It provided immediate jobs for 118 men who were paid 55 cents an hour, for seven-and-a-half hours a day, four days a week. Each man earned up to $100, then he was replaced and taken off of the relief roles. The CWA employees on the Fifth Avenue project were reduced weekly, from 164 to 55 men. By then, the project had helped many Hopkins families survive.

The CWA had been administered under the larger federal agency, the Public Works Administration. In PWA projects, a contract would be awarded for a certain job, the contractor would be required to employ men on or near relief, except for foremen and there was no $100 earning limit. Under PWA projects, Hopkins men built sewers by hand from Sixth Avenue and Excelsior to Interlachen Park.

In April 1934, the Federal Government decided to establish the rural Hennepin County office of the Emergency Relief Administration in Hopkins. The office, with a staff of 14 and with Joseph Vesely as secretary, was located above the Anderson Brothers store.

Government relief efforts continued throughout the 1930s, but the real heroes were the many individuals in Hopkins who gave of themselves to help their fellow citizens. Many businessmen, knowing they might never get paid, allowed customers to charge purchases.

Johnson Brothers had hundreds of dollars on their books and one businessman reputedly had $10,000 credit on his. Another told Feike Feikema in 1937 that not six months before, he and his family had been living on crackers and milk because what money he had earned at the store went to pay his wholesale warehouses. Einer Jorgensen recalled that, although he couldn't pay Ives for ice cream, no demands were ever made of him (and he did pay Ives after the depression). Mrs. Carlton Nygren, whose father, Thorvald Skottegaard, was a baker, would always give people bread when asked and his wife would add extra rolls to a bread order when she knew a large family needed it. Quentin

Krautkremer was just a boy when he was helping around his father's business. Gerard Krautkremer owned the West Minneapolis Fuel and Ice Company. Quentin remembers seeing men crying because they were out of work and his father would say "Can't let you freeze" and would send some coal to their homes. Krautkremer carried a lot of people through the depression and the majority of them eventually paid him back.

In addition to the compassionate store owners, many people were creative in helping themselves. Paul Stepanek is a good example. Laid off from Minneapolis Moline, he decided to sell snapping turtles. He caught 28 of them, went to see the chef at the Curtis hotel in Minneapolis. The chef bought them on one condition: he had to furnish ten pounds a day for thirty days before he'd be paid, at 35 cents a pound. In a month, Paul had caught 361 pounds of turtles and the money he made provided his living for almost a year.

When Minneapolis newspaperman Feike Feikema (Frederick Manfred) took a streetcar trip to Hopkins in June 1937, he reported the worst was over, but the evidence of the lean years was apparent. A drug store owner sadly told Feikema that quite a few family men were still workless and on relief: "Fine good men too, but the factory still hasn't enough business to take them on."

The hard times of the depression were difficult enough in Hopkins, but the shared suffering and common humility strengthened the community, for Hopkins had been tested, and had survived.

In Memory of Those Who Died in War

For many years the Hopkins High School Band would march from the high school to Grandview Cemetery on Memorial Day to honor the war dead. Today, there is a simple program in the Hopkins downtown park by the

The last Civil War veteran in Hopkins died in July 1943. Dr. Albert B. Sweet, 915 Excelsior Avenue survived the second-to-the-last Civil War vet, M.F. Maloney, by 11 years. Sweet was almost 96 years old when he died. Dr. Sweet served with Company F, 4th Minnesota Volunteer Infantry and was wounded in the thigh at Allatoona Pass, Georgia on October 5, 1864, while accompanying Sherman on his march to the sea. Dr. Sweet settled in Hopkins in 1892 and practiced medicine here until he retired in 1922.

war memorial to honor our town's soldier heroes.

To commemorate those from the Hopkins area who died in the service of our country, we are honored to print their names here, as several lists.

This first list is from the Grand Army of the Republic Memorial Day program of 1936 and a 1938 Memorial Day program from the George R. Wolff Post, Veterans of Foreign Wars and the John Wilbur Moore Post, American legion of Hopkins. It lists the men buried in the various cemeteries surrounding Hopkins from the Civil War, Spanish-American War and World War I.

Grandview Cemetery — Hopkins

Civil War — Daniel Drayne, John A. Hamilton, Norman B. Thomson, George E. Williams

Spanish-American War — Charles Anderson, Nels Nelson, Anton Werner

World War I — Joseph Cecka, Carl Eng, John Alvin Hausen, George H. Hawlish, Clarence G. Hayes, John Meebolt, Victor Miller, Wilbur Moore, Axel H. Peterson, Elmer L. Redeen, George R. Wolff

Bohemian Presbyterian Cemetery — Hopkins

(Also known as the Deephaven Junction Cemetery; now Faith Presbyterian Cemetery)
Civil War — Frank Bren, Sr., Joseph Bren
World War I — Jerry E. Bren, Arthur Edward Welsh

Shady Oak Cemetery — Hopkins

Civil War — Joseph Smetanna, John M. Chastek
World War I — Hans Anderson, Otec Chastek, John J. Chermack, Alexander Kriz, George W. Parks, Joseph Stodola, Edward Stodola

St. Margaret's Cemetery — Hopkins

World War I — John H. Miller, George C. Miller, Joseph J. Peshina

Hopkins World War II soldiers who died in the line of duty.

HONOR ROLL

Ensign John D. Arnot	Dec. 30, 1944
Pfc. Jasper W. Beardsley	Feb. 9, 1946
Lt. Donald Blake	Sept. 23, 1943
Cpl. Dean Dovenberg	Sept. 1, 1942
R.M. 1/c Edward L. Forster	Jan. 7, 1945
T/5 John Arthur Hams	May 5, 1943
Pvt. Willis Edwin Hutchinson	Aug. 25, 1944
Pvt. George Lauman	Oct. 16, 1944
S 1/c LeRoy Lembecker	Feb. 13, 1944
Sgt. Marvin E. Loock	July 23, 1945
Sgt. Albert E. Miller	Nov. 26, 1944
Pvt. Orien Nelson	June 16, 1945
1st Lt. Harold T. Novak	Aug. 19, 1944
Pfc. Robert D. Plehal	April 12, 1945
Lt. Douglas H. Puck	May 22, 1944
S/Sgt. Joseph L. Redpath	Jan. 15, 1946
S/Sgt. William H. Sloan	Nov. 20, 1942
Pfc. George F. Strachota	Nov. 8, 1942
Sgt. Carl J. Zobel, Jr.	Oct. 5, 1944

World War II

This list is from the Honor Roll published after *World War II*, which commemorates all those who served from the Hopkins area in the big war. There were nineteen young men from the Hopkins community who gave their lives in World War II, but there were many men and some women who played an important part in achieving the victory.

Korean War

We were unable to obtain a detailed Hopkins list.

Vietnam War

There were 1,072 Vietnam War dead from Minnesota.

A World War II draft contingent from Hopkins pose on 23 March 1942.

The U.S. National Archives and Records Administration web site of U.S. Military Personnel who died as a result of the Vietnam War (1957-1995) lists seven war heroes from Hopkins:

Herman John Baer (22 Sep 67), Eric Craig Egge (14 Oct 67), Carl Kollmeyer (5 May 68), Fred Chris Kraemer (26 Aug 70), David Thomas Nelson (13 Apr 69), Thomas Koenig Schaefer (3 Mar 69) and Dean Roger Zimmerman (16 Apr 67), all killed in South Vietnam.

In addition, six men were listed from Minnetonka and Eden Prairie: Andrew Ryan Barrett (27 Aug 70), Douglas Stanley Dressen (18 July 69), Richard Clayton Ewald (25 Oct 68), Robert Fredrick Gartner (27 Aug 71), Jonathon Lee Gens (27 Apr 68) and Dale Gene Granger (3 Oct 68).

Modern Challenges

Every generation has some issues it has to deal with in order to survive and prosper. Hopkins has had its share of modern troubles, but it has had plenty of successes, too. A survey of newspaper articles touches on many situations Hopkins city leaders have had to face during the latter half of the twentieth century.

Landfills and Garbage

Those early settlers in Hopkins could not have imagined that "explosimeters" would be installed in homes to monitor the release of methane gas emitted from former landfills. Many Hopkins residents can remember "going to the dump" to get rid of their junk. In Hopkins, there was a dump near Justus Lumber Company south of County Road 3, now called Excelsior Boulevard.

Another was once located by Nine Mile Creek in south Hopkins near where the Westbrooke Patio Homes were built in the early 1970s. A third landfill was on the old Hennepin County Fairgrounds site and was filled in the early 1960s. Central Park is located over this landfill. The largest landfill, stretching 37 acres along the city's boundary with Minnetonka, northwest of the intersection of 17th Avenue (Hopkins Crossroads) and Minnetonka Boulevard, was finally closed in 1980. It still is used to dispose of yard waste.

These old dumps still create problems for us today. The Minneapolis newspaper of December 26, 1990, explained that the "explosimeters" were placed in and near some of Westbrooke's townhomes that were built near a landfill used in the 1950's and 60's. The City of Hopkins needed to invest $1.3 million for an elaborate methane remediation project, on top of already spending $500,000 trying to solve the problem with that site.

Dealing with trash, landfills, garbage collection and maintaining clean air and water is a continuing problem for all cities, and Hopkins' problems are not unique or unusual. Besides dealing with their own trash, Hopkins citizens have repeatedly had to fight off being the dump-

> "We called it a dump. Every low spot on the south side was probably used as a landfill...at one time, it seemed to be the economical thing to do in all communities."
>
> —Don Milbert, former mayor of Hopkins

ing ground for Hennepin County, too. In 1985, a fight began to keep a waste-transfer station out of Hopkins, then a proposed hazardous waste transfer station became a battle in 1986. A proposed temporary storage site to store ash from the downtown Minneapolis incinerator was fought off in 1989. A vigilant citizenry and strong civic leadership have kept small Hopkins from taking the brunt of the big cities' problems.

Planning and Zoning

An issue was faced in 1994 when a sex-oriented book and video store started to operate in a building on Mainstreet near St. Joseph's Catholic Church. Hopkins' adult-use ordinances prohibited sex-oriented businesses from operating within 300 feet of a residence and within 1,000 feet of a playground, church, school or park, so the owner was asked to vacate that property. The owner moved to an industrial area of Hopkins, but took the city to court. After almost two years of legal wrangling, Hopkins won in Hennepin County District Court, which affirmed that the city was within its constitutional rights to restrict where such businesses could open for business.

Diversity and Poverty Issues

The schools are the first to notice when individuals enroll that do not have English as their primary language. The government authorizes reduced school lunch prices for students coming from low-income families. In 1990-91, 128 students in the Hopkins schools had limited English proficiency; in 2000-2001, this number had increased to 437. Students eligible for free or reduced price lunch increased from 8% of the school population in 1990-91 to 10% in 1999-2000.

True to form, the school district and community have rallied to support those in need of special services. The school district has translated forms and important documents into both Somali and Spanish to help the most recent immigrants to the area. They host English-proficiency classes for all ages.

The Hopkins Area Family Resource Center, located in downtown Hopkins, is a collaborative effort of the school district, the Cities of Hopkins and Minnetonka, the faith communities, foundations, area businesses, agencies and individuals to provide the connecting link between families and individuals in need and community services. It provides referral services for food vouchers, financial, employment and transportation assistance, health access information, adult education

and tax preparation help. Teens Alone, the School Supply Drive in August, Holiday Toy Chest collection and Fathers' Resource Center are other special services of the Family Resource Center.

Preserving Green Spaces

Being so small, available land is a precious commodity in Hopkins. Developed land brings needed tax dollars into the city's coffers, yet what would a community be without some sort of green space? Early in the 1990s, a one-acre forest in Hopkins was saved from development when a small number of homeowners signed an agreement to pay the City of Hopkins $185,000 over a period of 15 years to save over 75 mature trees bordering Highway 7 at Cambridge Street and Hiawatha Avenue. The purchase price of $285,000 had been reduced by a $100,000 charitable gift to the city from developer Mark Z. Jones.

The Minnehaha Oaks Association, nicknamed the "Oak Folks," a nonprofit organization, raised enough funds to repay the City close to $12,000 annually since 1993 with contributions from donors in 21 states. The final annual payment is due in 2006 at which time the City of Hopkins will be fully paid for its initial purchase of the property. In June 1999, Patricia and Vernon Isaak of the Minnehaha Oaks Association, received the Paul Harris Fellows Award for Community Service from the Hopkins Rotary, made possible by a $1,000 contribution to Rotary International by Vivian Blomquist. The "Oak Folks" have an aluminum-recycling project to help raise funds and awareness of the importance of green space.

Keeping Downtown Vibrant

By the late 1960s downtown Hopkins was in trouble. A

The good ol' days are gone for Hopkins. In 1940, it had 4,000 people and was the only place around. Then, the late 50's and '60's, Miracle Mile, Knollwood and Ridgedale invaded. Hopkins fought back, turning the downtown section of Excelsior Avenue into a compact shopping district and adding Welcomall, with trees, bus bays and decorative lighting. The changes are attracting new businesses, but not the retail stores essential for town growth.

—*Minneapolis Star*, **Thursday, May 7, 1981**

number of buildings in the shopping district were over 70 years old and needed renovation. About a third of the downtown shops were vacant. By 1972, there were still 17 vacancies. Sidewalks and the streets themselves needed repair. Hennepin County rerouted its highways and traffic began moving past, not through, Hopkins.

In 1972, the city and the chamber of commerce launched a revitalization project whereby the strip of shops on Excelsior Avenue became a compact shopping district dubbed "The Welcomall." Excelsior Avenue was narrowed and curved, bus bays, decorative lighting, trees and a nice sidewalk were put in to give curve appeal to the town. Pedestrians were encouraged to stroll down Excelsior Avenue and shop from store to store, after they had parked behind the shops. Some of the businesses such as Northwestern National Bank, First Bank Hopkins, Tait's Super Valu and Hance Hardware were rebuilt north of Mainstreet on First Street North. The new post office and city hall were located in a government center complex south of Mainstreet.

On the surface, the improvements seemed to have a positive impact on downtown Hopkins. Over 30,000 square feet of new space was added for shops and older shops were subdivided to allow for smaller retailers. The problem was, retailers were not clamoring to open stores in Hopkins, parking was very inconvenient and service businesses were opening on Excelsior Avenue such as Kelly Services (a temporary employment agency), not merchants. The crowds envisioned by city planners did not materialize. The crowds were, apparently, at the malls where one-stop shopping was more convenient. But Hopkins still had a mix of businesses

One hundred years is young for a city. So Hopkins is really just beginning to feel its oats, as it were. New Horizons of the future serve not only to stimulate it to new accomplishments, but also to turn its attention for a moment on its past and recall the progressive strides which it has made over the years. With such a backward glance, the city can take renewed pride in itself and overcome whatever problems or obstacles are erected in its path to ever greater achievements.

—Jim Markham, editor of the *Hennepin County Review* from 1928-1954 and consummate Hopkins booster

such as banks, grocers, drug stores and specialty stores with good service that brought people to town. President of the Hopkins Betterment Association in the early 1980's, Sheila Block, put it this way: "…we seem to have gone through these cycles before when some businesses will leave and others will come in. Hopkins is kind of special and somehow it will survive."

Hopkins did more than survive, it actually began to thrive throughout the decade of the 1980s but it took some time and some more planning and revitalization. In 1982, the city hired the nonprofit Center City Development Corporation to direct its development and offered low-cost loans to downtown businesses willing to improve their building's exteriors. Market studies were done in both 1980 and 1988 and a Business Council was formed to implement the recommendations of these studies. One of their recommendations was for a realignment of the main street through town. Subsequently, in 1992, Excelsior Avenue through town was straightened back to its original shape and was renamed "Mainstreet," which is what everyone called it anyway.

Through the help of various civic organizations—Hopkins Community Promotions, Twin-West Chamber of Commerce, whatever the name of the merchants' organization at the time, Hopkins boasts a strong grass roots business community striving to keeps its city vibrant, clean and hospitable. Whether Hopkins is a suburb, or a small town surrounded by suburbs, or both, remains an unanswered question, but small-town personal service is one thing that sets the city apart from others.

Concluding Remarks

It has been our pleasure to reminisce about Hopkins through the publication of this book. Our only regret is that we could not tell more stories capturing the spirit of the people who contributed so much to the well-being of this town.

We now invite you to join us on a walk through downtown Hopkins either literally or figuratively. As you read Chapter 8—Hopkins Now and Then— imagine what Hopkins was like in the years 1956, 1941 and 1921 and compare it to today. Or, it is highly recommended that you take this book with you on a stroll through town on a nice day and think about or remember what Hopkins was like "way back when."

Enjoy!

This is an aerial view of Hopkins prior to 1935 sighting along Excelsior Avenue toward the east. Hopkins High School, 1510 Excelsior Avenue, is at center bottom.

CHAPTER 8

Hopkins Now and Then

They called them "The Good Old Days"

I was born in 1913 in a white frame farmhouse on the southeast shore of Shady Oak Lake... I remember "going to town" on Saturday nights was a ritual; it was a family affair. We dragged a big washtub in front of the kitchen range, winter or summer, and all had baths (separate of course, there were three of us siblings). Mom had scrubbed the kitchen floor and covered it with clean newspaper to keep it clean for Sunday. Mom baked fresh kolaches (mostly prune) and cinnamon rolls; the whole house smelled good including us kids.

We had a horse named "Brownie" and a buggy; Dad had a heavy anchor to set out on the sidewalk to keep Brownie in place when we went to town. Later we had a Model T Ford—1922—we bought in 1922 for $400 new; they were called "Tin Lizzies." We tried to park by a popular grocery store or on the corner of 9th Avenue and Excelsior Boulevard (now called Mainstreet) by Jorgensen's Confection Store where the "Holy Rollers" were in full swing. They were a religious group, singing, playing banjos, very demonstrative, loud and exciting to watch. Some of us would slowly ease ourselves up to their bucket and drop a coin in to get a bit closer....

When I was growing up in the early 1900s, we bought our groceries at a small store on the south side of Mainstreet. Most of the stores, Caroline Pharmacy, Hagen Real Estate, Hovanders, Anderson Dry Goods, Nelson Shoe Store, were all family businesses. The floors were wide, natural planks with barrels standing against the walls, full of flour, sugar, rice, coffee beans, etc. Everything came in bulk—cookies, cottage cheese, fruits and veggies, each weighed and packaged at the customer's request. Vinegar came in a huge barrel and customers brought their own gallon jug. There were wheels of cheese; you could buy any size wedge. After World War II, supermarkets sprang up and frozen foods were available. National Tea was our first. Merchants had refreshment barrels for their customers. It was easy to charge all your groceries and when you paid the bill, they gave you a gift or a premium. In town, you could

phone your grocer and order a week's supply of groceries and they were delivered two hours later, no delivery charge. The butcher knew how you liked your meat trimmed and threw in a bone for the dog...

The Royal Theater on Mainstreet (where Rapid Print is now) had "dish night" once a week. You got a different dish (your choice) with your admission. There were 112 pieces to a set so it took a while to collect a whole set. Sometimes they'd run out of the piece you wanted. On Sunday nights, the Theater had "Bank Night" with a cash jackpot. It brought in crowds from miles around. You got your 10 cents worth because an afternoon at the showhouse included a comedy, travelogue, news, previews and the feature...

—Dorothy Erickson, in a talk given to the Mizpah Seniors, February 11, 1998, with editorial changes

Excelsior Avenue, Hopkins, Minnesota, 1929. Minnesota Historical Society photo.

A Walk Through Hopkins in 2002, 1956, 1941 and 1921.

Many changes have occurred in Hopkins over the years. It is fun to reminisce about the way things used to be. In this chapter, we will take a walk through Hopkins and try to remember what was here "way back when" and compare it to 2002.

What is now Mainstreet used to be called Excelsior Boulevard, then was renamed Excelsior Avenue West. It was the only east-west route through town. Today, the primary route through town is Excelsior Boulevard (formerly County Road 3) and it bypasses downtown Hopkins to the south at approximately where Second Avenue South used to be. This was the streetcar route from 1905 to 1951.

When Highway 169 was (finally!) finished, the main street through downtown Hopkins abruptly ended at 3rd Avenue. Today, Mainstreet begins at 3rd Avenue and extends to Shady Oak Road. In our "walk" through downtown Hopkins, we'll start on Blake and Excelsior Boulevard, turn north at 5th Avenue, then "walk" down Mainstreet heading east to west.

The "East End"—From Blake Road and Excelsior:

2002:

- Blake School occupies the southwest corner.
- On the northwest corner is a small strip mall containing these stores: Blake Deli and Grocery; Blake Cleaners, Crumley's Lunchbox, Fit-Rite Tailors, Blake Antique Mall, Checker Auto Parts, China Royal Restaurant, Labor Now Temporary Services. A converted office warehouse building to the rear has Goodwill as its anchor.
- A typical address would be "8400 Excelsior Boulevard." This part of town has assumed the numbering system of Minneapolis and St. Louis Park; the rest of Hopkins has its own, unique numbering system.

As we approach Hopkins on Excelsior Boulevard, Blake School is south. In 2002, the Blake School grounds are undergoing huge changes with the construction of a large athletic complex. On the north is another strip mall (addresses in the 8500's): Schumacher Chiropractic Clinic, Preci-

In Hopkins, you can look one way and see a replica of any small town, U.S.A., a scene that might appear on a Saturday Evening Post cover. Turn around and the view resembles the sprawling industrial complex of South Bend or Pittsburgh. Hopkins is a community of paradox—old-new, big-little, fast-slow. It's a metropolitan main street, where the corner druggist might interrupt Sally Brown's hop-scotch game to give her an ice cream cone on a hot afternoon, while the wheels of big business and industry turn top speed just a few blocks away.

—Select Twin Citian, September, 1962

sion Nails, Ronn's Salon, Mac's Liquor, Hopkins Video, Better Care Medical, Transportation Electronics, Aqualand Tropical Fish, Midwest Water Sports, Anderson Mill Work Inc, Edco-Arrowhead (at 8700 Excelsior, set back from the road) and Foreign Affairs auto repair.

The Depot Coffee House. Photo compliments of the City of Hopkins.

Key to Street Numbers—Even numbers are on the **south** of Mainstreet (shaded); Odd numbers are on the **north** side and are not shaded.

Small businesses line Excelsior Blvd. The East End has traditionally been industrial in character, but it currently is undergoing a facelift. Just before we get to Highway 169, note the large Super Valu warehouse south of Excelsior Blvd. completed in 2001. North of this and north of Excelsior Blvd. and just west of the tracks is where the Harley H. Hopkins (later known as the Wade) and the Chester L. Hopkins homes were located. These two homes were torn down about 1946 to make way for a Red Owl store and bakery. Super Valu purchased Red Owl and used the "North Annex" building until 2002.

The little brown brick railroad depot, formerly the Minneapolis and St. Louis Railroad depot built in 1903, is now a coffee shop refurbished in

Northwest Corner of Blake and Excelsior in 1956—the first of many service stations in Hopkins and Ronny's Café.

1998 as a joint venture of the Hennepin County Regional Railroad Authority, who owns the building, the city, which leases the building, the community, which provided the funds, and the Hopkins high school students, who helped refurbish the building to be a chemical free, safe place for students to gather. The railroad track is gone now and has been turned into a pedestrian path that connects to the larger network of Hennepin County trails.

1956 (From Blake and Excelsior):

1131	Merle's Skelly Service; 1123 Ronny's Café.
1124	Shell Service station; Blake School grounds (south).
503	Bill Matchke's Mileage, service station
408	East End Grocery and Barber Shop
17	American Legion Hall
15-11	Electrical substation
10	Maetzold Skelly
5	Kinn Service, auto glass, motor tune up, trailers for rent
2	Justus Lumber Co, building materials, fuel oil

1941 (From Blake and Excelsior):

South-	Blake School	North-	Bob and Jen's Café
South-	East End Grocery	North-	Hopkins Family Homes
South-	Justus Lumber		

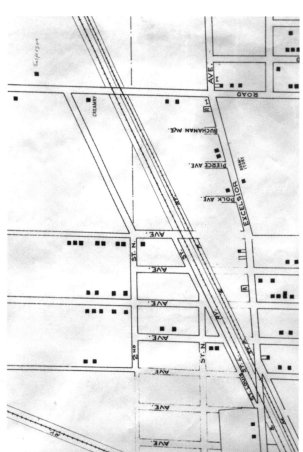

In 1948, the east side of Hopkins was still quite rural. Jasperson's Dairy farm and creamery can be seen in the upper right of map; the two Hopkins family homes can be seen on the large lot on the far left above the railroad tracks, although they were torn down about the time the map was made.

Mainstreet Hopkins

Mainstreet (formerly Excelsior Ave.) begins near a residential area west of Highway 169 (formerly Co. Rd. 18). To get to downtown Hopkins from Excelsior Blvd., we must turn north on 5th Avenue. When we get to 5th and Mainstreet, which many of us will recognize as the former site of the Hopkins Theater with its grand "Hopkins" marquis, we encounter two blocks of businesses to the east, then we'll turn west to take a mental "walk" down Hopkins' Mainstreet today (2002) and explore what was here in 1956, 1941 and 1921.

The construction of Highway 169 truncated the main street through Hopkins, alleviating huge traffic snarls at the former County Road 18 and Excelsior Boulevard and precipitating development along the new Excelsior Boulevard, formerly second street south, which bypasses downtown Hopkins.

1921 (From Blake and Excelsior): (Czech was still heard on the street.)

- South—Blake School Main Building (built 1907).
- At Van Buren north—"Beehive" tenement.
- At Monroe south—Market Grocery Store owned by Archie Kelly. (This building formerly was a saloon; later East End Grocery).
- W of RR crossing south—Sackrison grocery in 1915.
- W of RR crossing north—Hopkins family homes.
- Justus Lumber (south from Sakrison's to Washington Ave).
- NW corner opposite Justus—old, abandoned Burnes school (on Burnes farm field). School demolished by tornado in 1925.

Lee's East End Market, 408 Excelsior Ave. E., 1956.

The 1943-1948 map (left) shows that most of the merchants were located between 7th and 11th Avenues. The churches were close to Mainstreet. The streetcar line ended in a "Y" on 9th Avenue North. The large grain elevators gave Hopkins a rural feel. And the big theater marquis on 5th was a beacon that could be seen for miles around. Notice that what are now mostly commercial buildings south of Mainstreet formerly were rows of homes.

Mainstreet between 3rd – 5th Avenues

Street #	2002	1956	1941	1921
302 (S)		Evan & Hannah Peterson home	Charles Peterson home	The south side of Excelsior Ave. from Washington Ave. (now 169) to 6th Avenue had homes.
306	Walser Chrysler Jeep	Russell E. Welch home	Russell E. Welch home	
314		Town's Edge Oldsmobile (new location)	Joseph C. Lloyd home	
404	Vacant (Hopkins Car Care just torn down)	Fred Molzahn home	Axel F. Olson home	The north side was occupied by an open field of the Burnes Farm.
412		Hopkins Realty and Ervin Erickson home	Edw. J. Maleritsch home	
416	Creative Auto body	Walter Femrite home	Richard Ryshavy home	There was no 5th Ave. There was a large hill here.
420	Walser Bargain Lot	A & G Drafting Service	Hopkins Fruit Pckg Co.	
450	Vacant (Now Sports recently closed)	Select Service Oil Co	Select Service Oil Co	5th Ave from Excelsior Ave. to Hwy 7 was constructed by hand labor in 1933-34 with funds supplied by the Federal government's Civil Works Administration. Each man could work until he earned $100, then he would be replaced by another man on the relief roles. Such projects helped many Hopkins families survive the depression.
317 (N)	Walser Used Cars	F.S. Pollard home		
333		Comax Inc, Record Changers		
413	401 Burger King	Hopkins Milk House, food store	Farm Field – Burnes Farm	
415		Engler's Centre Liquor Store		
419	Burger King and the Honda Dealership take up the entire block. This used to be the Hopkins Theatre with attached businesses.	Labatt Business Equipment, office machines	Milk House	
421		Rogness Service & Sales; Schaefer Appliance	421 Hopkins Theater	
423		Hopkins Theater Florist, flower & Gift shop	This is a situation where the theatre did not move but the address changed when more businesses were added.	
425	499 Rudy Luther's Hopkins	Theater Café		
427	Honda	Industrial Credit Plan, Inc.		
429		429 Hopkins Theater		

The Hopkins Theater sign welcomed people to downtown Hopkins. The Theater stood on the northwest corner of Excelsior and 5th from 1941 until it was demolished in 1985. Saturday matinees and evening shows would be packed and a traffic jam would occur after popular movies as parents would wait to pick up groups of children. The theater had a great balcony, special seats for smokers and double seats for couples. An attempt was made to save the theater marquis in 1985, but not enough money was raised and it came crashing down with the rest of the building.

Mainstreet between 5th-6th Avenues

Street #	2002	1956	1941	1921
SW corner 5th	Rudy Luther's Used Car Lot	510 Texaco	500 Oil Station (T.M. Karrigan)	Railroad Track
SE corner 6th	Strip mall: (9) Army recruiting center; (5) Midnight Market; (3) Jim's Liquor; (1) Texaco	3 6th Ave S Pioneer Lumber; Coffman Realty, Package Homes Inc. Later, Weckman T.V.	Pioneer Elevator and Lumber Co	Pioneer Elevator and Feed Mill, also lumber
502			Whalen Nash Co., Auto sales	
22 5th Ave S	Dow Towers Apartments			
501 (N)	Sinclair Station			
517	517 Hopkins Park Plaza	24 5th Ave N	517 Leo Parent home	Home
519	14-46 5th Ave. N Tremont Plaza	Tremont Plaza Hotel	519 Frank Habeck home	Home
525	Mainstreet USA Used Cars	Direct Service filling station		

Robert (Bob) Bercheck was in the lumber business for over half a century. He worked for Hennessy Lumber at 610 Excelsior Avenue beginning in 1911 when he was 23 years old. He was the manager at Lampert Yards in Hopkins until 1955 when illness required he slow down a little, so he took an office position at Lampert Yards in Minneapolis. He retired in 1964. He remembered when lumber was transported by horse and wagon. Lumber for an average home in the Lake Minnetonka area would require 20 trips! Initially, lumber was northern pine from northern Minnesota. Later, lumber was western fir from Washington, Montana or Canada.

Mainstreet between 6th-7th Avenues

Street #	2002	1956	1941	1921
602 (S)		Superior Gasoline	Vacant Lot	(600-614) J.E. Hennessy lumber and garage. *Bob Bercheck was the colorful manager for many years.*
610	Hopkins Village Apartments, an 11-story high rise (entire block) with parking lot	Lampert Yards, lumber, coal and hardware	Lampert Yards, lumber.	
630		Hopkins Pure Oil Station	Pure Oil Station	Neider Restaurant and confectionery (1925). *Later, moved to 706 Excelsior Ave.*
611 (N)	Hopkins Honda – Used Cars	Northern Paper Company	Farm Service Co *Located along a railroad track, the Farm Service Co. handled feeds and grains for the local farmers. The structure was built of massive timbers, 18-24 inches across, to support the weight of tons of material unloaded from freight cars. The railroad bed is now part of the pedestrian trail system.*	(607-613) Minneapolis Gas Works
619		Keillor Heating Co.		615 Peshina home 617 home
621		Hopkins Self Service Laundry, also Eugene H. Cooper Co, machine & cutting tools		The berry box factory. Grain Elevator.
6 6th Ave. N	Hopkins Jaycees	Sivanich School of Music and Art		

Excelsior Avenue cuts diagonally through this aerial photograph looking northeast prior to 1935. 5th Avenue is only a small dirt road. Pioneer Lumber and Feed Mill is the business in the center of the photo. The large farm field is the Burnes farm. The large building in the lower left corner is Lampert Lumber (formerly Hennessy Lumber) and north of that is the Farm Service building, now site of Hopkins Honda Used Cars. 6th Avenue is in the foreground.

Farewell to an old block. The south side of Mainstreet between 7th and 8th Avenues was one of the oldest blocks in Hopkins. It was torn down in September 2002 to be redeveloped into townhomes above and businesses on the street level. Known as the "Koss block," the new block is named "Marketplace Lofts."

712 Excelsior Ave W. (The Eidam Building—Oldest Frame building on Mainstreet.) In 1895 Ed Eidam built this two story frame building and moved his grocery business from his prior location at 706 Excelsior Ave. W. (Before this, Eidam's store was located at Minnetonka Mills but due to it's failing economy, he had moved to West Minneapolis.) The Hopkins post office operated out of the store at 712 Excelsior Ave. W. from 1894 until 2-28-1899. When Ed Eidam died in 1900, his wife Anna took over the store and their son Louis took over when she retired. Wally and Lloyd Lindahl continued the grocery store

Mainstreet between 7th and 8th Avenues looking west during a 4th of July parade about 1901-1906. Mayor Paul Swenson is on horseback leading the parade. On the south side of the street are: Oltman's Furniture and Undertaking (702), Louis Berkowitz Grocer (704), Al Brown Barber (706), the two story building in the center of the block is Eidam's Grocery (712), west of that is Bren's Hardware (714) with a windmill behind it, and (partially hidden by tree) Marsh Drug Store (724). The building with the steeple is Mizpah Congregational Church on the southwest corner of 8th and Excelsior Avenues. The north (right) side has Knute Nelson's Blacksmith shop in foreground, and Swedberg Jewelry at 809 Excelsior Ave.

after Louis Eidam retired. Jim Exworthy lived upstairs and operated a paint and wallpaper business for many years called Andex Paint Co. A furniture stripping business was more recent. Lovelett's café was there in 1941. In 1956, Jimmy's Sporting Goods was in the building and in 2002, an employment service was there.

Imagine shopping in a store such as this. Photo at the left is the interior of Eidam's Store, 710-712 Excelsior Ave. about 1922-23. L-R 1 unknown, 2 Donald Jones, 3 Clarence Grover (salesman for Sunshine Cookies), 4 unknown, 5 Einar Lapic, 6 Alice Eidam owner, 7 James Eidam.

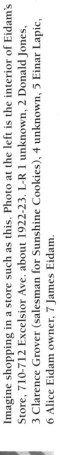

South Side of Mainstreet between 7th-8th Avenues

Street #	2002	1956	1941	1921
700	*Entire block will soon be "Marketplace Lofts"*	102 7th Ave S. West Minneapolis Fuel and Ice Co	102 7th Ave S. West Minneapolis Fuel and Ice Co	Gerard Krautkremer Garage, Fuel and coal, ice house. W. Mpls Fuel Co. Also Fahlstrom Barber shop
704	Suburban Feed and Supply (Previously was Champion Auto).	Hopkins Auto Lot		704 Neider Restaurant (1926). Earlier, D.E. Decker Barber Shop and pool hall; bldg. owned by Dr. Cath. Burnes.
706*		706 -708 Bursch's Liquor Store and Café	706 Neider's Café and Liquor Store. Became Bursch's in 1941.	Louis Berkowitz Grocery, Confectionery. 706 Al Brown, barber.
710	Vern's Barber Shop	Vern's Barber Shop		
712*	The Work Connection. *This was the oldest frame building in Hopkins.*	Jimmy's Sports shop, sporting goods, fishing; also Hopkins Café	Loveletts Cafe	Eidam Grocery. *They had a team of mules for delivering groceries. Store was owned by Mrs. Eidam & son, Lou.*
714	714 Storage for Koss Paint. *Koss Paint has been a family business since the 1940s. It moved to the east end of town prior to demolition.*	Bren Hardware & Implements. From 1959 to after 1989, Blunt Carlson Carpet was in this building.	Bren's Hardware, Mary Bren Hat Shop	712-718 Bren Bros Hardware & auto repair (insured 500 lbs dynamite in 1926). Previously was Kocourek & Bren hardware. *They sold horse blankets and handmade harnesses.*
720	Koss Paint	Koss Paint & Wallpaper. Also Frank Koss Insurance Agency	720-722 Koss Paint and Insurance	
722-724*	Vacant	724 Daniel's Photography Studio. *Ross Daniels was the one who encouraged BeBe Shopp to try out for a beauty pageant; she went on to become Miss America!*	724 Remer Drug Store	724 Bacon Drug Store. *This store was founded by C.A. Bacon's father-in-law, A.H. Marsh in the 1890s. See more below.*

706-708 Excelsior Ave.—Bursch's Restaurant operated in Hopkins for 48 years. It opened in the former Neider Restaurant in 1941 at 706 Excelsior Ave. It was a classic white-tablecloth restaurant with American fare: steaks, ribs and chicken. It served as Hopkins' primary business meeting spot having facilities for up to 300 people and was the site of innumerable wedding receptions and special occasion celebrations over the years. In 1959, a new Bursch's was built at 17-8th Avenue S. The son of the original owner, Arnie Bursch, sold the business to three Hopkins businessmen in 1986 and they changed the name to McThirsty's, which was a casual, contemporary restaurant. That eventually closed and the building was subdivided in 1996 into the various businesses there today—Blunt Carlson Carpet, Little Blind Spot and Studio 13 Hair Salon.

724 Excelsior Ave. was known as the Marsh Building, Bacon Building and more recently the Koss Building. Markham says it was built about 1893. W.S. Smetana says the building was there in 1897 when he came here. Charles and Nancy Jane Blomquist lived on the 2nd floor north from 10-19-1900 to 10-1-1903. The first occupant was A.H. Marsh, druggist, who lived on the south side and had the store on the north side. Sometime around 1900 the store was taken over by Marsh's son-in-law, C.A. Bacon. Dr. Catherine Burnes had her office in the rear of the building prior to 1900. Around 1920, Bacon sold to F.H. Hainert. Then followed drug stores owned by Remer, Prochaska and Floyd Alcott. Another outstanding tenant was Jack and Margaret Hines during prohibition days; it was a successful bootleg operation. Emil Lemke occupied the north apartment for many years. Daniel's Photography Studio was the first non-drugstore to occupy the building.

Koss Paint and Wallpaper, 720 Excelsior Avenue, 1956.

Looking west along Excelsior Avenue from the east corner of 7th Avenue, 1955.

Beginning at 706 Excelsior Avenue and ending at 724 Excelsior Avenue, in 1959 this block contained: Bursch's (which had just moved but the sign was still on the building; this became Champion Auto), Dewey's Café, Krahl's Sporting Goods at 712, Bren Hardware, Koss Paint, and Daniel's Photography. Photo compliments of Ken and Harriet Ahlstrom, of Daniels Photography.

Street Scene North Side of Excelsior and 7th

This photo was taken about 1916 during the time horses and buggies shared the streets with autos. Looking west from the corner of 7th and Excelsior, on the north (right) side is Shimota's Yellow Trail Garage; note the gas pump in front. Next is John Klopp's blacksmith's shop (with wagon wheels leaning against building), then Mike Schutz' Livery stable (with buggy in front), F.J. Shimota Paint (later to become Koss Paint before it moved across the street), then Hopkins City Hall and Fire Station (built in 1912), 8th Avenue, then Oltman's Furniture and Mortuary is on the corner of 8th and Excelsior. The two-story building on the left (south) of the street is Eidam's store. The power pole on the right has a gas light on it. Also note the telegraph poles on the left. Three to four feet above the sidewalk on the first telegraph pole on the left, you will note the stripes painted on the pole. The stripes were yellow—this indicated the Yellowstone Trail. There were no highway signs yet so one would follow the trail markings. The Yellowstone Trail, which went all the way to Yellowstone Park, was later to become Highway #7 but at this time, it went straight through Hopkins. The Jefferson Trail, which went to Fargo and farther west, also went through Hopkins. Its pole markings were blue and white stripes. When it rained, the street would become muddy and rutted and cars would get stuck in the middle of the street. In 1920, the streets were paved and a sewer system was put in, which was a great improvement.

In 1956, the same view shows Hopkins Motor Sales advertising Dodge cars at 703 Excelsior Ave. in place of the Yellow Trail Garage. The livery stable building was Suburban Business Machines in 1956. City Hall was still located in this block.

The same view of the north side of Mainstreet in 2002 with the Collision Center and Glenrose shops occupying most of the block.

North Side of Mainstreet between 7th – 8th Avenues

Street #	2002	1956	1941	1921
703	Hopkins Honda Collision Center, Used Car Showroom,	703 Hopkins Motor Sales, Dodge, Plymouth, also Machine Products Tools Mfg. Co.	703 Gerard Motors (Dodge, Plymouth, Chrysler)	Shimota Garage (the Yellow Trail Garage. *Excelsior Avenue used to be known as the "Yellowstone Trail"*
709		Gustafson-Fuxa, Inc., Electrical Contractors.	Jack Connely Tavern	Coyle blacksmith shop (formerly John Klopp's blacksmith shop)
711		Suburban Business Machine Co	Tip Top Ice Cream / Purity Dairy Store	George Burnes livery stable (Formerly Mike Schutz's livery stable)
715	GAH The Original Antiques Gallery of Hopkins	Club Café	Lil's Café *To alert the Hopkins Fire or Police Dept, you would call Lil's Café and someone would turn on a flashing red light to call in the volunteers.*	F.J. Shimota Paint
719	719 Specially Yours (gifts) and P Nathan Patries & Pieces of April Vintage Furnishings and Antiques.	717-719 Suburban Home Heating; state employment office	Herzan Bros. Food Market	
723	723 Glenrose Florist. *After the city hall was torn down, this was a parking lot until Glenrose built in 1997.*	Hopkins City Hall, Fire, Police, Water Department *The library was in the Dow House, not here.*	723 Hopkins City Hall, Fire, Police Dept, Library, Water Dept. *The fire, police and jail were on the ground level. The second floor had offices, a council meeting room and the Hopkins library. A steep, narrow flight of stairs led to the library on the second floor.*	723 City hall and Fire Barn built in 1912. *Called a barn because horses were used to pull the fire rigs.*

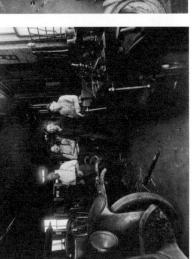
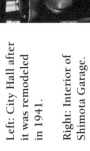

Left: City Hall after it was remodeled in 1941.

Right: Interior of Shimota Garage.

South Side of Mainstreet between 8th – 9th Avenues

Street #	2002	1956	1941	1921
802	Michaelangelo's Trattoria (Italian restaurant) *Previously Mr. Donut & Abe's Restaurant*	Standard Service Station	Standard Service Station	Hole from moving the Congregational Church
804	A and G Drafting	804 Harlen Jewelers. 804 1/2 Dentists L.E Hembre & A.E. Damerow, & Paul Slaton, Optometrist.	Burns Sandwich Shop	Truman Millinery *The Truman-Beckman Hat shop at the turn of the century employed four women to sew hats for Hopkins ladies.*
806	A+ Vacuum Cleaner Co	806 Shonka's Barber Shop	Shonka Barber Shop	Mashek Tailor
808		Hopkins Pet Supply	Mashek Tailor Shop	C.W. Grover, Bakery
810	Best Buy Liquor Warehouse	Mel's Hopkins Bakery	Malberg (Mel's) Bakery	Art and Jim's Haberdashery. *Formerly part of Anderson and Blomquist's store selling fine china, cut glass, silverware and kitchenware.*
812		Knutson's Liquor Store	Anton Olson Grocery	Shonka Variety Store. *Formerly the Charles Blomquist Grocery Store.*
814	Mainstreet Bar and Grill	Variety Store	Hopkins Variety Store *(Art Stevens sold this variety store to J.H. McKenna Co in November, 1941.)*	Restaurant/Saloon. Bowling Alley in basement. Jewelry Store. *Formerly Otis and Otis Fair Store, which sold a variety of items for the home.*
816 816 1/2	Dance and Sport Studio upstairs.	Sheehan's Inc. Sheehan's 908 Lounge (1957)	816 Shonka's Café 816 1/2 Old Opera Hall upstairs.	The Opera Hall

The Opera Hall was used for social events early in the century. The first Hopkins high School graduating class used it in 1902 for the ceremony. Organizations held dances and meetings here. The basement of the opera hall building had a bowling alley and boxing ring, along with Harry Blunt's barber shop and public bath. Later, the bowling alley was located on the second floor, where there were no automatic pin setters. This was done by kids earning money picking up the pins after the first roll and hoping the second ball would not come until they jumped out of the way! The pinsetters would sometimes get a bonus if they "accidentally" knocked down an extra pin or two!

818	Mainstreet Bar and Grill (cont.)	White Way cleaners. Apartments on second floor.	Planker's Food Market (Red and White)	Koblas Butcher Shop, formerly a saloon. 818 1/2 Hamack Tailor Shop
820		Bud's Music, records, TV, HiFi, band instruments, Dahlberg hearing aids	Federated Store, Mary Early, owner	McConaughey Restaurant
822	822 Bud's Music Center *Started by Bud and Dorothy Bast in 1952, then owned by their son-in-law Chuck Redepenning.*	Shirley's Ladies Clothing. 822 1/2 The Mirror Beauty Salon; Hopkins-LaSalle Dental Lab. Also apartments on second floor.	822 1/2 J.J. Hersman, dentist; Rose Beauty Shop; Selective Service Board #23	Saloon, later Olson's Grocery. In 1913, Martin B. (Punchy) Hagen had a laundry agency on the east 8 ft. of this building.
822-824*	Hoagie's Restaurant Pito's Barber Shop (rear)	Lea's Shoes, family shoes	824 Red Owl Store—groceries.	

*This building is the oldest brick building in downtown Hopkins, made from the last bricks produced locally by Hilmer Olson's brickyard. This also was the site where people voted to become the village of West Minneapolis in 1893.

Oldest Brick Building—822-824 Excelsior Ave.

The oldest brick building on Mainstreet is where Hoagies Restaurant is now located, on the SE corner of 8th & Excelsior Avenues. Through the years it has been known as the Olson, Anderson and the Hultin Building. Hilmer Olson came to Hopkins in 1887 and established a brick factory on the northwest corner of Shady Oak Road and Highway 7. He furnished brick for the first Minneapolis Threshing Machine Company buildings, beginning in 1887. By 1893, he had accumulated a surplus stock of bricks because the panic of 1893 had slowed development in the area.

Olson decided to use his surplus brick stock by constructing a building of his own. In 1893, he built 822-824 Excelsior Ave. W. as the first of a series of buildings. Olson told James Markham that he rented the first floor to his son-in-law. Other records show that John D. Helps operated a grocery store there and that Helps was the postmaster of the Bushnell post office at that address from 7-21-1892 until 8-15-1895. People voted to become the village of West Minneapolis at "Olson Hall," situate over the post office at Bushnell, Minnesota, and being on the third floor of the brick block on the corner of Excelsior and 9th

Avenue." [Note that another brick building built by Olson at 904-908 Mainstreet was also known as the "Olson Building" or "Olson Hall" in more recent years.]

Hilmer Olson lived on the second floor of 822-824 Excelsior Ave. from 1893-1902. Dr. George W. Moore lived and had his office on the second floor from 1903 until about 1942, when he retired. In about 1895, Charles Blomquist bought stock and fixtures from the bankrupt business Mandan Mercantile Co., which he housed at 822. Blomquist liquidated that stock and then started the Anderson & Blomquist Grocery store there. He operated there for 2-3 years before he moved to his own building at 812 Excelsior Ave. Martin B. (Punchy) Hagen started a laundry agency on the east eight feet of 822 in 1913. He moved into the main building in 1919. A news story of 8-28-1919 says Hiorth and Anderson had just bought Mrs. McConaughey's restaurant and was moving it to 822-824. Sam McConaughey had a restaurant at 822 in 1921-23. Johnson Jewelry occupied 822. Some time after Helps had the grocery store, 824 housed Warner's Saloon. Later, Anton Olson opened a grocery store there. It was Red Owl Grocery for a while. It has been Hoagies restaurant since August 1961.

Anderson and Blomquist store at 812 Excelsior Avenue West. You can see the corner of this building in the previous photograph on the far left.

This postcard looks west down Excelsior Avenue at the 800-block before 1917. From left—Chas. Blomquist Co, Otis and Otis Fair, Opera Hall, Saloon, Koblas Groceteria, Saloon, M.B. Hagen Laundry & Dry Cleaning, Hultin Building. On 900 block—saloon and lunchroom, Charleston Clothing and Shoes, and the State Bank of Hopkins. On the right—Swedberg Jewelry and Photography, Oscar Quist Shoes, Royal Theatre, Skottegard Bakery, John Erickson Billiards, I.O.O.F. (Odd Fellows) Building, and H.M. Peterson Confectionery.

A view looking east at the 800 block of Excelsior Ave., pre-1917. The oldest brick building (822-824 built by Hilmer Olson in 1893) can be seen on the right; this is now Hoagie's restaurant. The ladder on the side is a fire escape. W.R. Anderson is crossing the street diagonally. There is a hearse in front of the Odd Fellows building on the left. Note the street car "Y" and trolley cable on the dirt road. LEFT—S.E. Svec Grocery, Martin Beckman Confectionery, Skottegard Bakery, Brown & Spearing Barber, Royal Theater, Quist Shoes, Hopkins Theater, Oltman Furniture & Undertaking, City Hall (with tower). RIGHT—saloon, McConaughey Café, Hagen Laundry, saloon, Koblas Meat & Grocery, Shonka Saloon, Otis & Otis variety store, Charles Blomquist grocery store, Attorney Archie Miller, Molly Herman Hat shop, vacant corner, Caroline Drug Store.

821-823 (on right), the I.O.O.F. Building, was built in 1903. Stanley E. Svec conducted his grocery business in the corner store. He was followed by the Hopkins Co-op grocery store. John A. Althaus moved into 823 with the co-op when he left the Koblas building. Matt Weldon's Sweet Shop finally took over the whole corner store and the rear one-half of the east side. Howell's variety store followed Matt's. Frame Yourself was on the corner for many years. Twin City Leather and Boot is the 2002 tenant. John Erickson opened a pool room on the east side in 1904. J.M. Hogan had a barber shop with Erickson and also provided shower and tub baths in 1906. Erickson sold out to Martin Beckman in 1916. Matt Weldon bought Beckman's business in the early 1920s. When Matt's moved to the corner about 1930, A.G. Larson moved his clothing business from 812 to 821.

Imagine the muddy mess after a late winter snowfall! This photo looks west from 820 Excelsior Avenue in Hopkins before 1915. (This is where Bud's music is today; Hoagies at 824 would be on the SE corner). Photo was taken before M.B. Hagen Laundry located at 820 1/2 Excelsior Ave., and before Jack Shonka's Hopkins Theater moved to 805. Left (south) are saloons at 820, 824 and 900 Excelsior Ave. Right (north) at 819 is Jack Shonka's Hopkins Theater, Brown & Spearing Barber Pole at 821 Excelsior Avenue, Nelson's Confectionery at 901 has center entrance, not the later diagonal entrance. Note the streetcar cable support poles and the fire hydrant in front of 823 Excelsior Ave.

NORTH Side of Mainstreet between 8th – 9th Avenues

Street #	2002	1956	1941	1921
801	Quiznos Subs, Nails on Main	Gamble Store, hardware and appliances.	Gamble Store, hardware and appliances. Leo Priest Motor Co. in rear.	Oltman Furniture and Mortuary (The Oltman family lived on the second floor)
803			Blunt Barber Shop	Swedberg Jewelry and photography
805	Rapit Printing		Royal Theatre* owned by Abraham Engler	Royal Movie Theatre
809	Hopkins Best Steak House	Matt's cafe	Vacant Lot	
811	Sharpening Center	Quist Shoe Store	Quist Shoe Store	Quist Shoe Store
815	813 Back Door Tobacco 815 Redwing Shoes	Minneapolis House Furnishings Co.	National Tea Grocery Store	Harrison Theatre (They had live (girlie) shows as well as movies)
817	Couture Consignment	Bishop's Bakery, Kolstad's Jewelry	Skottegard Bakery; Theodore Lundman Jewelry	Skottegard Bakery
817 1/2	Vacant	Hopkins Beauty Salon, Minnie Ernst. Royal Finance Co,	Hopkins Beauty Salon, Minnie Ernst, owner	
819	Hopkins Tavern on Main	Blue Ribbon Bar	Blue Ribbon Bar	Until c. 1915 was Jack Shonka's Hopkins Theatre
821-823	823 Twin City Leather and Boot. 821 1/2 Hopkins Dance Center.	823 Howell's Ben Franklin, variety store ("Dime store"). 821 1/2 V.T. McHall, Dentist	823 Matt Weldon's Sweet Shop – restaurant. (Matt's Sweet Shop had tables and booths for dining and was popular for discussing hometown business.)	823 Martin Beckman's sweet Shop **A Pool hall was operated by John Erickson in the rear of the building. Svec grocery was here initially.**

The Independent Order of Odd Fellows (I.O.O.F.) built this building in 1903, mortgage paid off in 1915. They used the second floor for their lodge except for two front rooms used initially by Drs. Blake and Madden.

The theater at 805 Excelsior Avenue showed movies for 10-15 cents. Saturday matinees usually were western or adventure movies for kids. One night was bank night whereby a person whose name was drawn from the silver barrel received a cash prize. There were also dish sets given piece by piece with admissions. During World War II, the newsreels with Lowell Thomas updated us weekly. In 1941, the theater advertised "Air conditioned by Artesian Well Water." This theater burned down in 1953 or 54, but by then there was a newer Hopkins Theater located at 5th and Excelsior Avenues. In the early years, the movie price was 5 cents. They showed two-reel shorts that were serials; they stopped at the exciting part and one had to come the next week to see the climax. Initially this theater had vaudeville entertainment and silent movies.

SOUTH Side of Mainstreet between 9th – 10th Avenues

Street #	2002	1956	1941	1921
900	Clock Tower	900-902 Olson-Pfeiffer Pharmacy	Caroline Drug Store	Caroline Drug Store Formerly a saloon.
902				Hagen Real Estate and Phonographs
904	904-908 Edward Jones Investments. *This 3-story building is known as the Olson Building.*	904 1/2 Tremont Beauty Salon & apartments.	Jos. Lapic Food Guild Grocery 904 1/2 C.I.O. Local	904 Olson Restaurant *Formerly was a saloon that had an unusual feature: a shooting range.*
906		906 Jerdes, Men's clothing	Ray and Tony's Restaurant (Shonka's) (908 bar)	
908	Somewhere in Time Antiques	908 Nygren's, Ladies Apparel	Ediam and Smith Saloon	Johnson Bros Butcher Shop
910*	Martin's Hair Design 910 1/2 Suburban Tailors	Wee Moderns, children's clothing 910 1/2 E.C. Ernie Miller, State Farm Insurance & apartments	910-912 Hovander Brothers Groceries and Meats* 910 1/2 Dr. MacLaughlin, dentist	910 Johnson & Olson Stable and Garage. Also Seiwert Jewelry. *The Carl Seiwert family lived at the rear of the store. Carl Siewert had a private pool table in his basement for the entertainment of family and friends.*
912	Steve's Train City (antique trains and toys)	Hopkins Cleaners	910-912 Hovander Brothers Groceries and Meats	912 Swanson Grocery 912 Scandia Store, ready to wear (The Scandia supply co was operated by the Nelson brothers)
914	Hillary's Gift Shop	Thompson Jewelry & apartment	Thompson Jewelry & apartment	Charleston Clothing

(Left) Street Scene 900 block of Mainstreet, 1950s. The site of the Olson and Pfeiffer Drug Store is the Clock Tower Plaza in 2002. (Right) People bought bricks commemorating various families, individuals and organizations to help create this beautiful downtown courtyard dedicated July 9, 1992.

SOUTH Side of Mainstreet between 9th – 10th Avenues (Continued)

Street #	2002	1956	1941	1921
916	Mashek Cleaners	Smetana Drug and apartment above.	Smetana Drug and apartment above.	Smetana Drug with home upstairs.
918	(916 1/2) Tanning Parlor	La Beau Beauty Shop	Hage Radio and Refrigerators; Ernest Miller State Farm Insurance; Olson Watch & Key Repairs	918-920 Anderson Bros. Men's and Women's clothing. *Formerly the Anderson Dry Goods Store, featuring men and women's clothing and yard goods and notions.*
920	920-924 Party Crashers Photography	Fahlstrom Barber shop	Fahlstrom & Hodek Barbers	
922		Hopkins Tile & Linoleum 922 1/2 Apartments.	Premack's Dry Goods	Pre-1900 Knute Nelson's Blacksmith Shop
924		Nielsen Paint and Wallpaper		

5 9th Ave S	Pito's Barber Shop	Maddox's 9th Ave. Barber Shop		
9 9th Ave S	Parking Lot	Liberty Bar ("the Snake Pit")	Long's Bar	Bar
11 9th Ave S	Parking Lot	Hopkins Off Sale Liquor	Liquor Store	
15 9th Ave S	Vail Place	Drs. Allan J and James A. Blake, Dr. F.M. Madden	Dr. F.M. Madden, Dentist	
31 9th Ave S	Lutheran Digest	Hopkins Savings and Loan *Minnesota Federal (1961)*	Homes	Homes
16-18 9th Ave S	Parking Lot	Hopkins Post Office	Hopkins Post Office (*built in 1935*)	Homes
113 9th Ave S	Andrews Building	Hopkins Hotel	Hopkins Hotel	Hopkins Hotel
120 9th Ave S.	U.S. Post Office - Hopkins	Hopkins Public Library in Dow House	Suburban Hennepin County Relief Board & Dow Park	Dow Home

*910 Excelsior Ave. W. This building was built in 1894 to house the Nelson meat market that continued for many years. The Scandia Store occupied the east one-half of the building in the 1910s and 20s. When the Johnson Brothers (Alfred and Gust) got ready to retire, they sold the meat market to Waldo and Herman Hovander, their brothers-in-law. The Hovanders moved the business to the Hopkins Center area north of main street and changed it to a full-service grocery store. Tait's ran the grocery store there until 2001 when Driskill's bought the store—the only full-service grocery store that remains in Hopkins.

Corner of 9th and Excelsior Avenue about 1907 looking north up Ninth Avenue North toward the school. Photo compliments of Dean Empanger.

Our Store—Jorgensen's—was the teen hangout for many years… The store had a close connection to the school. Whenever a team won a trophy it would be displayed at the store before being taken to the school. The kids were always well behaved at the store. They knew they would be told to leave if they weren't. The back booth was reserved for the kids and they were allowed to carve their names and initials on the seats and backs. They didn't bother any of the other booths. After the different games, everyone raced to the store to get a booth. My dad would have to lock the doors when it got too crowded and then let more people in as others left. The store was sold in 1954 and my dad and uncle retired…

—Ruth Jorgensen Doyle

*9th and Mainstreet

A couple of "I remember when" oral histories of the early Hopkins residents say the building at 901-903 Excelsior Avenue originally sat a little distance north of Excelsior Ave. and upon a knoll and it was moved down to the street level at some unknown date. In 1906, Neil H. Nelson started a confectionery store on this corner but he continued to work at the M.T.M. factory until his store volume reached five gallons of ice cream a week. That happened in the first month. There were several changes of ownerships and in 1919, Pete and Einar Jorgensen took over after returning from World War I. They operated at this corner—known as Jeg's Corner—until 1954. The building was owned by the Westberg Brothers of Clear Springs at least as long as the Jorgensens were there.

Since that time, this corner has housed three drug stores, the *Hopkins News* newspaper office, two clothing stores (Meyer's and Lancer's) and finally antique shops have occupied this corner since 1988. Today, Mary Frances Antiques is the occupant.

In the photo, note the bell tower about the center of the block. This is one of the two school buildings located on 9th Avenue North. The old high school (with tower) was built from brick and the elementary school was wooden. Today, the former site of these schools is occupied by U.S. Bank and Hance Hardware.

The Twin City Rapid Transit Company ran a rail line to Hopkins in the early 1900s and what you see depicted here is where the streetcar waited to begin its run west to Excelsior or east to Minneapolis. The streetcar would turn west onto Excelsior Avenue, then back around the corner onto 9th Avenue North to await its run. Later, the "Y" turnaround was along the alley on 9th Avenue North. The city bus also stopped here, so many people would wait on the corner of 9th and Excelsior for their rides.

Jorgensen Brothers Corner Confectionary, "Jeg's Corner," was the meeting place after school and after ball games for kids. They had a restaurant menu and ice cream in all forms—sodas, sundaes and malts. A large glass front counter displayed penny candy of all kinds. Adults also patronized the store.

NORTH Side of Mainstreet between 9th – 10th Avenues

Street #	2002	1956	1941	1921
901	Mary Frances Antiques	Meyer's Department Stores, also attorney's offices	*Jorgensen Brothers Confectionary; also Paul Spearing Barber Shop *These stores served as the unofficial waiting station for streetcar patrons*	H.M. Peterson Confectionery *Formerly Nelson's Candy Store.* Brown & Spearing Barber Shop
903	Farmers Insurance Group	Montgomery Ward Catalog Order Store	Vacant lot	Vacant lot
905	Albert Pike Lodge 237 (Masons). *There was never anything else on this site. It was originally built as the Masonic Lodge. There has been some discussion of moving it to make way for a business, but it could only be moved back across the alley or down Mainstreet. To be moved down a side street a number of trees would need to be cut down. The Masonic Lodge rents a loft to an artist and also shares the building with another Masonic group.*			
911	Auntie M's Antiques	Vacant. *Nygren's women's apparel was here in the 1960s.*	Vacant lot	Vacant lot
913	Bethesda Thrift Shop	913-915 Paulson's Hardware *Hance Hardware was here*	913 Paulson's Hardware	Maetzold hardware and Garage
915	Cobblestone Court (Hopkins Area Resource Center, Adult Options in Education, more)	*before it moved to City Center.*	915 Hopkins Cleaners and Tailors. 915 1/2 LaBeau Beauty Salon	
917		Nelson's Shoes *Started in 1912; Mr. Nelson had started what became Jorgensen's Confectionery in 1906.*	Nelson Shoe Store	Nelson Shoe Store
921	Reigel and Assoc Ltd, Attorneys	Larson's Clothing for men	A.G. Larson Clothing	Post Office. *3 rural mail carriers used Model "T" roadsters to deliver the mail.*
923	Electric Dragonland Tattoo Parlor	Premack's Men and Boy's Wear. 923 1/2 Bill's Used Furniture and Upholstery	First National Bank	First National Bank

The site bounded by 9th Ave, 1st St. North and 10th Ave on the east half of the block was Hopkins' first downtown school, then it was a city park, now is U.S. Bank and Hance Hardware area. As a park, it had a tennis court, skating rink, swings, teeter-totter and a bandstand. On Saturday night, the Hopkins City Band would play concerts there. Today, a retail and professional services area exists one block north of Mainstreet between 9th and 11th. These are some of the businesses: Center Drug, Cheap Carpet, Trinity Bookstore, Hance Hardware. U.S. Bank, Driskill's Supermarket (formerly Tait's), Richard's Liquor, Snyder Drug Store and on 11th, the Hennepin County Public Library Hopkins Branch and U.S. West. Various professional, medical and legal offices exist in this central downtown location.

SOUTH Side of Mainstreet between 10th – 11th Avenues

Street #	2002	1956	1941	1921
1000-1006	1002 Photo Quick* Allstate Insurance. *William Strobeck built this building in 1908. Strobeck operated a furniture store and mortuary on the first floor. Hopkins Commercial Club maintained club rooms on the second floor for many years, The State Bank of Hopkins occupied the east half of the building beginning in 1910. The bank later expanded to occupy the entire building. In 1937, this building was remodeled for $8,000 and included offices, laboratories and waiting rooms for a group of professional men. A news article at the time stated Mr. Strobeck had built a splendid new monument to the enterprise he had shown as a business man and the faith he always had in his home town's future* 1006 Apartments above	1002 Northwestern Bank	1002 Security National Bank; also a liquor store	1000 State Bank of Hopkins. *Pres. of the Bank was Fred Kenaston, who was also the president of M.T.M. The vice president was Paul Swenson, the superintendent of M.T.M. The bank later affiliated with Northwestern National Banks of Minneapolis. It moved to 11th Ave and 1st St S. in 1974.*
10-10th Ave. S. Strobeck Building	Behind Photoquick on 10th S: El Sarape Supermercado, J.B. Hairitage)	Strobeck Professional Building: Feudner-Davidson insurance and real estate; Northern Contracting Co; Drs. A.H. & A.H. Jr, Malerich; Dr. H.E. Drill; Vesely and Otto law office; Whitney, Carroll & Perbix law office; Werness Insurance; Suburban Hennepin Co Relief Board. The Beauty Nook, Bess Hegland and Ruby Behrendt, owners.	1004 Gustafson and Fuxa Electric, 1004 Strobeck Mortuary (1941 advertised "lady assistant") Feudner-Davidson real estate; Dr. A.H. Malerich, dentist; Modern Beauty Shop (Bess Hegland); Joseph C. Vesely, & Frank N. Whitney, lawyers	Strobeck Electric and Mortuary. *Hennepin County Enterprise* Newspaper office

SOUTH Side of Mainstreet between 10th – 11th Avenues (Cont.)

Street #	2002	1956	1941	1921
1008	Hopkins Antique Mall	1006-8 Donovan's furniture & carpet. Apartments at 1006 1/2	1006-8 Donovan Furniture 1008 1/2 Div of Employment & Security (MN Unemployment Comp.); Dr. Smetana, dentist	Harry Leather's Ford Agency and Bicycle Shop. On the second floor was the telephone exchange for Northwestern Telephone Exchange Co.
1010-12	The Bed Shop	Dahlberg Bros Used Car lot	Dahlberg Ford – used car lot	Empty Lot
1014	Finishing Touches Antiques, also Francis Phelan, CPAs	Reeves-Cannon Co, appliance, heating sales & service	M.B. Hagen Electric (1941) 1942: Electric, Real Estate & Insurance	Tiroux Cigar Shop (3 or 4 men rolled cigars–Garde Royale and the Martellus brands.)
1016	Jack Yee's Restaurant	Karel's Restaurant, (Czech)	White System Lunch	
1020		M.B. Hagen Realtors	Rainbow Food Market	
1022	Decoys Restaurant	Archie's Bar	Glueck's Corner	Glueck Bry. Co. Saloon *Formerly the Last Chance Saloon, operated by DE. Dow.*
		This bar had the nickname of "Glueck's Corner" since the brewery owned the building and would not permit other brands of beer to be sold		

Nelson's Shoe Store window display for spring athletic shoes. May 15, 1935.

Nelson's Shoes interior, 917 Excelsior Ave., in 1930.

NORTH Side of Mainstreet between 10th – 11th Avenues				
Street #	2002	1956	1941	1921
1001*	1001-1005 Tropical Minnesota, also Accountant's Offices	Kokesh Hardware	Kokesh Hardware	Kokesh Hardware*
1005		Mashek Tailoring, cleaning	Daugherty Barber Shop / Mountain Barber Shop	
1007	Tamara's Antiques	Kucera, Frank Jos. M.D; also Mountain's Barber shop,	Dr. F.J. Kucera	Wolff Paint Shop and Residence
1009	Schatz Insurance	Hopkins Savings and Loan	1009 Hennepin County Review newspaper office, J.L. Markham, Publisher	Newspaper office
1011*	Outdoorsman Gun Shop	Hennepin County Review, newspaper office.		
1017	Beneficial Finance	1017-23 Dahlberg Bros. Ford.	Dahlberg Brothers Ford	Park. The first park in Hopkins began in the middle of the block and extended along the north side of Excelsior to 11th Avenue North. The park was developed by the Women's Improvement League, an organization determined to improve the quality of life in the growing community.
1019	Boston Garden Restaurant			
1023	Chez Francoise gift shop	After World War II, the garage portion was modernized and extended to the Hennepin County Review Building.		

The business district ended at 11th Avenue, with the exception of Torlief Larson's Blacksmith Shop at 12th and Excelsior.

*1011 Excelsior Ave—The Hennepin County Review was published here. It was the main newspaper for Hopkins, Eden Prairie and Minnetonka. The Review was the predecessor of the Sun and Sun-Sailor Newspapers. Much history of Hopkins can be found in the issues from the 1920s through the 1950s.

Kokesh Hardware

*1001 Excelsior Ave—A narrow wooden building stood here as Kokesh Hardware, built in 1903 by Frank J. Kokesh Sr. Kokesh Sr. Wooden steps led up to the main floor. It was a real hardware store—no gifts, dishes or anything that was not needed for building or farming. Merchandise was stored in the second story and basement of the building. Frank Kokesh Jr. and his son Frank J. Kokesh (the third generation), wanted to construct a new build-

ing without closing down. So, in 1958, the old wooden building was moved to the middle of 10th Avenue and stayed open from May through August while the new store was being constructed on the old site. After the new store was open, the old building was moved to Maple Plain by a longtime Kokesh employee, Don Meuhlberg, to be used as a corn crib and machine shed on his small farm.

The building was raised up on blocks ready for its move.

The old Kokesh Hardware building, 1001 Excelsior Avenue, before it was moved.

The new Kokesh building is almost done. The old building was not destroyed but moved to a farm.

Kokesh Hardware operated out of the old building in the middle of 10th Street North while the new building was constructed.

Mainstreet between 11th – 12th Avenues

Street #	2002	1956	1941	1921
1102* (S)	1106 Big Ten Restaurant	Lund Sinclair Service	1102 Lund's Sinclair Station	
1106			Suburban Chevrolet, Max Grossman, prop.	
1110	Pekoe & Java Coffee and Tea	Suburban Chevrolet, new and used cars and trucks	Lone Tree Vegetable Stand	
1114	Papa John's Pizza			
1118	Hopkins Theatre			
1120			Hazuka Mobile Service	1120 Sinco Gasoline Station
1101*(N)		Northwestern Bell Telephone	Northwestern Bell Telephone	
1105*			Selmer Johnson home	
1109*	Hopkins Center for the Arts	Suburban Chevrolet used car lot	J.W. Broz home	
1115*			Robert Zerban home	
1123		Al Benson's 66 Service		

They don't make them like this any more! The Sinco Gasoline Station on the SW corner of 12th and Excelsior Avenues.

*The block that is now the Big Ten Restaurant through the Hopkins Theatre used to be occupied by Suburban Chevrolet. In the 1940s, Just Lund's Sinclair Station was on the southwest corner. In the early 1900s, the first Hennepin County Fair was held on this corner.

*1101-1115 –This block had a telephone building and three homes in the 1940s. These houses were on a high bank above Mainstreet much like those between 15th and 16th avenues. The entire block was leveled for a used car lot for Suburban Chevrolet headquartered across the street.

Suburban Chevrolet's used car lot, 1111 Excelsior Ave., in 1956.

Mainstreet between 12th – 13th Avenues

Street #	2002	1956	1941	1921
1200 (S)	Carpet Resources	Typewriter Sales & Service	Bob and Jen's Tavern	
1202	Henderson and Associates	Servisoft, Home Softener Service		
1204		Anton's Beauty Salon		
1206	Monkabean's Coffe and Ice Cream shop		Elmer's Ice Cream & Elmer Schedin home	
1208	American Security Corp & Marsden Building Maintenance			
1218	Vacant	1218 Economy Refrigerated Lockers*	1218 Economy Refrigerated Lockers*	
1222			Richard Berger home	Blacksmith
1201 (N)	Custom Wheels (Firestone)		1201-1203 Texaco Service Station	
1205		Gils Tire and Auto Supply; also Hopkins Auto Parts		
1207	Jeff's Barber Shop	Hopkins Specialty Co; Ted's Barber Shop, Nicollet Cleaners and Dyers		
1209	Gopher Cash Register	Milbert's Confectionery & Grocery	Milbert's Grocery	
1213	1213 Home	A.F. Marx home & others. *This was moved here from across the street.*	Marx rooming house	
1221	Mark Apartments	Apartments (9)	Charles Anderson home	

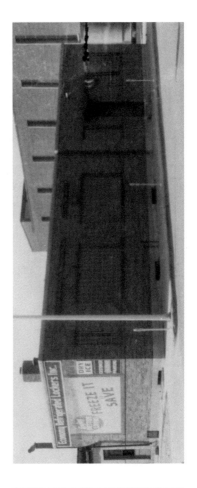

Before electric refrigerators were widely used, most homes used an icebox in summer for food storage. Winter was no problem. Economy Refrigerated Lockers was built to provide freezer lockers for rent. These were used by individuals to freeze and store beef, pork, venison, ducks, chickens and garden vegetables for longer storage than an icebox could provide. One could buy a side of beef and the locker people would cut, trim and package it and then store it in their rental "lockers." Photo shows the Economy Refrigerated Lockers at 1218 Excelsior Ave.

Mainstreet between 13th – 14th Avenues

Street #	2002	1956	1941	1921
1310 (S)	St. Joseph's Church	St. Joseph's Catholic church	Vacant lot (church not there yet)	
1320	John Ireland School	St. Joseph's Catholic grade school	St. Joseph's Church and School (same as school building now)	
1301*(N)	Raspberry Ridge Apartments and Hopkins Activity Center*	South Junior High entire block; behind that is the athletic field (Maetzold Field) taking up the entire block between 13th and 14th Avenues and 1st and 2nd Streets N.	Hopkins School District 19. Elementary east side; Jr. High west side.	

*1301–Built in 1925, this was both the elementary and junior high school for many years. The west wing was 7-8-9 and the school district office. The east wing was K-6. The central area had an auditorium, theatre, basketball court and library. The Hopkins Activity Center at the north end of the west wing was school space added in the 1950s. The Hopkins Historical Society is located in the former band room of this wing. The school was

known as "South Junior High" after the high school was moved to Highway 7 and North Junior High was built. A World War I cannon used to sit in the center of the school's front yard but was used for steel in a World War II scrap metal drive.

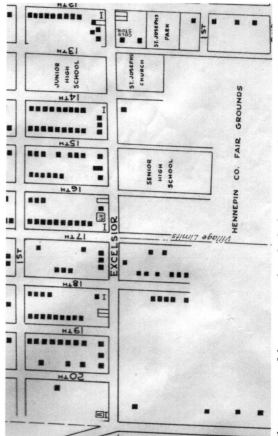

The west part of downtown Hopkins had a large amount of open space prior to 1948 and very little commercial property.

Milbert's Grocery at 1209 Excelsior Ave. was a favorite snack stop for students from South Junior High. 1956 photo.

	Mainstreet between 14th – 15th Avenues			
Street #	2002	1956	1941	1921
1400 (S)	Washburn-McReavy, Strobeck-Johnson Funeral Chapel & Cremation Services	1400 Strobeck-Hauge Funeral Chapel "Serving the Hopkins community since 1910"		
1402		Home for several teachers.	Leslie Hall home	Home
1404-	Central Park Square: Suburban Feed & Supply (1404), Noah's Ark Child Care, Information Bionics, Electric Craftsman (light shop), Rehab Dynamics, Star Wok Chinese Restaurant and Dominoes Pizza. To the south is Central Park.	1410 W Country Club Market	Vacant lot / Hennepin County Fairgrounds was to the south.	Vacant lot
1401 (N)	Tooth by the Lake Cosmetic Dentistry. AAL – Aid Association for Lutherans	Automobiles, Inc & Great West Discount Co, auto finance. Kranz King of Kars Hopkins Marine Sales	Ben Miller Mobile Oil	Charlie Hersman Oil Station
1409		Hubert Wolf home	Hubert Wolf, Sr. home	
1413	Harmon Auto Glass	Bloomie Mountain home. 1413 1/2 Mamie Milbert	Bloomie Jenstad home & Ed Rasmussen res.	
1419	Antiques West			
1421	Tidal Pool Tropical Fish	Matteson Home	John Matteson home	

Kranz King of Kars in 1956 advertised "Cadillac, Oldsmobiles, Buick Hdqt's, we are specialists in beautiful automobiles and genius financing."

Country Club Market in 1956, 1410 Excelsior Ave. Now this is Central Park Square.

Mainstreet between 15th – 16th Avenues

Street #	2002	1956	1941	1921
1510* (S)	Central Park Manor Apartments (entire block)	Hopkins High School	Hopkins High School *Football Field was to the south.*	Hopkins High School
1505 (N)	Jeff's Auto Service		Cecil Sundquist home	
1513	Windmill Imports	Bernard Ewest home	Bernard Ewest & Anna Sullwold residence	
1515	Merry Maids	LeRoy Blunt home		
1517			Mrs. Emil G. Souba home	
1521	Westside Natural Health	Jos. H. Baker home		

*In 1908, the first Hopkins High School was built here. Behind were tennis courts and a football field where coach Russell "Butsie" Maetzold won many championships. Mr. Tanglen became superintendent of schools in 1946 when the school system consisted of the two downtown buildings plus Harley Hopkins. He was instrumental in the growth of the district to the size it is today. The old high school was known as the "Annex" in its later years.

Mainstreet between 16th – 17th Avenues

Street #	2002	1956	1941	1921
1600 (S)	Katherine Curren School	Katherine Curren School	Hennepin County Fairgrounds	
1601 (N)	Jasmine Garden Chinese Restaurant	Berglund's Grocery & Confectionery also the "Big Little Store." Donald A. Berglund residence.	OM Hippe Grocery. Bertin Brurs res.	
1605	Romen's Interiors	Gustafson residence	Carl E. Gustafson home	
1607		Henry A. Bartels res.		
1609	Kiwi Cycle (motorcycles) Parts and Accessories	Gustafson's Hopkins Greenhouse	Gustafson and Son Florists	
1615	Minnetonka Life-Care Pregnancy Help Center			
1617	Perfect Image Styling Salon	Pure Oil Station 1617 Carroll Hutchinson fam, Elmer Meisner res.	Edel Gas Station (Tydol Products) 1617 Harry Goede res.	
1619	Woodlines			

This was the last block of Hopkins. After you crossed 17th Avenue, you were in Minnetonka Township.

*Part of the Hennepin County Fairgrounds' land was used for Katherine Curren School. The Fairgrounds included two grandstands and horse race track in the vicinity of Central Park. Also, the county shops were where the Hopkins shops are now located to the south of Katherine Curren school.

Mainstreet between 17ᵗʰ – 18ᵗʰ Avenues

Street #	2002	1956	1941	1921
1714 (S)	Bell-Mobile			
1718			Willis Hutchinson home	
1728	Kentucky Fried Chicken			
1701 (N)	Hopkins Auto Service		Frank Stodolka home	
1715	Digital Media Express	Home	Carl Realander home	
1719	R. Ralston Collectibles & Antiques	Bren Radio & TV Service and Hobby King Handicraft, art supplies	Patrick Shaughnessy home	
1721-25	Metro Elevator Inc. (*This was the site of the first frame home in Hopkins.*)		1721 Vassar home	

17th Avenue was the western boundary line between Hopkins and Minnetonka Township.

Mainstreet between 18ᵗʰ – 19ᵗʰ Avenues

Street #	2002	1956	1941	1921
1800 (S)	Dairy Queen			
SW	A small strip mall containing: Speed Queen Coin Laundry, Hopkins Thrift Bakery, MN Trophies & Gifts, Karina's Hair Design.		Conoco Oil Station	
1842	NAPA Auto Parts	Anderson Bros, farm implements		
1801 (N)	Dale Feste Automotive	Ace Super Service, gas station, Kleven Oil Co, Bulk storage	Gas Station and C.M. McCloud res.	
1819	As You Like It Ceramic Studio	Dot's Cafe	Gary Hutchinson Feed Store	Feed Store
1821	Valvoline Instant Oil Change			

The west end of Hopkins about 1958; Excelsior Avenue from 17th Avenue to Shady Oak Rd. The Pines Trailer Court had 122 mobile homes. The Super Valu building at the end of Excelsior Avenue burned May 3, 1988.

Mainstreet between 19th Avenue & Shady Oak Road				
Street #	2002	1956	1941	1921
19th Ave to Shady Oak Rd	The Oaks of Mainstreet Condominium homes	Trailer Park*		
2012				
2100		Pines Grocery Store Johnson's Super Valu grocery. Bobbie's Bake Shop. (*Burned down in 1988.*) Dorholt Printing.	Otto Mantel home	
1901	D.J. Sales and Home	Duemke Res, Kilbourne res, and Rose Skottegard home	Dumke Res & Rose Skottegard home	
1909	Private home	Fitz home	Edwin Scheunenman home	
1917		A.J. Slamen home	Mrs. Lena & Muriel Redpath home	
1919	Brandstetter and Boyat Dentists			
2011	Smith Auto Import Repair (entire block)			
2021		Frank Hardin Standard Gas station	Standard Station and Nitehawk Café	

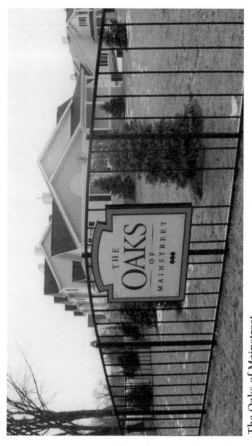

The Oaks of Mainstreet.

*Pines Trailer Court

Shortly after World War II, the H & H Pines Mobile Home Park was built in Minnetonka Township. It provided cost-effective housing for many people. Some units were owned and some were rented. When they were first used, they were the peak of modernity and space-saving ingenuity. Hopkins annexed the Pines in 1966. By 1996 when the last residents were asked to vacate the property to make way for a new housing complex, the Pine's owner was living in Arizona and the Trailer Park had many health and building code violations. Through bond sales, the city paid $1.1 million for the land, and gave owners an average of $3,000 for each unit plus provided $1,950 to every tenant for moving expenses. This is now the Oaks of Mainstreet.

References

The following abbreviations are used throughout these notes:

HCA   *Hopkins Centennial Album 1887-1987*
HCR   *Hennepin County Review* Newspaper
HHS   Hopkins Historical Society
MHS   Minnesota Historical Society
STRIB   *Minneapolis Star, Minneapolis Tribune,* or *Minneapolis Star-Tribune.*
SUN   *Hopkins* or *Minnetonka Sun, Sun-Sailor,* or various other names of the west-suburban newspaper that served the Hopkins area.

All referenced documents and photos are from the HHS archives unless otherwise noted.

Manuscripts and Unpublished Sources

Bates, Don, *Music in Hopkins*, HHS Talk, 9-25-1994.

Blomquist, Clint, various unpublished manuscripts. Blomquist was the first curator of the HHS and wrote many articles for publication in the local newspaper or for talks he gave to various civic groups. These are identified by a numbering system he devised, with the help of former Hopkins librarian Mary Heiges, and are located in the HHS archives filed by topic or surname.

___Blomquist's writings include: *How Hopkins got its name, The Bohemian Settlers of Hopkins and North Eden Prairie, Churches in Hopkins Parts 1 and 2, Levi Longfellow, Early Years of Theater in Hopkins, Harmony Hill, Father Vacek (Hopkins Review 11-21-1979), First Hopkins Harvest Festival Becomes County Fair, Hennepin County Poor Farm, Postmasters and Location of Post offices, Tosteson-Hutchins, Daniel Dow, Short History of Hopkins (Hopkins Review 5-30-1979)* and more.

Chicago, Milwaukee, St. Paul and Pacific Railroad Co, Chicago, IL, *The Milwaukee Road in Minnesota.*

Craig, Bill, *Hopkins History*, manuscript 8-5-1998.

Donovan, Frank P. Jr., *Hopkins First Railroad: The M.&St.L. Railroad.*

Elmshauser B. and Driscoll, J., *Draper Family Genealogy.*

Feltl, Katherine, Stephen, Stanley, Cyril, Mary and Margaret, *History of the Pioneer John Joseph Feltl Family in Minnetonka and Hopkins, Minnesota 1867-1974.*

Frear, Dana W., *History of early post office, Minnetonka Town.*

Firmage, Hugh, *History of First Settlement of the Area Known as South Minnetonka and North Eden Prairie*, manuscript.

Godfrey, Allan Downing, *A Historical Study of the Organization and Consolidation of School District 274 Hopkins, Minnesota*, paper for Master in Education degree, 1965.

Hamilton, Wallace E., *A Historical Sketch of Mizpah Church*, from original by Robert Mayo, presented Sept. 18 and 19, 1938, at the 50th Anniversary of the congregation, updated in 1952.

Harley Hopkins Graduating Class of 1950, *The Growth of Hopkins and Vicinity, A Territorial Centennial Project.*

Hopkins School District Athletic office, dates of high school state championships, posted on wall of Lindbergh Center.

Houser, John R. III, *What Hopkins Had: A Brief History of Hopkins, Minnesota, 1852-1939,* unpublished manuscript, HHS, 1976-78. John Houser, funded by the Urban Corp and the HHS, started to write a book about Hopkins, but sadly, he died before his book was published. His unfinished manuscript remains and some of his material was used in HCA as well as in this book. References from Houser were invaluable because Houser had listened to all the HHS oral histories done in the 1970s in addition to reading many of the documents in the early HHS collections.

Interlachen Park Association, *Our History, Homes and Humor,* 1985.

Interlachen Section Minneapolis Needlework Guild, *Minute Book,* 1925-1934.

John Hus Presbyterian Church Historical Sketch from their 75th anniversary brochure.

Kucera, Dr. Frank, *Memoirs* of this long-time Hopkins physician are located at the HHS.

Matchke, William, *A Tribute to Chermack,* 1991, scrapbook, HHS.

Markham, James L. *Hopkins, the First Hundred Years,* unpublished manuscript. Jim Markham was the editor of the HCR for many years. He wrote the editorial column *From the Grumble Seat,* which contained much Hopkins history.

___Markham states that the Hopkins family was the first to know about Shakopee Massacre. This editor thinks this is speculation only. It apparently was Sioux not Ojibway who were on Hopkins' land when discovered sharpening knives. In the final battle, it was the Chippewa/Ojibway attacking the Sioux at Shakopee. Perhaps the Hopkins family witnessed the Sioux following the Chippewa back to Mille Lacs sharpening their knives, or more likely, this was a different situation altogether.

___*Church of St. Joseph: A Brief History. Hopkins Bands*, others. Clint Blomquist stated that over 650 type-written pages were donated to the HHS that Markham had written about 1949-50 in anticipation of publishing a Hopkins history book, which he was unable to accomplish before he passed away. Some works attributed to Clint Blomquist here may in fact have been initially written by Markham.

Marshall, Ceil Robertson and Stewart, Marion "Shorty" J. *The History of Glen Lake, 1982*, booklet.

Mayo, Robert Johnston, *Early Days in the Hopkins Neighborhood*, personal manuscript of R.J. Mayo, superintendent of Hopkins Schools from 1913-1937 and one of the organizers and an early director of the Hennepin County Historical Society, author of *History of Hennepin County* and *Adventures in Minnesota History*. Manuscript was given as a speech before the Women's Improvement League on March 19, 1940, was in the possession of Mr. Mayo's sister-in-law, Miss Berdie Chalgren and was submitted as a Senior History Paper in 1970 by Jeffrey L. Wagner.

Mayo, R.J., *Hi-Crier* (Hopkins high school paper), dated 1933, in which Mayo interviewed members of the Miller family. Also early teachers.

McDermott, Marjorie, *History of Mizpah Church*.

North Star Abstract and Title Guaranty, Inc, *An Ordinance to Change the Municipal Name of the Village of West Minneapolis to the Village of Hopkins* 3553468, Adopted July 7, 1928, Filed July 28, 1965, Book 1013 of Misc., page 131.

___*Charter of the City of Hopkins, Hennepin County, Minnesota*, 2484585, Adopted December 2, 1947, filed January 8, 1948, Book 544 of Misc., page 281.

Olson, Deloris M., et.al., *Recollections of Life in Hopkins*, Contributors: Florence Sween, Mary Boucher, Jerre Miller, Elfreda Addy, Donald Milbert, Jim Shirley, Ruth Doyle, Margaret Lapic.

Phelps, Fred T., *A Brief Sketch of the Beginnings and Development of Interlachen Park, Hopkins, Minnesota*, April, MCMLXX, booklet.

Portner, Florence (Stenzel), *The Beehive I remember*, Jan, 1978.

Severson, Svante, *History of Hopkins Banks*.

Schmitz, Iva B., donor, *Record of Minnetonka Township Original Purchases of Land from Federal Government*.

Shorba-Manfred, Maryanna, stating that James L. Markham said men were begging for work from him during the depression, in an interview in 1953. From p. 91 Houser.

Sidla, Adolph, notes on railroads going through Hopkins.

Sidla, Anton J., *History of the Catholic Workman Branch 141 of Hopkins*, 1976.

Stubbs, Avery, *Historic Minnetonka Mills, 1852-1862*, manuscript compiled 1925-1985, p. 19 re Shakopee battle and aftermath. John P. Miller building Harrington Hotel and widow Gordon working there from pp. 134 and 138. Also p. 62 (from *MN Republican*, Feb 12, 1857)—"John P. Miller is erecting a hotel."

___Chair and bedstead manufactory at Mtka Mills p. 65. Bustling town in 1855 from page 64 quoting George H. Day memoirs, *Minnetonka Record of Excelsior*, Mar 15, 1918.

___Native Americans demanding meat p. 102, story by Atwood and others.

___Demolition of Burnes' blacksmith shop at Minnetonka Mills, p. 118.

Territorial Government, *A Bill for a Territorial Road from Minneapolis to Glencoe*, Hennepin County History Museum.

Vavra, Helen Mary & Kranz, Albert James, *The Dvoraks of Minnetonka Township, Minnesota, 1988* about Shady Oak School, Bryant School and St. Margaret's Church.

Books and Periodicals

Atwater and Stevens, eds, *History of Hennepin Co*, Vol II, 1895, p. 1214: "In the spring of 1852, was the advent of the first settlers. At that time James Shaver, Jr., and Simon Stevens took claims, holding their homes as squatters, as the Indian title was not yet extinguished. Mr. Shaver located on the south shore of Wayzata Bay. His wife was the first white woman to make her home in the town.

Later in the same year, came James Mountain, Mrs. Mary Gordon and five sons, John McGalpin, George Andrews, John Bourgeois, and others."

___ "During 1850 the most desirable lands near the river had been claimed and were maintained until by the reduction of the reservation in 1855, they were regularly entered. Next after Colonel Stevens came J.P. Miller who staked out a claim and built a house on the tract now known as Atwater's Third Addition. Edward Murphy claimed the tract adjoining that of J.P. Miller, below and along the river."

___ pp. 1463-64, includes photos of John P. and Catherine Miller.

Bailey, Bruce, "Doc Kate –The Lady in Black." The *Hopkins Historical Society News*, Summer 2001.

Baldwin, Rufus J., "Indian Occupation and Wars." *History of Minneapolis and Hennepin Co.* ed. by Col. John H. Stevens and Judge Isaac Atwater, 1895 re Sioux-Ojibway discord.

Berry, Joan, *With Grace and Grit, Hopkins United Methodist Church, 1885-1985.*

Burns, Debra K., "A brief history of raspberry growing in Minnesota," *Northland Berry News*, Sept 1989.

Chastek, Jan M., story published in *Amerikan Narodni*, 1905, Chicago, IL, translated into English by Betty Uherka, donated to the HHS by Paul Makousky.

Donovan, Frank P. Jr., *Mileposts on the Prairie, The Story of the Minneapolis and St. Louis Railway*, Simmons-Boardman Publishing Corp, New York, 1950. From Dean Empanger.

Faith Presbyterian Church of Minnetonka, *Centennial Edition Church Directory*, 1987, Pastor Moore History of the church.

Friends of the Hopkins Community Library, *Library News*, October 2001.

Gilman, Rhoda R., "Territorial Imperative: How Minnesota Became the 32nd State." *Making Minnesota Territory 1849-1858*, special issue of *Minnesota History* 56 (Winter 1998-99): 154-67. Extensive quote used by permission, Minnesota Historical Society Press.

Hallberg, Jane King, *Minnehaha Creek Living Waters*, Expanded Edition, Cityscapes Publishing Co, Minneapolis, 1995, p. 34; States Calvin Tuttle built the second house on the west river bank, p. 33. pp. 37-38, originally from Owens, Col. John P., *The Minnesotian*, Saturday, September 11, 1852 (See discussion under Atwater).

Honeywell, Inc., *Defense Systems Division Review*, 25th Anniversary Issue, September and October 1981, compliments of Jim Zdrazil.

Hopkins High School Alumni Directory, *A Brief History of the Hopkins School District (1850-1996).*

Hopkins School District 270 Parent Extra May 2002, about Ronald B. Davis Community Center.

Kuralt, Charles, *On the road with Charles Kuralt*, Ballantine Books, 1986, p.237.

Long, Barbara Beving, *Historic Resources of the City of Minnetonka*, Volume 1, 1993, p. 27 re Minnetonka Township.

Mechlenburg, Virginia, *The Public As Patron*, College Park, MD, The University of Maryland, 1979, p. 66. On-line version from HHS files.

Minneapolis City Directory, 1893-94, from the Hennepin County History Museum.

Morris, Lucy Leavenworth Wilder, ed., *Old Rail Fence Corners, Frontier Tales Told by Minnesota Pioneers*, reprint edition, Minnesota Historical Society Press, 1976, First published in 1914, Daniel Dow story p. 62-64. Chester Hopkins story p. 101.

Neill, Rev. Edward D. and J. Fletcher William, *The History of Hennepin County and the City of Minneapolis*, 1881, p. 238.

Old Rail Fence Corners, see Morris.

Olson, Russell, *The Electric Railways of Minnesota*, Excerpts found at HHS.

Patera, Alan H. and Gallagher, John S., *The Post Offices of Minnesota*, Burtonsville, Maryland, 1978.

Raabe, Editor, *Hopkins Historical Society News*, Spring 2000 re Justus Lumber.

___1937 *The Cultivation of Raspberries Mural on Display at the Weisman Art Museum, Hopkins Historical Society News*, Spring, 2002.

Select Publications, Inc, *Select Twin Cities* magazine featuring Hopkins, September 1962.

Shutter, Rev. Marion Daniel, *History of Minneapolis*, Vol I, S.J. Clarke Publishing Co, Chicago, 1923, pp. 574 & 575 re Mary Gordon being member of First Baptist Church of St. Anthony.

Skold, Betty Westrom, *100 Lighted Candles, Gethsemane Lutheran Church 1890-1990.*

Tufford, Garrie L., "Steam Train to Lake Calhoun," reprinted from *The WEDGE*, a community newspaper of the Lowry Hill East Neighborhood Assoc. of Mpls. Originally published April and May 1976.

Wagner, Jeff, Editor, *Hopkins Centennial Album 1887-1987*. The basis of this book is from HCA, which did not include references, so in some cases, the actual source is not known. Changes to HCA were recorded and have been incorporated into this book.

Weisman Art Museum Newsletter, *Historic Mural Restored for Current Exhibition*, University of Minnesota, Winter 2002.

White, Bruce M., "The Power of Whiteness or, the Life and Times of Joseph Rolette Jr." *Making Minnesota Territory 1849-1858*, special issue of *Minnesota History* 56 (Winter 1998-99): 178-197. Re Population, used by permission, Minnesota Historical Society Press.

Interviews, Oral Histories and Talks

Bates, Don, *Music in Hopkins*, talk to the HHS, 9-25-1994.

Chicago and North Western Transportation Co, letter of Jan, 1973 states: "The line from Minneapolis to Merriam, through Hopkins, was built in 1869 by the Minnesota Valley Railroad Company, which later became part of the Chicago and North Western."

Cohen, Rabbi Norman M., of Bet Shalom Congregation.

Constans, George, Bren, Duffy, Werness, Mel, HHS talk 5-15-1994 about the VFW.

Elmshauser, B. and Driscoll, J., *Draper Family Genealogy*: Land Records Doc. 548 Hennepin Co MN, SE S25 T117N R22W N5th PM. Issue Date 4-2-1857—according to affidavit given by Rufus E. Draper, Mary Draper settled the land the 7th of July 1855, was widowed with 5 children; phone conversation with Elmshauser 11-12-2001; states that the Draper family had land deals in many states from coast to coast.

Erickson, Dorothy, *They called them the good old days*, manuscript of talk to Mizpah Seniors Feb, 1998, revised, Jan 13, 1999.

Hamilton, Lyman, description of Hopkins in 1915, from Houser, chapter VII.

Heiges, Mary J. letter about founding the HHS, 6-9-1995.

HHS meeting first Historic Homes awards given, 10-28-2001.

Isaak, Patricia, Minnehaha Oaks Association, Update 8-17-02.

Kloss, Cecil, *Homebuilding in Hopkins*, talk to the HHS, 3-16-1997.

Makousky, Paul donated the story of Jan M. Chastek to the HHS.

Rappaport, Gary, phone conversation re Venturian and Napco, 4-10-2002.

Romportl, Chuck, *History of St. Joseph's Church*, talks to the HHS, 2001.

Senn, Debra (Winter) Renfro, talk to the HHS 1-20-91 on Harley H. Hopkins.

Shirley, Jim, talk to the HHS 10-28-2001 about the Albert Pike Masonic Lodge.

Supervalu publicist, phone conversation, 4-1-2002; also corporate publications.

U.S. Post Office, Hopkins, Minn, *Dedication Program* Nov 23, 1968.

Western Bohemian Fraternal Assoc of Cedar Rapids, IA (ZCBJ) Letter to J.C. Vesely, from 1958 with attachment *A Brief History of Western Bohemian* by Roman L. Hruska, published in the convention program of 1947.

Wigfield, Vern, local railroad historian, provided much of the railroad and streetcar information.

Woodside Cemetery Caretaker Christine Randall letter: "380 sets of no name remains are buried at Woodside cemetery, 10 Hillcrest Dr, Tonka Bay, MN 55331, from the Hennepin County Poor Farm, burial permit dated 6-10-1955 by John Huber."

Newspapers

Blake, Laurie, *Growth of rental units changes Hopkins' flavor*, STRIB, 5-20-1982.

Coleman, Becky, *Mashek's celebrates its 70th*, SUN, Jan 25, 1984.

Draper, Norman, *Hopkins Wins Case Against X-rated Bookstore*, STRIB, July 20, 1996.

Flanagan, Barbara, *Hopkins Centennial*, STRIB, 7-6-1987.

Freeborn, Dan, *Spotlight on Hopkins*, STRIB, March 6, 1993.

Fuller, Jim, *Venerable Bursch's in Hopkins gives way to upscale upstart*, STRIB, 12-23-1988.

Furst, Randy, *Protesters, authorities plan tactics at Alliant*, STRIB, October 7, 1998, and *65 Antiwar Activists arrested at Alliant Plant in Hopkins*, STRIB, November 2, 1999.

Harmon, Tom, *Butsie Maetzold Recalls Hopkins' Glorious Years*, SUN, 3-25-1971.

Harvala, Eileen, *Decade of growth rejuvenates Hopkins*, SUN, Dec. 27, 1989.

___*Fire Department Celebrates Centennial*, SUN, August 4, 1993.

Harwood, Markie, *Raspberry Grower to lead fest*, SUN, 7-14-1976.

Hennepin County Enterprise, "Hopkins-Little City of Excellent Schools, Beautiful Homes," 10-14-1915.

Hopkins News of July 26, 1906 devotes entire issue to Hopkins, with photos.

Hennepin County Review (HCR), *Blaze Damages Dow House Halts Repairs* (10-13-1938). This article states the Dow home was built in 1888. *Bids Out for City Hall, Dow House Demolition*, (3-11-1965). *Take a Last Look! The Dow House was torn down Wednesday without much fanfare*, (4-15-1965). *Splinters are all that's left of the Dow House late last week and by Tuesday, there wasn't a sign of the once mighty structure*, (4-22-1965).

___regarding: Katherine Curren (5-29-1952), Anne Campbell Borland (3-1-1956), Alice Smith School (1-29-1951 and 6-21-1951), first school basketball team (10-27-1938), Assemblies of God Church (7-15-1965), ZCBJ (1-5-1933), Burwell School (1-9-1947), Lions club (11-21-1957), Jim Markham Retiring (3-18-1954).

___*Workmen wreck Burnes House, landmark built 77 years ago* (4-20-1939).

___*Last look before the old City Hall on 8th and Excelsior becomes a thing of the past this week*, 5-13-1965.

___*Hopkins as "Raspberry Capital" Is Revealed in New Post office Murals*, 10-22-1936.

___*Artist Hanging PO 'Raspberry Murals,' Back From Two Eastern Art Exhibits*, 2-4-1937, indicates murals were completed in fall of 1936 after a year of work.

Hopkins-Minnetonka Weekly News about Tanglen (8-27-1987).

Hopkins Review, A series of Hopkins historical pieces, many written by James L. Markham or Clint Blomquist, were published in the late 1970s.

Horner, Tom, *Those magnificent young men and their flying machines*, SUN June 6, 1974.

Johnson, Betty and Nagel, Marge, *Early Burwell Student remembers the school*, SUN, 5-20-1981.

Johnson, Kristi Lee, *Hopkins Close-Up: A Mainstreet Success Story*, STRIB Adv. Suppl., July 6-7, 1995.

Kaszuba, Mike, *Trash from the past is haunting Hopkins*, STRIB, 12-26-1990.

___*A Suburb's poorest residents move on*, STRIB, November 25, _____.

McBee, Duchess, *Hopkins' eager archivist, historian*, SUN, 10-8-76.

Mack, Linda, *Arts Center to Expand the focus of downtown Hopkins*, STRIB, 4-23-1997.

Moll, Virginia, *Hopkins' Own 'Mr Music', J.J. [Chermack] was born with talent*, SUN, 8-7-1969.

Northwestern Democrat, Jan 19, 1856, re Burnes' blacksmith shop at Minnetonka Mills: "At the present the miscellaneous business of Minnetonka City is confined to a large dry goods and grocery store of Levi Eastman; the blacksmith shop of Mr. Burnes and the Lake House kept by A. Green."

Unknown newspaper clipping. Obituary of Mrs. Sarah Bassett of Hopkins, 1911. "Charles Bassett and his family left New York in 1853 and after looking around for a suitable site, settled in West Minneapolis."

___*Shocking accident, a fatal collision on the Minneapolis & St. Louis RR yesterday; Miss Minnie Reeve of Hopkins scalded to death and two engines wrecked*, unk date.

Reilly, Katherine, re school demographics, SUN, 2-27-2002.

___*New homes for old things in downtown Hopkins*, SUN, 8-29-2001.

___*Proclamations presented to owners of historic homes*, SUN, 11-7-2001.

___*Hopkins Library to Close March 2*, SUN, 2-27-2002.

Shaughnessy, Mike, *Hopkins teams bring home 5 state titles…so far*, SUN, 2-22-2002.

Shipman, Catherine, "Hopkins Strategic Redevelopment," *Minnesota Real Estate Journal*, 9-21-1987.

STRIB regarding–*Dr. Sweet, last civil war vet* (obituary July 7 and 8, 1943), *Hopkins Bank Held Up by Gang* (11-7-1933), *Butsie Maetzold* (obituary 4-22-1982),

SUN regarding–*Hennepin County Poor Farm* (5-2-1974), *Hopkins Senior Club* (10-31-2001), *Fairview Lutheran Dedicates New Church* (6-6-1974), *Retired fire truck* 10-16-1969), *J.J. Chermack* (2-3-1972), *At 73, Bloomie Mountain to End Library Career* (unk, but about 1962), *Raspberry History: Festival's roots linked to depressed prices* 7-4-1988.

Thompson, David, *Hopkins Planning Grant Okd*, STRIB, 7-27-1967.

Towley, Carl, *These are your schools*, HCR 10-10-57.

Wathen, Mary, *Mashek family business grows with 70-year history*, SUN, September 12, 1983.

Websites

Cross of Glory Church; Gethsemane Lutheran Church; City of Hopkins; Raspberry Festival; US Post Office; Sokol; Supervalu.

Hopkins School district 270 website, Eilene Harvala, Communications Office.

Minnesota Historical Society *Place Names*. Minnetonka Township was organized May 11, 1858.

Startribune website, "2000 Census."

U.S. Junior Chamber of Commerce website.

U.S. National Archives & Records Administration, 700 Pennsylvania Avenue NW, Washington, DC 20408, website regarding Vietnam War dead.

Index